Football in France

Global Sport Cultures

Eds Gary Armstrong, *Brunel University*, Richard Giulianotti, *University of Aberdeen*, and David Andrews, *The University of Maryland*

From the Olympics and the World Cup to extreme sports and kabaddi, the social significance of sport at both global and local levels has become increasingly clear in recent years. The contested nature of identity is widely addressed in the social sciences, but sport as a particularly revealing site of such contestation, in both industrialising and post-industrial nations, has been less fruitfully explored. Further, sport and sporting corporations are increasingly powerful players in the world economy. Sport is now central to the social and technological development of mass media, notably in telecommunications and digital television. It is also a crucial medium through which specific populations and political elites communicate and interact with each other on a global stage.

Berg publishers are pleased to announce a new book series that will examine and evaluate the role of sport in the contemporary world. Truly global in scope, the series seeks to adopt a grounded, constructively critical stance towards prior work within sport studies and to answer such questions as:

- How are sports experienced and practised at the everyday level within local settings?
- How do specific cultures construct and negotiate forms of social stratification (such as gender, class, ethnicity) within sporting contexts?
- What is the impact of mediation and corporate globalisation upon local sports cultures?

Determinedly interdisciplinary, the series will nevertheless privilege anthropological, historical and sociological approaches, but will consider submissions from cultural studies, economics, geography, human kinetics, international relations, law, philosophy and political science. The series is particularly committed to research that draws upon primary source materials or ethnographic fieldwork.

Previously published titles in the Series:

Gary Armstrong and Richard Giulianotti (eds), *Fear and Loathing in World Football*

Tony Collins and Wray Vamplew, *Mud, Sweat and Beers: A Cultural History of Sport and Alcohol*

John Bale and Mike Cronin (eds), *Sport and Postcolonialism*

GLOBAL SPORT CULTURES

Football in France
A Cultural History

Geoff Hare

Oxford • New York

First published in 2003 by
Berg
Editorial offices:
1st Floor, Angel Court, 81 St Clements Street, Oxford, OX4 1AW, UK
838 Broadway, Third Floor, New York, NY 10003-4812, USA

Berg is the imprint of Oxford International Publishers Ltd.

Library of Congress Cataloging-in-Publication Data
Hare, Geoff, 1945–
    Football in France : a cultural history / Geoff Hare.
      p. cm. – (Global sport cultures)
Includes bibliographical references and index.
    ISBN 1-85973-657-2 (cloth) – ISBN 1-85973-662-9 (paper)
  1. Soccer–Social aspects–France–History. I. Title. II. Series.

GV943.9.S64H37 2003
796.334'0944–dc21

                                                                    2002155815

British Library Cataloguing-in-Publication Data
A catalogue record for this book is available from the British Library.

ISBN 1 85973 657 2 (Cloth)
          1 85973 662 9 (Paper)

22352376

Typeset by JS Typesetting Ltd, Wellingborough, Northants.
Printed in the United Kingdom by Biddles Ltd, Guildford and King's Lynn.

Contents

Tables

Acknowledgements

'No man is an island.' A single authored book – a non-fiction book more particularly – can rarely be entirely the work of one person. There are first of all the multiple sources – written and human – that have been consulted over a number of years (and which hopefully have all been properly acknowledged). There are particularly those writings of others that have proved full of inspiration and fired enthusiasm for the subject. There are those organisations that have believed in the project enough to give financial help for travel. There are those information professionals in libraries and documentation centres who have found or ordered books and articles. There are those friends who knowingly or not have been engaged in conversations about some aspect of the work that the author was trying to clarify. There are others who have kindly agreed to read parts of the manuscript, have commented on it, and thus helped excise embarrassing errors or clarify an argument. The series editor and publishers are always well focused in this kind of contribution. There are those who have taken a more distant interest in the work itself perhaps, but who none the less have offered moral support and kind encouragement. From time to time there is some inspirational music. And then there is one's nearest and dearest, who does more by just being there, but knowing when to keep out of the way, than she knows. For there comes a time when the author has to shut himself away and finish it off, complete the second or third drafts of the more rebarbative chapters, bring it up to date, and take full and final responsibility for the whole, knowing it could be better, but knowing too it is no good to anybody until it is published.

It is invidious to pick out some people for one type of help and others for another, and to put them in any order other than alphabetical. They generally know how they have helped. I shall just list them below therefore. I make an exception for my wife Cathy who deserves pride of place, more than ever, for her love and support, and to whom I dedicate this book.

My thanks to: Pierre Bourdieu, Agnès Chauveau, Hugh Dauncey, Kathryn Earle, Alan Fidler, Gloria Gaynor, Richard Giulianotti, Chrystel Hug, Samantha Jackson, Claude Journès, Françoise Lebrun and friends, Daniel Leclercq, Christian Lépagnot, Jo de Linde and the *Financial Times* Paris Office, Patrick

Acknowledgements

Mignon, Hélène Pérennou, 'Loulou' Pérennou, Dave Place, Jessica Plane, Nick Swingler, Marie-Pierre Toulet, Andy Young; also to the staff of the Bibliothèques André Malraux and Mouffetard (Ville de Paris); the Institut National de l'Audiovisuel; the Documentation Centres of the CSA, the INSEP, the Institut Français de Presse; Robinson Library (Newcastle University); and for financial help, the Institut français d'Ecosse, Newcastle University Small Research Grants.

Geoff Hare
August 2002

Glossary

AJA	Association de la jeunesse auxerroise (Auxerre football club)
AS	Association sportive
BEES 1	Brevet d'Etat d'éducateur sportif 1er degré (first-level State coaching qualification)
BEES 2	Brevet d'Etat d'éducateur sportif 2ème degré (second-level State coaching qualification)
BEES 3	Brevet d'Etat d'éducateur sportif 3ème degré (third-level State coaching qualification)
CFA1	Championnat de France amateur Division 1 (French football's fourth division)
CFA2	Championnat de France amateur Division 2 (rank below CFA1)
CFI	Comité français interfédéral (umbrella body bringing together competing federations of football clubs in early twentieth century)
CFO	Comité français d'organisation de la Coupe du monde (1998 World Cup Organising Committee)
CLT-UFA	Compagnie luxembourgeoise de télévision (Luxembourg and German [Bertelsmann] broadcasting holding company)
CNFE	Centre national de formation et d'entraînement (girls' national youth football coaching centre at Clairefontaine)
CNOSF	Comité national olympique et sportif français (French national Olympic committee)
CNRS	Centre national de la recherche scientifique (national research funding body)
CPEF	Centre permanent d'entraînement et de formation (local State-funded sports coaching centre)
CRS	Compagnies républicaines de sécurité (French riot police)
CS	Club sportif
CSA	Conseil supérieur de l'audiovisuel (French broadcasting regulator)
CTD	Conseiller technique départemental (county coaching adviser)
CTR	Conseiller technique régional (regional coaching adviser)
D1	Division 1 (called Ligue 1 from season 2002/03)
D2	Division 2 (called Ligue 2 from season 2002/03)

DATAR	Délégation à l'aménagement du territoire et à l'action régionale (State-run regional economic planning body)
DEF	Diplôme d'entraîneur de football (qualification to coach at highest amateur club level)
DEPF	Diplôme d'entraîneur professionnel de football (qualification to coach at professional club level)
DNCG	Direction nationale de contrôle de gestion (financial regulator of French professional clubs)
DTN	Directeur technique national *or* Direction technique nationale (national technical director of coaching, or national technical directorate)
FAS	Fédération des associations de supporters (federation of football supporters clubs)
FC	Football club (in both French and English)
FCAF	Fédération cycliste et amateur de France (early French federation of sports clubs)
FFF	Fédération française de football (French football's governing body)
FFFA	Fédération française de football association (earlier name of FFF)
FGSPF	Fédération gymnastique et sportive des patronages de France (early Catholic federation of sports clubs)
FIFA	Fédération internationale de football association (world football governing body)
FLN	Front de libération nationale (Algerian National Liberation Front)
FN	Front national (J.-M. Le Pen's extreme-right political party)
FNDS	Fonds national pour le développement du sport (national sports funding body)
INF	L'Institut national du football (national football coaching centre at Clairefontaine)
INSEP	Institut national du sport et de l'éducation physique (national training and research centre for elite sportsmen and women)
JPP	Jean-Pierre Papin
LFA	Ligue de football association (an early federation of football clubs)
LFP	Ligue de football professionnel (the French professional football league, from 2002/03)
LNF	Ligue nationale de football (name of the French professional football league 1981/2002)
LNFA	Ligue nationale du football amateur (the body running French amateur football, under the FFF)
LOSC	Lille Olympique Sporting Club (Lille football club)

MNR	Mouvement national républicain (extreme-right party, founded as a break-away from the FN)
OAS	Organisation de l'armée secrète (underground movement opposing Algerian independence in the 1960s)
OL	Olympique Lyonnais (Lyon football club)
OM	Olympique de Marseille (Marseille football club)
PMU	Pari mutuel urbain (national horse-race off-course betting organisation)
PSG	Paris Saint-Germain (Paris football club)
RC	Racing Club
SA	Société anonyme (limited company)
SAEMS	Société anonyme d'économie mixte sportive (a type of mutual company available to sports clubs in French business law)
SAOS	Société anonyme à objet sportif (a type of limited company available to sports clubs in French business law)
SASP	Société anonyme sportive et professionnelle (a type of limited company available to sports clubs in French business law)
SEM	Société d'économie mixte (a mutual company in French business law)
STAPS	Sciences et techniques des activités physiques et sportives (sports science courses)
STO	Service du travail obligatoire (compulsory work scheme for Frenchmen in Germany in Second World War)
TF1	Télévision française 1 (the major French commercial independent television channel)
TGV	Train à grande vitesse (high-speed train)
UCPF	Union des clubs professionnels de football (French professional club chairmen's union)
UEFA	Union des associations européennes de football (governing body of European football)
UNECATEF	Union nationale des éducateurs et cadres techniques de football (French coaches' union)
UNFP	Union nationale des footballeurs professionnels (French players' union)
US	Union sportive
USFSA	Union des sociétés françaises sportives et athlétiques (early French federation of sports clubs)

1

Introduction: Studying French Football

Why Study Football in France?

Why is it important to study French football? Isn't France supposed not to be a sporting country? A few years ago interest in sport and in football as indicated in attendances at Division 1 (D1) matches, was about half that of England, Italy or Germany. French football clubs are consequently financially impoverished and its top players go abroad, under the freedom of contract offered by European legislation (essentially the Bosman ruling), to earn the kind of money their British, Italian and Spanish equivalents are paid – indeed the exodus is not confined to their internationals, but affects their second rank players too, now to be found sitting on the bench in various English stadiums. Numbers of French professionals playing abroad were: 75 in 1998/99, 87 in 2000/01, and 113 in 2001/02 (Chaumier and Rocheteau 2001: 656–699), and of the French Euro 2000 squad, eight plied their trade in England, six in Italy, two in Spain, two in Germany, and only four in France. However, readers don't need to be reminded that the top two English teams of 2001/02 were managed by Frenchmen, that France won the 1998 World Cup, and then indeed in 1999 they gave the English inventors of the game as big a footballing lesson on the Wembley turf as that inflicted by Puskas's Hungary in 1953, and finally rounded off two marvellous years with the last-ditch victory over Italy in the 2000 European Championship. Such a run of success had to end at some stage, even if the manner of France's ignominious early exit from the 2002 World Cup was a shock. Time will tell whether it was just a blip or whether it heralds a more serious decline.

The 1998 World Cup victory underlined that a mere sport, as mediated through television, can suddenly move a whole nation in various ways. The saga of 'les Bleus' has had a galvanising effect on reappraisals of French identity, crystallised a renewed national self-confidence, and confirmed France's position in the world through global TV exposure for its success stories (high tech industrial products, luxury goods, cultural tourism). From Anderson's notion of 'imagined communities' and Hobsbawm's 'invention of tradition', we know that sport and national identities have long been intertwined. Sport (especially male sport), and its mediation through the national press and TV, has played a crucial role in the construction and representation of national identity. Just as English defeats on the cricket field in the last decade or so have been represented as symbolic of the nation's decline (Maguire 1999: 177), so French football victories have been seen as the revelation of the opposite. The French National Front leader Jean-Marie Le Pen, in 1996, had challenged the artificiality of the French team, saying that some players had chosen French nationality as a matter of convenience (Marks 1999: 50), pointing the finger at Desailly and Vieira, for example, born in Ghana and Senegal respectively. But the growth of the Extreme Right was slowed down (temporarily at least) after the World Cup victory, which moved on the debate about the legitimacy of the place of ethnic minorities (to use the British terminology) within the French nation. Given the team's ethnic mix, the only way the national team's achievement could be celebrated, the only way the nation could identify with the victory, was by equating the nation with the same diverse ethnic mix as the team. The French white establishment could identify with a balding Kabyle born in a poor Marseille *banlieue* and with a tall shy Guadeloupean, on equal terms with a shaven-headed goalkeeper of Spanish extraction; they could identify with all of them equally as representatives of the nation; and Blacks and Beurs (second and third generation North African Arab immigrants) all over France could be proud of their community's contribution to a French national achievement. Without forgetting of course the unassuming, middle-aged ex-factory worker with the Corrèze accent who as national team manager came to represent all the values of 'la France profonde' and of *la République: solidarité, travail, droiture, professionnalisme* (solidarity, work, honesty, professionalism). In short, football became, for a privileged moment at least in the summer of 1998, the major focus for integration and solidarity in a Republic where the terms have a founding value.

The wider popular impact of football in France following the two cup wins is also clear, for example, from the result of the *Journal du Dimanche* opinion poll of the Top 50 French people (6 August 2000: 1, 30). In summer 2000, for the first time since it was inaugurated in 1988, it was topped by a footballer, Zinedine Zidane. The ex-Maoist intellectual Philippe Sollers commented in the same issue: 'I am an unconditional admirer of Zidane, Anelka, and Trezeguet. I jump up when France wins, not just at football, but everywhere and increasingly often.' This is merely one example of equating the French national football team with a wider idea of the whole nation winning. Indeed we have seen this idea gain currency in the immediate aftermath of France 1998 in the form of the transformation of the French 'Astérix complex'[1] into the metaphor of 'une France qui gagne' (France as a winner). In other words, a French national inferiority complex being replaced by a belief in French effectiveness – a new national self-confidence. Football has become a common metaphor for an upsurge of general national self-belief, a recognition – a perhaps still fragile recognition – that France is emerging from a long period of depression as the nation has come painfully to terms with its war-time collaborationist past, with decolonisation, with loss of status in a world now dominated by 'Anglo-Saxons' and the English language, and with an economy and society bedevilled by high unemployment. Through football, the French have discovered they are not eternal losers.

This is new. French football history abounds with accounts of heroic defeats (1958 and 1982) and of national coaches basing tactics on the essential individualism of their players. This recurrent national self-image purveyed through football equates to the Astérix complex. This refers to the expectation of ultimate defeat for 'les petits Français', just like the Gauls led by Astérix against the Roman legions, while, importantly, emerging with honour safe and some small victories of clever and stylish individualism against overwhelming odds. This Astérix complex has proved durable, especially since the 1982 and 1986 World Cup semi-final defeats by Germany. The only way French football and its national history could be celebrated – until 1998 – was if style was considered more important than effectiveness. If victories could not be expected on the European or world stage, then at least France could play 'champagne' football, à la Platini or Kopa. The same might have been said for other aspects of French life: the intellectual Raymond Aron had said something similar in the 1950s regarding the French not being winners: that they preferred to be right, or to do things properly, even at the price of defeat.[2] Or at least there was a time when the received idea was that France enjoyed world renown in luxury goods, perfume, fashion, wine, in culture and the arts, but not in business and industry or high technology. The recent French footballing victories have laid this ghost, certainly in the context of football and, some people would argue, possibly more widely. The 'World Cup effect' has not entirely disappeared – certainly not in terms of the increased interest in football, as seen for example in increasing numbers of spectators in stadiums.

The contention of this book is therefore that football is important in France, and that it can be used as a window on French society more generally; that the way football is organised, played and watched reveals interesting, wider differences between France and Britain. Indeed, how sport has or has not been a legitimate object of study within France may also prove revealing.

One aspect the author has regrettably had to omit, for lack of knowledge and space, is women's football, which is just starting to grow in importance and deserves a subsequent study to itself.

The Academic Study of French Football in France and Britain

In Western Europe today, sport may be seen as a 'total social phenomenon', to use Marcel Mauss's term, in that it traverses and affects the whole of society, and therefore reveals all its dimensions. In this respect, studying sport in general, and football in particular, involves looking at the physical, mental and social behaviours of its actors (practitioners [players, administrators, managers], financiers, and audiences), in an attempt to establish some coherent interpretation of all its components, be they historical, sociological, economic, cultural, or ethnographic. Any study that has the ambition to understand sport in its totality will be enriched by the inclusion of a mosaic of analyses from these different angles of view. Following Roger Caillois's claims that the sociology of a given civilisation is directly related to the particular configuration of 'games' ('jeux') existing within it, and Norbert Elias's contention that sport is a privileged site for understanding social relationships and their evolution, Pociello sees the study of sporting practices as offering insights into society, from the psychology of participants and spectators to the socio-political analysis of national or multinational organisations running professional sporting events. Indeed the two poles of his approach cannot be divorced: any analysis of commercial sporting institutions, for example the football World Cup, must take into account the common grass-roots sporting culture, the ethics, feelings and values that are shared by its audience and that are a key to the sport's resonance within society. Given the growing impact of sport in contemporary society, sports studies are inevitably led therefore to pose questions about the norms and values that a given sport carries, and about the social and political functions that the sport comes to assume within a given society (Pociello 1999).

While it is accepted that football is a multi-faceted social phenomenon, with social, cultural, political, and economic dimensions that must be explored, the overarching theme that will emerge in this study, in an attempt to give the book its coherence, is the issue of the values that football carries. A major question posed by Patrick Mignon (1998: 8) in this context is whether the values carried by football are simply the expression of identifiable collective cultures, or whether we are dealing with a process of top-down construction of values by the State or the media. Our study will not necessarily resolve this wider issue of sociological theory. However, the hypothesis adopted is that these values are not static or constant, but are subject to change, and that football is one of the most visible sites of tension between old and new values, between competing cultural and social models; in other words, that football is an ideological battleground. The last years of the twentieth century have been particularly productive of change in this respect.

Pierre Bourdieu had a particular view of the direction that sport has been evolving in the last two decades of the twentieth century. This view started from the idea of Elias and Dunning, who showed that what characterised modern sport at its outset was its autonomy as a social sphere within civil society, its ability to organise its own practices in its own terms for their own sake – not for financial gain, and free from State control. This remained true for a long time after different sports moved out of their exclusively amateur period into the professional era. Then, from the 1980s onwards, as business practices have entered different sports at club and international level, sport has gradually been losing this autonomy. Its ludic, non-material values have been under attack from business logic. In Western Europe the sport at the forefront of this erosion of autonomy has been professional football, and its self-regulation is being broken down. The Trojan Horse of business logic, to use Bourdieu's image (1999: 16), is television, which has transformed football from practice into a new kind of spectacle. Indeed one could go further and conclude that the influence of television as a marketing tool has turned football into a commodity to be bought and sold. And as was seen in 1998, the ultimate TV entertainment commodity is the World Cup, although professional club competitions (like the new World Club Championship and the European Champions League) are also subject to this trend. France is not alone in undergoing this evolution in its national league at club level, although France's particular national cultural specificities have apparently mediated its effects in certain ways, differently certainly to Britain.

Within the hypothesis of football as a battleground of cultural values, it will be asserted that although French and British football are more and more subjected to the same commercial pressures that Bourdieu identified, the cultural histories of the two societies provide a different balance of power in this same ideological battle of cultural values. Certainly both countries are subject to increasing standardisation of European law (the Bosman ruling is a key landmark in professional sport), and are experiencing the same globalising economic pressures bringing increasing standardisation of consumption and ways of life as major European or global groups are formed by fusions of hitherto national companies. There are, however, certain differences of political culture and of institutions that mean that the liberalisation and commercialisation that are changing British football have met greater resistance in France from strong values of public service and statism. These values have governed the growth and organisation of sport in general and of the media companies that, on both sides of the channel, are building a symbiotic relationship with major professional sports clubs and events.

A further historical difference is that French football differs from its British counterpart in its organisational structures. Its regulatory system and its governing bodies and clubs have been shaped by the French State's concept of the public service, of Republican and democratic values, and of centralist interventionism, as opposed to laissez-faire individualism (Miège 1993).

These French specificities are to do with the particular tradition of French statism, and the different speeds of development of national broadcasting systems. On the one hand, France moved initially much more slowly than Britain from an exclusively public broadcasting sector and heavily State-regulated sector to a mixed public and commercial broadcasting system, and then moved much more quickly to a pay-per-view subscription TV system. On the other hand, in the tradition of French statism and public service, the special relationship between sport and the State in France has protected its values better than in most other European Union countries. One could add that until the victory in the World Cup no one could have argued that this protection had significantly helped the international competitiveness of French teams, whether at club level or national level.

The Ubiquity of Sport in Contemporary Culture

There is no doubting the growing social importance of sport within late modern society. Many analysts have drawn attention to its development, not only in western countries but across the world from South America to emerging African and Asian nations. Sport is the flavour of the decade and football the flavour of the moment. The 1990s have been called the age of sport. Even the Queen, in one of her annual messages to the Commonwealth, in 1998, noted the importance of sport as a carrier of important modern *values (Daily Telegraph,* 9 March 98: 1), unwittingly echoing a former editor of *Marxism Today,* Martin Jacques, who claimed we are witnessing the 'sportification' of our culture:

> Almost all of us, whatever our age, wear trainers. No designer label is complete without its sportswear collection. Sports personalities have become cultural icons, sought after by sponsors and advertisers alike. And where sport was once low-brow, now it is the stuff of serious literature. Sport has become ubiquitous. It is the metaphor of our time . . . [J]ust as rock became the dominant cultural form of the Sixties and Seventies, so sport has become dominant in the Nineties, invading areas of life where previously it had no presence: sport as fashion, as showbiz, as the body beautiful, sport for health, sport as a new source of value, sport as business. (Jacques 1997: 18)

Jacques is not sure the sportification of society is wholly a good thing. Looking at similar social phenomena, but with more positive conclusions, French ethnologist Christian Bromberger, à propos of the 1998 World Cup, talked about the 'footballisation' of French society (Losson and Villepreux 1998). One unexpected aspect of the impact of France 98 was a legitimisation of sports studies in French intellectual circles, whether among sociologists, economists or cultural historians. The French serious daily press gave the World Cup major coverage, where football had not previously merited more than a few column inches from time to time. The newspaper of reference, *Le Monde*, read by French political, economic and intellectual elites, carried a daily 8-page World Cup supplement for the month of the competition. Subsequently football coverage (and sports coverage in general) has noticeably increased from pre-1998 norms. In the month preceding the 1998 World Cup, two major (international) academic conferences dealing with football were held in Paris: one, entitled 'Football et cultures', was hosted by the organisation funding and managing all State-directed research, the Centre national de la recherche scientifique (CNRS) (see Lenoir 1998); the other, on 'Football: jeu et société', was organised by the National Institute for Sport and Physical Education, Institut national du sport et de l'éducation physique (INSEP). Their sponsorship by the three ministries of Youth and Sport, Education, and Research showed how football was coming to be seen as part of mainstream culture.

Hitherto, the serious French studies of football that existed were often characterised by a long-standing academic and intellectual elitism towards the analysis of popular culture. In the French academic world especially, this elitism was difficult to break down. The liberal intellectual attitude to football was that it was a *pointless* activity, and so not worthy of study. For the structuralist-functionalist analyst, football was seen as conducive to social disruption and came under deviance studies. To the Marxist intellectual, football was ideologically suspect, a part of the dominant ideology of capitalism, inhibiting the development of a revolutionary consciousness among its supporters (football as opium of the people). Jean-Paul Sartre was aware of this attitude among his fellow contributors to *Les Temps modernes*. He remarked: 'Ha! Football ! can you just see their faces at *Temps modernes* if I went to watch a match?'[3] This disdainful attitude to football that Sartre, to his credit, appears to have found amusing still finds expression from time to time, as in a piece in April 2001 by Robert Redeker of *Les Temps modernes*, where he argues that the wave of interest in football is 'cretinising' the French (Jeffries 2001).

Early studies on the sociology of leisure and sport, published in France or elsewhere, by Dumazedier (1962), Weber (1970, 1971), Pierre Bourdieu (1980) and Elias and Dunning (1986) can now be seen as seminal. Through their analyses the legitimacy of the study of football as social practice has been established, its economic ramifications recognised, and its status acknowledged as a useful window on social and cultural change, offering particular insights into cross-cultural differences, as the sport becomes globalised, and into cross-national divergences that persist. In his articles written in the 1970s Eugen Weber drew attention to the social and political significance of French sport. Innovative work on sport and leisure such as Dumazedier's *Vers une civilisation du loisir* (1962) has helped demonstrate the centrality of practices previously thought insignificant. Pierre Bourdieu and some of his research team (notably Faure and Suaud 1994a, 1994b, 1999), have turned their attention to the sociological analysis of sporting practices. Bromberger (1987, 1995, 1998) has brought his ethnographic approach to bear on the place of football in the daily lives and culture of inhabitants of Marseille for instance. The sociologist Alain Loret (1996) shows how the organisation of sport reflects much deeper economic structures and social values: his analyses of new individualistic, 'fun' sports (surfboarding, rollerblading) showed how they were a protest against established, mainstream (team) sports such as football, taken up in France in the late nineteenth century and moulded around Pierre de Coubertin's ideas. He shows how highly regulated competitive sports express the values of industrial society: performance, results, classification and how they may be being overtaken by recent innovations in alternative physical leisure practice. The French national institute for elite sportsmen and women, the INSEP, has a research department which, in addition to studies of sports science (bio-mechanics, physiology, and psychology), has a sociology unit headed by Patrick Mignon who has published extensively on fan culture. Indeed, since sports sociology is a compulsory part of the training on STAPS courses (Sciences et Techniques des Activités Physiques et Sportives) for physical education and sports teachers, coaches, managers and administrators, there exist a number of French sports sociology textbooks (e.g. Pociello 1999). Historians too have provided valuable source books on football, such as those by Alfred Wahl (1989, 1990a, 1990b). Useful summaries of the institutional, regulatory and legal framework of sport in France have emerged from Miège (1993, 1996) and Thomas (1991), finding different patterns of approach between the northern and the southern European states. A good source on the history of French sports policy is Callède (2000).

Within the context of rapidly changing communication technologies and the liberalisation of media industries (and their globalisation), the recently growing economic importance of sports such as football has stimulated several socio-economic analyses of French sport. Jean-Marie Brohm (1992, 1998), in the Marxist tradition of condemning professional sport as exploitative, has studied the political sociology of sport. Bourg (1986, 1991, 1994, 1997), Maitrot (1995), Poiseul (1992, 1996a, 1996b, 1998) and Halba (1997) have examined the economics and business practices of contemporary sport. Finally, French media studies specialists have just begun to take an interest in the symbiotic relationship between sport and major press and television companies (Thomas 1993; Ferran and Maitrot 1997).

From the English-speaking world, Richard Holt's *Sport and Society in Modern France* (1981) was important in creating more interest in analysing the social context of French sport. Other British-based work has come from Philip Dine (1995, 1996, 1997a, 1997b, 1997c, 1998a, 1998b, 1999, 2001), Richard Giulianotti (1999), Pierre Lanfranchi (1994), Dauncey (1999), Dauncey and Hare (1998a, 1998b, 1998c, 1999a, 1999b, 2000) and Hare (1999c, 2003). Policy studies, such as those by Dine (1997b, 1998a, 1998b), have looked at the way the French State has intervened in the selection and coaching of elite athletes in order to use success in international sports competitions for domestic and diplomatic purposes. The Frank Cass journals and monograph series, under the guidance of J. A. Mangan, have taken an interest in European sport, including French sport. While one or two other English-language monographs have appeared in the 1990s, often with short chapters on a number of countries, usually including France, by Williams and Wagg (1991), Giulianotti and Williams (1994), Armstrong and Giulianotti (1999), and the remarkable summum *Football. A Sociology of the Global Game* by Richard Giulianotti (1999), there has been a relative impermeability of British and French sports studies – until the recent conferences. While Elias and Dunning have been much cited and influential in France (their work *Quest for Excitement. Sport and Leisure in the Civilising Process* appeared in French translation in 1994), many French specialists have appeared relatively unaware of other work emanating from British analysts. One exception is the English-speaking Patrick Mignon, whose work shows close familiarity with that of British sports academics (see his *La Passion du football* (1998) and his chapter in Finn and Giulianotti (2000). Equally, French-speaking academics such as Richard Holt, Pierre Lanfranchi and Philip Dine have managed to get their work recognised in French research circles. The major barrier on both sides has apparently been linguistic. One of the aims of the current work (along with previous work in collaboration with Hugh Dauncey) is to act as a cultural interpreter between the two research communities, and to build bridges of understanding between different cultures. This book may thus be situated within intercultural studies.

From Community to Commodity? Social and Cultural Change and French Football

The same cultural history approach that brought Jacques, Bromberger and others to see sport as a metaphor for late twentieth century life, and to see football as revelatory of wider social and cultural change, has led analysts to apparently contradictory conclusions. On the one hand, football has been seen as exacerbating (and indeed organising) rivalries between individuals, social groups, towns, regions or entire nations, leading to violence ('football hooliganism'), while on the other hand, more positively, it has been seen as creating social bonds and relationships, collective identities and a sense of belonging or community. The same event has been seen to stimulate both violent confrontation and social cohesion, as in European Championship competitions or the World Cup. Pociello (1999: 4) indeed sees sport's contemporary importance in societies such as our own, disrupted as they are by economic globalisation and threatened by 'social fracture', as this dual ability to organise confrontation while at the same time reinforcing a sense of community. His view would lead to an interpretation of English fans' violence during the 1998 World Cup and 2000 European Championships as being a desperate attempt to (re)create a national identity and a sense of personal value that had been lost during the socio-economic changes of post-imperial Britain, while Scottish fans' studied avoidance of violent behaviour in France 98 reflected a sense of national identity that defined itself precisely in contradistinction to English identity. Similarly, within the context of French football, past extremes of behaviour by fans of two of France's most passionately supported club sides, Saint-Etienne and Lens, have been interpreted by Mignon (1998) as the last defensive throws of old industrial communities being torn apart by the restructuring of the French economy in the 1980s.

Key words used in this book, 'community', 'spectacle' and 'commodity', refer to the dominant values of the three overlapping phases of the social and cultural history of French professional football, as I see it. As everywhere else in Europe, football has undoubtedly helped forge links between people who had no cultural or social identities other than the fact of belonging to a certain urban space. Football's early development in France has something in common with the creation of a shared sense of place in emerging working-class communities in cities across Western Europe, albeit on a smaller scale than in England, reflecting the smaller scale of the French industrial revolution. Yet French football differs in its organisational structures and in the input of the middle classes and their values. Its system of self-regulation and governance owes much to the French civic tradition of public service, of Republican and democratic values, and of State interventionism, as opposed to British laissez-faire individualism (Miège 1993). There was in the period up to the 1960s, both a growth of small town clubs that represent the community within the nation and an official recognition of sport as a public service.

In the period between the two world wars, new and older urban communities founded identities around the local football club. The entertainment value of football as spectacle grew in importance as professionalism, a national league and a transfer system developed and there were pressures to attract crowds and gate income. Differences in scale of support between England and France are attributable to their different socio-economic development in the nineteenth and twentieth centuries and to the later and more fragile implantation of football in the working-class consciousness in France. French public service television became the natural mediator of this spectacle for the nation – at least for matches of national importance – not only the national team, but just as importantly French club teams playing in Europe. Indeed football as national spectacle in the Gaullist era (the 1960s and early 1970s) feeds a sense of national identity.

The slower evolution of professional football in the direction of commercial-isation in France than in England is to do with a more general French attachment to public service values (or the values of amateurism), community control, and rejection of free-market economic solutions (that the French call 'liberalism'). The under-development of French football (low income and punitive social taxes on clubs) led, after the 'Bosman' deregulation of national protectionist contracts, to an exodus of a hundred or more of France's top players to England, Italy, Spain, Germany and elsewhere. They have been replaced by imports from Africa, South America and smaller European countries (Hare 2003). As deregulation has been imposed on football, after many other sectors of social and economic life, through the process of Europeanisation and globalisation, there has been local French resistance to this creation of a global marketplace.

However, there is growing pressure for France to harmonise (i.e. liberalise and commercialise) its practices regarding professional sport with the rest of the European Union. The newly elected French League management committee, backed by the financially stronger clubs, indeed promised in 2000 – in the name of 'modernisation' – to align the structures of French football with those of England, Italy and Spain within two years (Caffin 2000). One tool they are using is television rights. The struggle for control of broadcasting rights to French football between the subscription channel Canal+ and the commercial, free-to-air channel TF1 has had the effect of massively increasing income to football clubs. French football has become, as in other countries, a 'commodity whose media value is determined by the size and composition of the audience it can deliver to potential advertisers and sponsors' (Maguire 1999: 152–153). For the first time, in 2002, the French professional league has attached the name of a commercial sponsor to its title. What is happening then, as France enters the new century, is the increasing commercialisation and commodification of football. Top clubs are being re-branded to catch a national and international audience of consumers of a lifestyle associated with a club. A significant example in this respect is Olympique de Marseille's promotion of itself as OM, deliberately separating its new brand image from its original geographical reality and identity, in order to give itself a national or international audience. In the era of globalisation of markets, commodity is squeezing out community.

Globalisation, with its pressures for harmonisation, is affecting France. But globalisation and Europeanisation have not passed without local resistance. France's position within the global economy of professional football has been brought face to face with its own under-development (in business terms) or, to look at it another way, with its semi-peripheral position in the global media–sport complex, as Maguire (1999: 19, 91–93) has called it. French clubs have seen their best players poached by core European footballing nations. This deskilling of French football has been most keenly and controversially felt by the loss of the most talented products of the famous French youth footballing academies, the *Centres de formation* that all professional clubs are obliged to finance by their national Federation.

Nicolas Anelka was one of the first to be poached – from PSG by Arsenal for half a million pounds in January 1997 – to be sold on two and a half years later to Real Madrid for £22 million. The fact that, in summer 2000, PSG bought back Anelka from Spain for 218 million francs is ironic and redolent of the spoliation and dependency that French clubs see in the current situation. Since PSG, in order to pay the transfer fee, were helped by Canal+ and Nike (MD 2000), it is certainly evidence that French football is being further removed from local community control to become a 'corporate sport' owned by the sports-media complex.

Europeanisation and globalisation have meant a growing commercialisation of football that has gone a long way to breaking the links between community and sporting spectacle. Commodity values have begun to replace the sporting ethos at the heart of football. If French football is still in some ways French, it is in the sense that the governing bodies and the French Ministry of Sport, for example during the French presidency of the European Union, have tried harder than elsewhere in Europe to put the brakes on this headlong rush into greater commercialisation whereby sport is increasingly 'handcuffed to television' (Barnett 1995). This is in the tradition of French sports administrators from Coubertin and Jules Rimet onwards who have played key roles in spreading the sporting ethos across Europe and the world (see Chapter 2). This local resistance by the French authorities and governing body to the ideological process that is globalisation has been interpreted by some as a rejection of modernity or modernisation. Others defend it as another French exception.

The successive chapters of the book will weave the argument outlined above into a social and cultural history of French football, beginning, in Chapter 2, with a brief history of football in the French national consciousness, covering the importing of English sports by French elites in the late nineteenth century within a divided nation, its popularisation and the 'incomplete professional-isation' of football in the 1930s, and the evolution of notions of administering sport as a public good and the implication of the State and municipalities in the national organisation of professional football. Chapter 3 looks at the socio-economic geography of football as reflected both in the nationalisation of the game and in its promotion of local and regional identity through the growth of its professional clubs, initially in small industrial towns, before the current trend for the growth of the big city club. The special case of Paris, with its periods as a football desert, will merit a separate section. The symbiotic relationship between club and supporters leads us directly into Chapter 4, which situates key moments in the development of fan culture. In a sociology of the French football public, we examine the growth of the modern supporter from the success of Saint-Etienne, the special relationship of the fans and the city of Marseille, the growth of the French 'Ultras' and their particular form of identity within football support, and again the special case of the recent creation of a fan culture around Paris Saint-Germain, the club that everybody loves to hate. Chapter 5 focuses on French coaches and coaching systems, including the special place of the French youth academies, that are credited with the flourishing of the current generation of French players. A sixth chapter, on the players themselves, is held together by the theme of national identity, with a section on imports and exports of players at club level (including Waddle and Cantona), but focusing more on the national team, 'les Bleus', and its heroes, from Kopa and Platini to the Zidane era, when the multiethnic team took on important symbolic value for the nation. Chapter 7 is devoted to football as a television spectacle, from the transformation of the TV–football relationship with the creation of the pay-TV channel Canal+, its purchase of PSG, and the impact of digital TV. The business side of club football is addressed in Chapter 8, covering the links between businessmen, politics, and the commercialisation of football. It will examine various 'affaires' involving club chairmen such as the larger-than-life Bernard Tapie, and contemporary corporate involvement at club level. The final chapter, after a glance at the fall-out from Korea 2002, will assess the strengths and weaknesses of French football and the current state of its commodification: players as commodities, the post-Bosman exodus, and the issue of neo-liberalism versus the public good as it is perceived in France.

Notes

1. The term was first used by Alain Duhamel in a wider social and political context (Duhamel 1985).

2. Raymond Aron, in *Le siècle des intellectuels*, programme 4: 'De Sartre à Foucault 1958–1980' by P. Desfons and M. Winock, France 3, 1999.
3. Source: http://www.france.diplomatie.fr/culture/france/biblio/folio/sport/sport26.html (accessed 10 May 2001).

2

Establishing Football in the French National Consciousness

In France the vocabulary of 'le football' (or 'le foot' for short) is still partly English, revealing the sport's origins. Whereas 'le goal' (goalkeeper) is now more commonly called 'le gardien', the French quite happily cry: 'Penalty!' or 'Corner!', and talk of 'un match', 'un club', 'la Ligue' (League), 'le coach', 'un short' (shorts), 'le transfert', 'les fans', 'un tacle', 'un dribble', 'shooter' (to shoot). It was from Britain, where Association Football as a sport was already established with firm organisational and regulatory foundations, that football and other modern team sports were imported into France in the late nineteenth century. The first English clubs had been founded in the 1850s, a national regulatory body, the Football Association, in 1863, and by 1885 there was already a national professional championship in England. The first 'French championship' (amateur still) did not exist until 1894, and even then only six clubs entered and it was national only in the sense that the Paris press is called national, since all were based in the capital. It took until 1932 for a national professional league to get off the ground.

In the late nineteenth century and the early twentieth, class and religious divides that split the nation played their part in the slow establishment of football as a national professional sport, as well as the aristocratic values of the French sporting ethos promoted by Baron Pierre de Coubertin, the founder of the modern Olympic Movement. However, French football enthusiasts played a determining role in the early internationalisation of the game, and have continued to do so in more recent times. International regulation, the establishment of the international governing body FIFA (note the combination of French and English in the name, Fédération internationale de football association), the World Cup competition, UEFA, European Club competitions, the European Nations Championship, all owe much to celebrated French administrators of the game.

A French tradition of central State regulation was also influential in the above developments. It has certainly played a role in the establishment of a particular set of values associated with French football that have only recently come under serious threat: these are values that take for granted the necessary intervention of the State and publicly accountable authorities in order to establish democratic principles and ensure the public good in the organisation of the sport, from grass roots to the elite clubs.

The Adoption of Football and French Ideological Divisions

Sport became part of a national mission after the military invasion and defeat of France in 1870/71 by Bismarck's new Germany and its annexation of Alsace and almost half of Lorraine. The new and fragile Republican regime promoted physical fitness among the nation's youth in order to counter the idea of French national decline and to prepare the nation's youth for a war of revenge. Gymnastics, shooting and semi-military activities became popular with the more nationalistic practitioners. For individual participants, however, enjoyment and the social aspects outweighed the militaristic and moral values the organisers put forward (Holt 1981: 58). Competitive team sports as an alternative form of physical exercise and leisure activity were imported initially by British expatriates. The first French football club was founded in Le Havre as 'Le Havre Athletic Club' in 1872 by Oxford and Cambridge University men working in shipping and transit companies (Holt 1981: 65). Today the professional Le Havre team still plays in light-blue and dark-blue halves. However, just as multi-sports clubs were in vogue in France, the club was not devoted exclusively to association football – rugby football and a combination ball game were also played. Other English expatriates founded the short-lived Paris Association Football Club in 1887 as the first exclusively soccer playing club. In about 1889 some of its members transferred allegiance to the new Standard Athletic Club. In 1891 two significant soccer clubs were founded: White-Rovers (by English workers) and Gordon FC (by Scots). The first truly French association football club seems to have been Le Club français (1892), whose title implies the existence of other British or at least British-inspired clubs. One or two other of the Parisian multi-sports clubs established association football sections, including the Racing Club de France and Le Stade français, founded by pupils and old-boys from exclusive Parisian *lycées* (Holt 1981: 65–66). By 1893/94 football had a significant enough presence that clubs were allowed membership of the USFSA, a multi-sports federation presided over by Baron Pierre de Coubertin. The USFSA created the first (amateur) 'national' competition between six Parisian clubs in 1894. It was called *le championnat de France*, but unlike today's championship, it took the form of a knock-out competition.

In these early days, before the First World War, football was played by an urban social elite in imitation of its elitist amateur British roots (à la Corinthian Casuals) with an estimated 2,000 players in France by the turn of the century (Bourg 1986). A fascination for all things British – Britain was seen as the home of modernity, free trade, and sportsmanship (*le fair-play*) – encouraged the adoption of football by some of the aspiring middle classes as a way of distinguishing themselves from the working class (Lanfranchi and Wahl 1998). Football was perceived as less nationalistic than gymnastics (as seen in the club names). While Paris and the Channel ports were the first to feel the English influence, football also spread to Mediterranean ports like Marseille and Sète. British workers played amongst themselves, then the French joined in. French students who studied in Britain also helped import enthusiasm for the game, especially to Paris. The existence of a similar traditional game, *la soule*, in Brittany and Normandy helped the game spread in the north-west of France. During this period football had difficulty getting public recognition, papers tending to favour other sports. The widely read sports paper *L'Auto* generally devoted its front page to rugby. This despite the fact that by the turn of the century association football had 350 registered teams and rugby only 141. Growth was such during the *belle époque* that by 1911 about 2,000 football clubs flourished (Thomas *et al.* 1991: 108–112; Wahl 1990a: 126–129).

Football was inevitably affected by political and social events in its early history. Following the establishment of the Republican regime as Napoleon III's Empire collapsed in the debacle of the 1870 war, football could not remain immune from the major ideological divide in French society between the secularising Republican left and the Catholic traditionalist right. The Republican leader of the 1870s, Gambetta, had pointed the finger at Clericalism as the real enemy of the Republican conception of France, and the Republicans first recovered secular influence over education in the 1880s, before separating Church and State in 1905. Parallel development of football and other sports clubs on each side of the ideological divide took place, and is sometimes still visible, as for example in the market town of Auxerre in Burgundy, where alongside the D1 club A J Auxerroise is Le Stade Auxerrois, still in the regional leagues that its neighbour emerged from in the 1960s. Le Stade was founded as a secular sports club whereas A J (*Association de la jeunesse* or youth club) was the Church sports club. Some older supporters of Le Stade reportedly still refuse to set foot in the Division 1 stadium across the way (Sowden 1997: 10–11).

Four major national sports federations (governing bodies) had grown up, divided ideologically (lay or Catholic), and also distinct in that two were omnisport federations, and two solely devoted to football: Union des sociétés françaises sportives et athlétiques (USFSA), Fédération gymnastique et sportive des patronages de France (FGSPF), Ligue de football association (LFA), and Fédération cycliste et amateur de France (FCAF) (Thibert and Rethacker 1996: 34). Henri Delaunay, after a playing career with L'Etoile des Deux Lacs, became Secretary-General of the FGSPF, founded by the Catholic Church as a proselytising tool. The French Catholic clergy, seeing themselves deprived of influence over French youth by the secular educational reforms of the Republican governments of the 1880s and the organisation of a universal free State educational system from which religious teaching was banned, reacted by creating through local 'patronages de quartier' new places for young people's out-of-school or post-school activities, under the FGSPF as the national co-ordinating body. Influenced by association football's popularity with the Parisian middle classes, the patronages chose to concentrate on soccer rather than rugby in promoting a team sport, and they helped spread the game to other parts of the country (Augustin 1990: 101).

Army service also helped spread the game. In the period from the 1880s to the First World War, compulsory national service brought most young men into the army, where football became a common recreation, with inter-regimental and inter-regional games. However, in the course of the interminable Dreyfus Affair (1894–1906) attitudes to the role of the army were sharply divided both inside and outside the ranks. The army itself was torn between the traditionalist, Catholic ideology of its officer class and its Republican duties to the State. A simple incident is illustrative of the effect on soccer of these various rifts cutting through society as a whole, and reflected in disputes between the different federations vying with each other over regulating and organising football. These disputes had led to the resignation from FIFA of the lay multi-sports federation USFSA, which happened to be the only federation recognised by the French army. In February 1912, the French international team selected to meet Switzerland included a certain Triboulet, a left-winger, doing his national service in Cholet. He asked for a 36-hour pass to enable him to play. However, while the army gave him leave, they forbade him to play, since the French national team were playing under the banner of FIFA. Triboulet caught the train to Saint-Ouen in the northern Paris suburbs with the firm idea of sitting in the stand to watch the game, but no replacement had been arranged, leaving France with only ten players. Under pressure from fellow players and spectators, he was persuaded to take the field, and turned out to be the star of the match. He scored the second goal and made two others in France's 4–1 victory (a rare enough occurrence in those days). The next day a proud comrade sent a newspaper cutting to Triboulet's commanding officer, and the national hero found himself serving a week in an army gaol for disobeying orders (Thibert and Rethacker 1991: 32–33).

In the face of these divisions, in a 'climate of sectarianism' (Holt 1981: 201), Henri Delaunay of the FGSPF was instrumental in founding an umbrella body (Comité français interfédéral – CFI) bringing together the federations that were in competition with each other for running football in France. Delaunay (a known Anglophile as his nickname of 'Sir Henri' showed) had attended the English Cup Final at Crystal Palace in 1902 and was inspired to set up something similar in France, partly for its own sake, but also to unify the warring federations. However, it took until the end of the First World War to organise a national knock-out competition open to all clubs irrespective of their governing body. The success of the French Cup ('la Coupe de France') increased football's popularity and unity at the top. By overcoming ideological divergence, internal politics, and personal rivalries, it also led to the transformation of the CFI into a single French Football Federation in 1919 (Thibert and Rethacker 1991: 40). While the 'Union sacrée' (Sacred Union) had helped the nation put aside its differences to face the First World War, these social and ideological conflicts were to continue to structure political and social relations up to and beyond the Second World War, as they became complicated by and gradually overshadowed by class and political conflicts opposing capital and labour. The resolution of differences within football's governing bodies as early as 1919, then, is a tribute to the unifying power of the sport, which was becoming the nation's mass sport with its own specialist press such as the magazine *Football* founded 1910, and *France Football* in 1923 (Wahl 1989: 352).

Football, Social Class and 'Incomplete Professionalisation'

It was between the wars that football really spread to the French industrial working class, and also to the countryside, since large numbers of ordinary soldiers had come across football in the trenches (Wahl 1989: 137–139). The press carried reports of heroic footballers at the front and tributes to football's martyrs. Indeed, the French Cup was named after Charles Simon, founder-president of the CFI, killed in action in 1915 (Wahl 1989: 132–133; Pickup 1999: 30). There were press campaigns to raise money to send footballs to the troops (Wahl 1989: 134). Those who were fortunate enough to escape the carnage found that, back home, paternalistic employers started actively to encourage football as a way of structuring the lives of their workforce, while at the same time bringing physical and moral education to them. As a team sport, football seemed to fit the needs of a big factory better than individualistic activities such as gymnastics, which had lost popularity. Alsace and Lorraine had been recaptured, the War of Revenge had been won, and at such a terrible price in human lives that the belligerence of neo-military sports could be put aside with a clear conscience. The values inherent in football were thought to foster teamwork, leadership, as well as local pride – indeed pride in the factory through its team (Fridenson 1989). The history of the industrial worker tells us much about football players and spectators in France, but with certain differences from England, as will be seen in more detail in following chapters.

Jacques Marseille (1990) hypothesises that French football embodies the particular shape of the French industrial revolution of the twentieth century, industrialisation that was based on the small and medium-sized enterprise (rather than on big companies) and on the long-standing strength of the family firm – firms that have been closely linked to football clubs from small to middling-sized towns: Roubaix, Sedan, Sochaux, Reims, Saint-Etienne.

It was this industrial link to football that led to the sport's eventual professionalisation in 1932, although it was preceded by a period of shamateurism ('amateurisme marron'), and followed by a period of 'sham professionalism'. True amateurism was being eroded as regular competitive games were established. From about 1,000 clubs in 1920, the number almost quadrupled in five years, and by the later 1930s there were 6,000 (Holt 1981: 70). The number of players registered with the FFF (created in 1919) multiplied: in 1920, 30,000; 1926, 100,000; 1931, 130,000. Paying spectators increased correspondingly: 10,000 at the 1919 Cup Final, 30,000 in 1928 (Lanfranchi and Wahl 1998). As spectator interest grew, especially through the French Cup competition, certain club directors saw an opportunity for financial or social gains to be made, and a market for players (i.e. transfers) came into existence. First, some players' transport expenses were reimbursed, and kit was provided free. Well-paid or undemanding jobs were found in the club chairman's company. This attracted moral condemnation from those who frowned on the transformation of sport as practice into sport as entertainment or spectacle. The Federation tried to ban transfers by imposing a year's exclusion from first XI's for those who moved club, but then exceptions to this rule became the majority of cases. The idea of transfer fees was raised to compensate clubs losing players. Supporters of professionalism argued that it would help improve the standards of French football and presented the issue as a battle for the modernisation of the sport. By the time the FFF agreed to set up a committee to look at the issue in 1929, professional leagues existed not only in England and Scotland but also in Czechoslovakia, Austria and Hungary, and Italy had established a 'non-amateur' player status. Gabriel Hanot, and a fellow journalist named Gambardella, argued not for a fully professional league as in England but for a mix of professional and amateur players within clubs belonging to a national league. The FFF eventually found its hand forced by the wealthy automobile industrialist Jean-Pierre Peugeot, who, imitating Agnelli at Fiat, invested heavily in his local team Sochaux and merged it with AS Montbéliard, making it openly professional. In a challenge to the governing body of the sport, he invited the eight teams most in favour of change to compete in his Coupe Sochaux. The FFF, in order not to lose control of the sport, accepted professional player status, while retaining the amateur status of clubs; that is, they were still to be run as non-profit-making associations with unpaid officials. Thus the first professional championship was able to start with the FFF's blessing in autumn 1932 with 20 clubs playing in two geographically divided groups of ten. By the 1933/34 season there were 35 professional clubs, divided into a First Division (14 clubs), a Second Division (North) and a Second Division (South) (reflecting the English system – except that in the latter it was the Third Division that was divided on regional lines).

This decision did not create a proper profession overnight. Clubs kept control of players, imposing a maximum wage, powers of suspension, and a contract that was a retain-and-transfer system for the playing life of the employee (*le contrat à vie*). Importantly, in differentiating the French and English situations, 'professional' players in France could keep another paid activity, thus enabling students and other 'semi-professionals' (as we might now call them) to stay in the game. Professional football was not seen as an exclusively working-class profession as in England – nor did it move in that direction. Lanfranchi and Wahl (1998) give the example of the 1934 championship winning team of Sète that included players listed as: literature graduate, law student, two medical students, alongside an Algerian Arab labourer and a Parisian jeweller. All had signed professional forms but had another regular activity. Some professional soldiers also played for pro teams. In the mining town of Alès, miners tended to choose the best amateur clubs that could get them stable office jobs rather than opting for professional status. Even as late as the 1950s Raymond Kopa recalled that he had seen professional football as a way of getting himself a training as an electrician to avoid going underground in the mine, and had never contemplated being able to devote himself entirely to football. Lanfranchi and Wahl comment that the situation constitutes a French exception in a sport that had seen the English middle classes voluntarily exclude themselves from a sport they saw as the 'people's game' as soon as it turned professional. However, that had been half-a-century before, and social class differences were lessening in 1930s France. There was now a less impermeable barrier between the workers and the middle class, especially in France where there were fewer (and smaller) industrial conurbations, and no equivalent to the homogeneous working-class communities of the size of Birmingham or Manchester.

Already at this time foreign players were imported into French football, which has been cosmopolitan since its inception. English and Scottish imports were especially popular for their robust game, and passing and heading abilities. A centre-half, Jock McGowan (Olympique lillois, 1932), is described as 'built like a wardrobe, broad, powerful, as strong as an ox, solid on his bow legs and using beer *à gogo* as his training regime'. Those coming towards the end of their career often tried it for a year, but adapted with difficulty being unable to integrate because of problems of language and being from a different social and cultural background. A certain Jack Trees's contract was torn-up by his club when he 'contracted a malady that had nothing to do with football'. Hungarians and Austrians had more success.

Studies by Faure and Suaud (1994b) and Lanfranchi and Wahl (1998) use the term 'incomplete professionalisation' to describe the situation. Clubs (chairmen and directors) and players, as well as the Federation (national administrators of the game), acted out an amateur model of football, refusing ('obstinately', add Lanfranchi and Wahl) to apply fully the rules of the free market to football. They use the term 'dilettantism' and 'improvisation' to describe pre-war relations between the stakeholders. Football was seen as 'pin money' and neither players nor directors generally were fully committed to the sport. This is confirmed by the use of the term 'professionnalisme marron' (sham professionalism) by one player of the time. It was not uncommon for professional clubs to revert back to their amateur status after two or three years as professional. The players may have turned professional, but the clubs had stayed amateur and had been run as such. Only a small number of wealthy industrialists had committed themselves to clubs. Other club chairmen were local notables looking to improve their local celebrity and symbolic capital through sport. Only Sochaux had a full-time 'directeur sportif' in charge of recruitment of players.

Lanfranchi and Wahl (1998) interpret the process of professionalisation in France as follows:

> Whereas in England or Austria, professionalisation emerged out of the conjunction of a strong demand by urban populations for sporting entertainment and the industrialists' plan to control the masses, in France the introduction of a professional league was a response to the desire of those who ran football to regulate the market and control players' wages. It was not to make profits, that was anyway forbidden by the law of association [under which the clubs were run]. (Lanfranchi and Wahl 1998: 322)

All this suggests that French football professionalised around amateur values. None of its stakeholders, whether players, clubs or governing bodies, applied business logic to the sport; rather they applied family values. There emerged from the change a hybrid system significantly different from the models being set in place elsewhere in Europe.

The Set-back of the Second World War: the Ideological Cul-de-sac of the Vichy Years

General mobilisation in the autumn of 1939, the rapid defeat of France in the spring of 1940, occupation by German troops, the symbolic handshake between Hitler and the new Head of State Marshal Pétain that introduced the collaborationist regime, the loss – again – of Alsace-Lorraine and the division of the rest of France into Occupied Zone (northern half plus the western seaboard) and so-called Free Zone – all this was bound severely to disrupt the recently formed professional league. The ideology of Pétain's Vichy regime was anti-Republican, authoritarian, traditionalist, corporatist, and founded on a feeling of betrayal and national decline under the preceding Republican regime and especially under the socialist-led government of the Popular Front (1936–38). Nostalgia for a golden age of pre-urban France, where the strongest values were those derived from provincial France and 'la terre' (the soil), saw the national slogan 'Liberty, Equality, Fraternity' replaced by 'Travail, famille, patrie' (Work, Family, Motherland). The regime's determination to effect a 'national revolution' in all areas of French life did not bode well for the 'business' of professional football.

The domestic competition had already been inevitably affected during the 1939/40 season, not least by loss of players and spectators following army call-up. Then, under direction from the Vichy government, the national competition was divided into three (later two) zones. Travel was not easy in the Occupied Zone, but separate championships were contested annually in the *zone Nord* and the *zone Sud*. A national perspective was retained by having *la Coupe* (the French Cup), which, until the Liberation, reverted to its original name, the *Coupe Charles Simon*, contested by the winners of the two respective zones at Colombes (in the Paris region). Standards of play reputedly fell through loss of players and general disruption.

Vichy attempted to reform the whole of sport. Its Commissariat général à l'éducation nationale et aux sports went back to the old idea of the need to use regimented gymnastic training to develop the physical fitness and moral fibre of the country's youth. The Commissariat required footballers 'to practise a trade outside football', effectively abolishing professionalism. The tennis star Jean Borotra, new *haut-commissaire aux Sports* (High Commissioner for Sport), developed a rationale for the new role for sport in French society that had echoes of the elitism and purposeful idealism of Coubertin: it was based on the idea that playing sport was morally superior to watching it for the purposes of entertainment. The logical consequence of this sport-for-all policy was amateurism. Pickup (1999: 33) quotes Borotra as shunning professionalism 'because it was associated with financial gain, whereas sport should be "chivalrous and disinterested"'. Borotra believed that shamateurism was 'the principal cause of the moral weakness noted in recent years in some sporting circles and of the disrepute into which certain sports had fallen'.

Apart from ideologically inspired policies, there were other rather gratuitous changes such as reducing playing-time to 80 minutes (it returned to 90 minutes in 1942 after Borotra's departure). Such decrees had one significant consequence for the continuity of French football's governing bodies after the Liberation: the resignation of Jules Rimet as President of the French Football Federation (Pickup 1999: 34). This will certainly have helped French football and its administrative organs to recover from the collaborationist period and indeed escape the sometimes brutal 'épuration' (literally 'cleansing' of collaborators) at the Liberation, since Rimet's resignation signalled a refusal to collaborate.

Vichy's attempts to outlaw professionalism went through various stages. A form of professional status was reintroduced in 1942, but hedged around with various conditions: no transfers were allowed; professionals had to play for the club they were registered with before the war; and no club could have more than seven professionals on their books. Delaunay *et al.*'s history of French football interprets the compulsory fielding of four (inevitably local) amateur players by clubs as a desire to create genuinely 'regional clubs' (Pickup 1999: 34). In 1943 the High Commissioner decreed that all clubs would have amateur status, whilst professional players would become State civil servants (*fonctionnaires d'Etat*). Further, they would play for one of 16 federal teams, each representing a region. Pickup says these federal teams did allow a degree of continuity for professional football and were a haven for those players who were able to avoid deportation to Germany through the *Service du travail obligatoire* (STO), the compulsory labour scheme which operated while France was occupied. However, the French international Fred Aston recalls that, playing during the Occupation for the Paris Capitale team, he and other former professionals were given civil-servant status and were sent into schools to justify their pay, and indeed to prevent them from being sent to Germany under the STO (Brochen 2001c: 17). Vichy's radical reform never really became bedded in. Initially the federal teams were scarcely 'regional' in character, the federal competition was not properly financed, and the competition was interrupted by the advancing allied forces that gradually liberated France in the course of the summer and autumn of 1944 (Pickup 1999: 34).

The general desire of the Resistance-inspired governments that replaced Vichy to sweep away the dead-end of Pétainism allowed French football to return reasonably speedily to its former shape, especially as there had in fact been little change of personnel in the running of the clubs; nor was there any huge 'épuration' (Wahl 1989). By the end of 1944, a national championship was organised for 24 clubs split into two groups, one North and one South (transport infrastructures were inevitably in disrepair). It took until the 1946/47 season to come back to one national First Division of 20 clubs. There was understandably a feeling of starting again to build professional football that had undergone an incomplete (or even false) professionalisation only shortly before the interruption of the war and was therefore in a stage of development that lagged even further behind that in Britain.

Sport, Freedom of Association and Public Service Values

Given the initial refusal to adopt business values in the early years of professionalisation and the war's interruption of the professional system, an essential component of French football is its link to the voluntary sector, municipal life and participatory democracy. Post-war the State has guaranteed the public service values that pervade sport in France by adding regulatory and funding frameworks that tie grass-roots and elite sport together – ties that recent developments in the commercialisation of sport are threatening to put asunder.

We have seen how French clubs professionalised in the 1930s, very late compared to Britain, and only half-heartedly, whereas Newton Heath – later to change their name to Manchester United – was paying its players legally by 1885. Most English clubs formed themselves into limited companies in the nineteenth century to protect their founders from financial liability from any club debts, and, although under FA rules they were not able to be used as tradable speculative companies, they were none the less businesses from the start (Conn 1997: 32). French clubs on the other hand have developed under the structures of a very French institution, the so-called 'association 1901' or 'association à but non lucratif' (non-profit-making association). The law of 1901, establishing the freedom of association, was seen at the time in France as a major advance in democratic rights. For the first time in its history the French State authorised any group of citizens to come together legally to undertake a common activity of their choice. At the height of the secularisation and Republicanisation of French civil society, the measure was partly to make it easier for secular and Republican groups to come together in order to challenge the grip of the religious congregations on social activity (Collinot 1997: 4).

In France, in the early century when sports clubs were mushrooming, the 1901 law was the natural statute under which to create small-town amateur clubs like the Association de la Jeunesse auxerroise sports club in 1905. When such clubs turned professional, the club's officers found that the 1901 law provided all the necessary legal protection for club officials, while allowing them to trade on behalf of the club, and pay employees. In the spirit of non-profit-making, whether religious or secular, and of the sporting ethic inherited from Coubertin and the tradition of *bénévolat* (voluntary work by local notables deriving social status from time invested in the service of local sport), it was unknown for the *Société anonyme* (limited company) model to be used for professional clubs. The 1901 law guaranteed that, in principle, the association's officers (President, Secretary, Treasurer, and other executive committee members) did not profit personally or even get paid, that no dividends were distributed to members, and that the club was run according to open democratic principles, meaning all club officers and committee members were subject to election by club members. Organisation of a football club was, then, essentially unpaid voluntary work, and therefore community based and public-spirited.

The 1901 law also protects club members and the public by imposing a statutory duty on such an association to respect health and safety regulations, employment law and so on. If it is found they infringe any of these rules they can be closed down (Miège 1993: 48). Of France's 730,000 associations active in 2002, 170,000 were sports clubs, counting about 13 million playing members (French Sports Ministry website). At the point of the sport's professionalisation, 30 years of voluntary public service in running football clubs on this basis was bound to militate against adopting a private business ethos. Today's modernisers would say the same thing in a slightly different way: that the amateur ethos of French football club structures based on the Association 1901 structure (that turned out to be highly resistant to true professionalisation) has slowed the development of the professional game.

Local Municipal Involvement

Another aspect of public sector involvement in football resides in the financial support provided for local teams by municipalities. Town councils have seen it as part of their public mission to subsidise sports activity. Local mayors have also seen the political capital to be made out of supporting the town's team. This remains the case today: even at D1 level, French football clubs are still supported financially by local authorities through the 'subventions' system which in the season 2000/01 represented on average 4 per cent of D1 clubs' income and 15 per cent for D2 clubs (Grandemange and Cazali 2002). Even Paris Saint-Germain, the richest club, was nervous about the possible effect on their municipal subsidy of the change of the Paris mayor following the 2001 municipal elections, which saw, for the first time, a left-wing majority on the Paris City Council.

This sense of public mission and local political involvement extends to French professional clubs making use of the local municipal stadium, although a governmental decree clarifying the law on this in 2001 means that professional clubs now have to be charged a realistic rent for its use (Lagarde 2002: 4). With the single exception of that of AJA, grounds still remain the property of municipalities who are required to pay for maintenance and reconstruction. Funding for the upgrading and redevelopment of the ten World Cup venues in 1998 came from a mixture of private and public sources, but the football clubs themselves (who are essentially tenants) did not have to pay even a symbolic franc (see Chapter 3).

A sense of community and a sense of local public involvement have been strong and enduring features of French football, which has become a key tool in local politics, used, sometimes corruptly (see Chapter 8), by local political figures to further their local and national careers. The fate of the local football club can often be an election issue. The extent of a city's involvement can be gauged from the example of Marseille, where the municipality used to give 5 million francs subsidy per year to OM and charge nothing for the use by the club of the municipal stadium (Samson 2000). This gives the mayor significant influence within the club. The mayor, plus his number two, their hospitality guests, and various councillors are always to be seen in the Presidential Box at home matches, alongside the club's top officials. In one of the darker moments of OM's 2000/01 season, with both relegation and municipal elections looming, Mayor Gaudin publicly commented that the club's major shareholder, Robert Louis-Dreyfus, would have to get more directly involved in running the club. The plight of the club was worrying, especially since the mayor had been influential in bringing Louis-Dreyfus to OM in the first place, after the downfall of Bernard Tapie. The municipality seems to have most direct influence on the non-professional side of the club. The non-profit-making association (OM Association) that exists alongside the professional SAOS to run the amateur and youth sides of OM is chaired by a close friend of the mayor, under the influence of the mayor's number two R. Muselier. It receives 5 million francs annually from the city council and 3 million from the Conseil général (the local county council) to look after a few hundred amateur players. This compares very favourably with a municipal grant of 180,000 francs per year to the local Post Office sporting club that has 7,000 members. The city takes OM much more seriously, then, than its other local sports clubs and presumably expects to exercise influence in proportion. In this respect *Le Monde* has commented that the dream of the top people in the Mairie is to run the club (Samson 2000).

Professional football in general is still reliant on municipal subsidies, and this aspect of the 'French exception' has come into conflict with European developments and France's wider national ambitions to create 'a strong France in an independent Europe', as French clubs, essentially non-profit-making organisations operating within the context of high taxation and exceptionally high social costs falling on all French employers, have come to terms with the European Single Market and the commercial realities of European competition law, as expressed in the Bosman ruling. Sports federations and sports clubs can be considered as businesses if they undertake economic or commercial activity and so come under European competition law (Treaty of Rome articles 85–86 guaranteeing the free working of competition and the raising of all barriers to trade on the internal market [Miège 1996: 87]).

The right-wing free-market Balladur government of 1993–95, in the bluff shape of Minister Charles Pasqua, recognised that local authority subventions to professional clubs were illegal, more particularly for clubs that were trading commercially in the form of SAOS (Société anonyme à objet sportif) or SEMS (Société d'économie mixte sportive) (therefore '*à but lucratif*'). Henceforward they could only get sponsorship from French regional authorities (Echégut 1994: 21). Maximum allowable town hall support for D1 clubs in 1996/97 was 30 per cent of budget, in 1997/98 20 per cent, and in 1998/99 10 per cent (Miège 1996: 94–95; Bayeux 1996: 103–104). First division clubs had long derived over 15 per cent of their income from local authorities, and Second Division clubs over one-third. Martigues (who were to be relegated from D1 in 1996) relied on the town for half of their budget (van Kote 1994). Local authority subventions have been considered by towns to be part of their image promotion and a reinforcement of their local identity, an instrument for attracting inward investment. Now it was becoming seen by Brussels as a means of discrimination through illegal public subsidies destroying fair competition, coming under article 92 of the Treaty of Rome which bans help given by states or public authorities where this creates unjustified competitive advantage. Whereas the European Commission and the European Court had been indulgent towards sport on this matter, the European Parliament has taken a harder line.

The 1984 law has been modified by a further article in August 1994 (Balladur government) and a decree of 24 January 1996 (Juppé government) gradually phasing out subsidies from town halls to clubs (whether SAOS, SEMS, or *Associations à statuts renforcés*), with a complete ban having been envisaged by the end of 1999. However, the Sports Minister of the left-wing government (1997/2002), Madame Buffet, managed to delay the implementation of this. She attempted, however, to define the areas in which such support can be given and tried to tighten accountability structures. Her sports reform bill of 2000 attempted to protect clubs' municipal subsidies. This reflects her own and the government's stronger ideological attachment to public service values and public involvement in local life. A governmental decree of 2001 set out that local authority subsidies to professional clubs could only be in support of activities of 'general [public] interest' and up to a ceiling of 2.3 million euros per club per year. This mainly concerns the coaching and educational side of the club's youth academy. All such subsidy needs to be rigorously accounted for. Regarding municipal services to a club, these have a ceiling of 1.6 million euros per season or 30 per cent of income. This can be for buying advertising space, use of a club's logo as part of the town or region's public relations activities, and match tickets that are given out free to local amateur clubs or schools or for other hospitality purposes. The local authority cannot guarantee loans, nor offer help from members of staff paid by the town hall etc., and can no longer give the professional club (as opposed to its association) free use of the municipal stadium, but must charge a rent (Grandemange and Cazali 2002).

Sport as a Public Service Needing Republican Regulation

French institutional and legal structures, then, traditionally reflect a view of sporting activity as part of the public service mission of the State and of local authorities. The ethos of the Republic is that the State is responsible for the improvement of the general well-being of its citizens and for efforts to integrate all citizens into the nation ('la République une et indivisible'). As Mignon (2000: 236) points out, a law of 1920 obliges municipalities to offer facilities for sporting recreation. This notion of sport and recreation being a Republican public service mission may also be traced back to Coubertin's Olympic ideal (taking part is more important than winning), seeing sport as a philosophical and ethical approach to life, 'promoting the development of the physical and moral qualities that are the basics of sport', and 'through sport, educating young people in a spirit of better mutual understanding and friendship, thus contributing to the building of a better and more peaceful world' (Miège 1993: 9). It has also been reinforced by the idealistic, socially progressive governments of the Popular Front (1936) and of the Liberation (1944), when much was done to widen access to leisure activities and sport.

French theorists have identified a more general typological split between northern and southern European nations in their approach to State–sport relations (Miège 1993: 99). Indeed, France may be seen as the archetypal example of the Latin model (with Italy as the exception that proves the rule). The northern liberal model, as in Great Britain, treats sport as essentially dependent on individual initiative, and its organisation and regulation are left to national federations as the sports' governing bodies. This extends to such important matters as the building and financing of a national stadium, even if they are patently failing to do this. British sports organisations appear totally independent of the State, which merely ensures the material conditions needed to allow a given sport to prosper through public grants or other form of help in building infrastructure and facilities. Public investment in the organisation of Euro 96, the European Nations Cup held in England in 1996 (admittedly a smaller event than the World Cup), was limited to £100,000. The French government subsidised the World Cup by the equivalent of £190 million. In Britain, government has even handed over the responsibility for awarding grants to sports clubs and associations to a non-governmental organisation, the National Lottery. In France funding is allocated by a public body, the FNDS (Fonds national pour le développement du sport – National Fund for Sports Development), some of whose money comes from the Loto sportif (State-run football pools) and the Loterie nationale (National Lottery), both of which are public bodies. In the southern European interventionist model the promotion and development of sport are seen as public services, for which the State takes some degree of responsibility. Where the State does not take direct responsibility for organising or regulating a given sport, the sports authority concerned is at least under some degree of public control (Miège 1996: 10–11, 1993: 99). In France a mechanism of official recognition (*agrément*) by the Sport Ministry allows, for instance, the imposition of model statutes on sports governing bodies to ensure democratic functioning and accountability (Miège 1993: 48). This means having an Annual General Meeting of club members who approve the annual budget (or not), and electing a management committee for four years that cannot be paid and which elects an executive. Clubs therefore have wide representation, and freedom of opinion is ensured within the club, which must operate ethically with no illegal discrimination (Miège 1993: 48).

In return for this State 'tutelage' and official recognition of the sport's public service mission as being of 'public utility', a sporting body or affiliated club becomes eligible for official grant aid, in proportion to their number of members (Mignon 2000: 237). The Ministry delegates to the French Football Federation (FFF – equivalent to the English FA) the monopoly of organisation, regulation and representation of football in France. In turn the FFF delegates the right to organise a professional league to the LFP. Whereas for the first four decades of the league the professional clubs were separated from the amateur game, since the early 1970s the professional league has been even more closely linked into the nation-wide practice of football by a pyramidal system of promotion and relegation involving national divisions (semi-professional in Division 3) down through the amateur regional and local district divisions. The tutelage exercised by the State is real and allows supervision of the legality and fairness of a federation's decisions, for example in respect of disciplinary measures. The State can in theory withdraw official approval of the Federation's position as the governing body of football, since the FFF's authority has simply been delegated by the State on behalf of the nation's citizens. Although the French State is becoming more interventionist as legal complexities increase, it systematically consults the French Olympic Committee (CNOSF), the highest sports governing body in France, on policy (Miège 1996: 18–19).

The system may not work perfectly, as a recent parliamentary report (the Asensi report – see Potet 2000a) pointed out. However, the State's interest in ensuring democratic functioning and accountability in sport is shown by its desire, through the Asensi report, to expose where it is falling down in practice – which is often at the level of the national federation. The report found a lack of transparency, self-perpetuation in terms of social class amongst the leading officials, and a lack of opposition voices on national committees. It remains to be seen whether the political will is there to bring reform to the top of the political agenda.

Of Western European countries, France has the strongest State intervention in sport. Comparisons established by the Council of Europe in 1993 found that France was the top of the European league for public finance for sport as a percentage of the whole of sports spending, and spending from the central State budget was ten times that of the UK (Table 2.1). The French Republican State justifies this level of intervention in terms of the need to 'ensure the general interest of sport prevails over the multitude of private interests that traverse it' (Miège 1993: 68).

Table 2.1 *National Spending on Sport (1993), in Millions of Dollars*

	State budget	Local authorities	Public finance as % of GDP	Private firms	House-holds	Betting pools, loto etc.	Public finance as % of whole
Germany	119.8	5,767.9	0.35	828.3	14,954.3	190.2	27.2
UK	132.1	2,486.8	0.24	835.8	13,035.8	5,366.0	15.9
France	1,333.0	1,334.5	0.42	665.1	8,542.6	6,499.5	38.1

Source: Council of Europe in Vuori *et al.* (1997: 2).

There are particular reasons for the French State's support for sport. After the Second World War, State and government took an increasing interest in sport, both in terms of developing an elite of competitors (seen as a necessary condition for figuring honourably in international competitions), and in terms of encouraging sport for all (see Dine 1997b, 1998b). The latter corresponded to powerful aspirations on the part of the centre-left governments emerging from the Resistance movement to spread access to leisure activities to the whole population (democratisation) and improve the nation's health and fitness. Through the ordinances and laws of 28 August 1945, 25 October 1975 and 16 July 1984, the State has therefore gradually spread its authority over an area of activity that had previously been run by private non-profit-making associations. The collaborationist Vichy regime started the State's intervention in French sport with its Sports Charter (December 1940). After the Liberation of France, the federations never regained their autonomy. The 1945 Act introduced the notion of delegation of power from the State to federations and sporting groups. The 1975 and 1984 laws further structured relations by recognising the power of the federations to regulate their own sport, under the tutelage of the Minister, and by imposing certain types of common statutes on them, while recognising the federations' 'mission de service public' (public service mission).

Since the decentralisation laws of 1982 there has also been more intervention in sport at the local and regional levels. Two types of organisational structure now exist in parallel: firstly, sporting institutions themselves (sports clubs, departmental and regional committees, and national federations, hierarchically structured, and democratically accountable), and, secondly, State administrative structures dependent on the Ministry for Sport, again at departmental, regional and national level. See Chapter 5 on the French coaching system, which brings the two sets of structures together.

Organising the World Game: France and the International Politics of Football

As regards the development of an elite of competitors to represent the nation, and to use sport more generally as an instrument of public policy for national aggrandisement, President de Gaulle is often credited with being hugely influential in setting the tone and in laying down infrastructures in a strategic way. He was appalled at the poor performance of French competitors in the 1960 Olympic Games and resolved to do something about it. However, Dine (1998b), in his analysis of the role of the State in French sport in the post-war period, demonstrates how Gaullist policies borrowed heavily from structures set up under Vichy and that French politics and sport have been intertwined for far longer than the period of the Fifth Republic. He does confirm that since 1960 sport has come increasingly to be seen as an instrument for maintaining and increasing French grandeur. Contrasting the success of French competitors at the Atlanta Olympics of 1996 with France's failure in Rome in 1960, his analysis underlines the success of the policy of associating international sporting events with politics, describing how, particularly during the Fifth Republic, the State has organised and funded 'une France qui gagne', in a peculiarly French approach to sport via State management ('l'Etat gestionnaire'), a 'middle way' between State control typified by former Eastern-bloc countries and the 'organisational and financial autonomy (and, increasingly, the entrepreneurialism) characteristic of the United States and Great Britain' (Dine 1998b: 310).

Hosting the World Cup finals in 1998, heavily subsidised by the State and the host cities (see Dauncey and Hare 1999b), reflected not only a French tradition of public commitment to sport at home but also an equally important use of sporting events for wider political purposes. In football, despite the fact that up to then French success at European club and international levels had been somewhat muted, France's long commitment to the world game also owes much to the tradition of individual unpaid enthusiasts in the French sporting federations and clubs. In particular, a small number of prominent administrators have worked enthusiastically to set up international structures to govern football and thereby integrate French football into the wider world game. Equally important, but perhaps with motives closer to home, some prominent sports journalists have also played important roles in organising international competitions.

Over the years, French administrators have been at the heart of moves to give an international dimension to football. FIFA, the World Cup, and various European competitions owe their existence to French initiatives. In 1904, in the teeth of English opposition, a world governing body, FIFA, was created on the initiative of French and Dutch representatives. The then President of the French Football Federation, Jules Rimet, was elected as FIFA President in 1920. The concept of a World Cup competition was the brain-child of Henri Delaunay, secretary of the FFF, and Rimet, whose name was borne by the original trophy. France was one of the early hosts when it hosted the third World Cup finals in 1938 (see Sinet 2002).

The idea of a European club competition came from Gabriel Hanot, editor of the famous French sports daily *L'Equipe*. After English champions Wolves had beaten Moscow Spartak and Hungarian Champions Honved in 1954, the *Daily Mail* claimed that they were world club champions. The editor of *L'Equipe* was sceptical and proposed a more structured way of deciding Europe's top club. UEFA had only just come into existence and refused initially to take responsibility for organising a competition. So *L'Equipe* contacted the relevant clubs, rules were agreed and FIFA authorised it. UEFA agreed to organise it from September 1955 onwards, once Paris had offered a venue for the final, which brought together the French champions Reims and Real Madrid.

The European Nations Championship is another major international competition owed to the work of a Frenchman, Henri Delaunay, who, sadly, did not live to see the first finals take place, again in France, in 1960. France hosted the finals a second time in 1984.

Football's sixteenth World Cup finals were of course held in France in 1998. Decisions about the World Cup, from the highest level of the State, for example in choice of site for the new national stadium, through the multilateral relations linking the State to the Organising Committee (CFO), the FFF, and the clubs and the host towns, followed the tradition of the way sport in France, whether participatory or spectator sport, has been seen as a matter of public interest and as a legitimate concern of the public authorities since the Popular Front of 1936. The strongly presidentialist regime of the Fifth Republic has continued a tradition of using a range of sporting and other cultural manifestations as instruments of world politics, to compensate for France's relative lack of military or economic power, even into the current period when French economic, industrial and technological power is far greater in world terms than in 1960. French football administrators like Rimet and Delaunay, following in the footsteps of the founding father of the Olympic movement, Coubertin, have been among the most influential visionaries of football as a world game. Importantly, they helped move football beyond the national context to internationalise the playing and governance of the game, at times when its English inventors, with an insularity that went wider than the sporting domain, were reticent about the internationalisation of football and reluctant to become involved at the heart of European or world football until there was no alternative and most decisions were irreversible.

Conclusion

Football was imported into France quite late from England and Scotland by the middle classes, as a reaction against the regimented and militaristic gymnastics promoted by the new republican regime of the late nineteenth century. The sport spread geographically across the nation in the early twentieth century, particularly in the period of the Great War. The adoption of football as France's national sport in the inter-war period has echoes of the way working-class communities elsewhere in Europe (but earlier) forged leisure habits and a local identity around the sport. None the less, compared to Britain, French football's development took place on a much smaller scale and with a much stronger and more persistent middle-class input, both on the playing side and in its organisational structures. This reflected, firstly, the different scale and timing of the French industrial revolution and its consequent urban geography. Secondly, dominant social values were at stake. In Britain, football is essentially dependent on individual initiative and its organisation and regulation are left to autonomous bodies which operate independently of the State. British professional football clubs are run as businesses outside of local government control, they are generally proprietors of their own grounds and are free to enter the stock market as public limited companies. On the other hand, French football's regulatory system and its governing bodies and clubs have been shaped by the French State's concept of the public service mission and voluntary community service and civic values, and by Republican and democratic values, and centralist interventionism, as opposed to laissez-faire individualism.

This ethos is now very much in tension with current trends in the global sport-media complex. As deregulation has been imposed on more and more sectors of social life, often in the name of 'modernisation', there has been local French resistance to this creation of a global marketplace. However, there has been growing pressure for France to harmonise its practices regarding professional sport with the rest of the European Union. In summer 2000, backed by the financially stronger clubs, the French League management committee promised – as in 1932, in the name of modernisation – rapid alignment of the structures of French football with their European neighbours. By this they meant greater commercialisation and the transformation of the major club structures into limited companies quotable on the French Stock Exchange (Caffin 2000; Psenny 2000, Brochen 2000). As football moved into the twenty-first century and issues of doping and regulation of players' contracts within EU employment legislation require European-wide not to say global solutions, the French Sports Minister Mme Buffet, for her part, attempted to take the lead in defending 'l'exception sportive', arguing that free-market business values cannot be allowed to destroy traditional sporting values. Football as a world game, in its organisational structures, its regulation, and its international competitions, then, owes much to France, and French football has consistently looked outwards and seen itself as a part of a wider sporting world, as well as seeing football as part of the wider social and political context.

3

Towns and Cities: a Socio-economic Geography of French Football Clubs

This chapter looks at the socio-economic geography of football as reflected both in its development into a national game and its promotion of local and regional identity through the growth of professional clubs, particularly in small industrial towns, but more recently in France's handful of big cities. The special case of Paris, with its periods as a footballing desert, will deserve a separate section.

The Emergence of a National Game based in Small Industrial Towns

Jacques Marseille (1990) has argued that the geography of French football reflects the French industrial revolution of the twentieth century. Patrick Mignon (1998), too, argues that the aspects which characterise French football culture are attributable to the slow development of cities and urban cultures in France. French peasant society resisted industrialisation far longer than in England, and this has left its mark on the structure of French football and its clubs. Unlike Britain, there were no enclosures which drove people off the land and into cities at the end of the eighteenth century. There were never the real equivalent of huge nineteenth-century industrial cities like Birmingham, Liverpool, Sheffield and Manchester or Glasgow where football represented the core of social life for working men and where watching and talking about the local professional team was handed down from generation to generation as part of young people's socialisation into the adult world. In France the industrial revolution of the nineteenth century was not a massive upheaval of population and a spawning of major new cities. Rather than concerning the whole country, it affected pockets of population, mainly in the north around Lille (including Roubaix, Tourcoing, and Lens), the north-east (Alsace-Lorraine – Strasbourg, Metz, Nancy), the centre and south-east (e.g. Saint-Etienne, and the Lyon area), around the Marseille conurbation, and the Paris region. It was also more gradual, rather than quickly changing the balance of power between town and country. The rural exodus did not really accelerate until the 1950s and the real modernisation of France was effected only in the post-Second World War period of economic growth up to the 1970s. There was still a third of French workers employed in agriculture in the late 1930s.

A further difference between France and Britain is that the working-class districts in cities were less deeply rooted and more heterogeneous than in Britain. The growth of big towns in France was less uniquely linked to industrial development. In cities like Lyon and Paris the industrial working class constituted only part of the working population, many of whom were still employed in small workshops and were distributed across the conurbation, mingling with other social groups, so that the large urban centres that did exist were not uniformly made up of the industrial working class On the other hand, industrialisation elsewhere spawned a number of scattered small, one-industry towns. Shortage of manpower here had meant that employers, as far back as the mid-nineteenth century, encouraged a contingent of worker peasants into the factories as well as recruiting immigrant workers for the hardest jobs. This, plus a paternalistic management style in heavy industry, favoured a particular type of working-class environment, the 'ville-usine', a one-factory town, more the size of a large village indeed. In this context, football teams having the support of a big factory infrastructure began to have an advantage over the more middle-class, big-city sports clubs that were less tightly organised. All the local talent was channelled into such factory or company clubs, as the huge majority of the small town population was made up of industrial workers and no other leisure activities were available. This again was a contrast to the situation in Paris. Individuals like Raymond Kopa, after he had lost two fingers in an industrial accident, saw football as a potential escape from the mine and felt that status acquired from local soccer would help him get an apprenticeship and an electrician's job (Beaud and Noiriel 1990: 83–87). Also, large tracts of France were relatively untouched by industrialisation, in particular the south-west. Compared to Britain, then, a different relationship between the development of professional football clubs and urban geography was inevitable in France.

By the time of the expansion of football in the 1920s (a quadrupling of registered players and a tripling of spectators) and the run-up to profession-alisation, the geography of football reflected the new economic geography of industrial France. The distribution of clubs across numerous small or medium-sized towns worked against the growth of large urban support such as existed in Britain and Italy. French industrialisation was initially based not on the rapid development of big companies but on the small and medium-sized family-run firm. Such firms have been closely linked to football clubs in small to medium-sized towns, as in the north Lille, Roubaix and Tourcoing, in the east Sedan, Sochaux, Reims, in the south-east Saint-Etienne (Marseille 1990: 72). During this period that saw the beginnings of football's adoption by the masses, the biggest clubs were often directed by industrialists and businessmen whose names remain associated with the success of their teams or with the stadiums: a brewer from Lille, Jooris, played a key role at the head of LOSC; the textile magnate Prouvost was president of FC Roubaix; the Laurant brothers, heads of a small drapery firm, ran Sedan; the wealthy grain merchant Le Cesne directed Olympique de Marseille from 1909 to 1922. These sponsors provided equipment, dealt with transfers and bonuses (illicit until professionalisation in 1932) and often gave clubs a stadium, responsibility for which was often taken over by the municipalities during the 1920s, when the teams became symbols of the whole town and not just of its founding firm (Bromberger *et al.* 1995: 180–181). In the professional era, the best-known examples of successful clubs that owe their origins to this type of environment are FC Sochaux-Montbéliard and AS Saint-Etienne. The latter was founded in 1919 by the Guichard family, owners of a large grocery chain (now the Casino hypermarket chain) based in Saint-Etienne and still sponsored by the Guichard family. FC Sochaux was run by the town's main employer, the motor magnate Jean-Pierre Peugeot, who created a factory-sponsored team that became openly professional before regulations permitted, taking it from the Second Division of the regional Burgundy League in 1929 to become national professional champions in 1935. Clubs from small towns like these were highly dependent on a wealthy local industrialist who acted as sponsor. The attractiveness of such a club to players was obvious: as cup winners in 1937 each Sochaux player received a Peugeot coupé 201 as a bonus (Wahl 1989: 284). With the decline of industry it is no coincidence that Sochaux and Saint-Etienne have yo-yoed between Division 1 and Division 2 since the 1990s. Elsewhere, in non-industrial France, in market towns like Auxerre in Burgundy or Guingamp (Brittany), local notables, often with political ambitions, sought to promote themselves through football.

The paternalism of such bosses was often criticised by inter-war trade unions. Wahl (1989: 189) quotes a union leader: 'Capitalist football's exploitative bosses excite their workers on the pitch just as they push them to increase their work rates in their factories.' Unions also worried about the transformation of the company clubs into town clubs when the FFF was formed in 1919, which they saw as diluting class consciousness as players from different social classes came together in the same team (Bromberger *et al.* 1995: 182). Company owners certainly expected football to add value for their firm's image. But their influence on football was more in terms of its organisational structures, which were modelled on those of French companies: they were very hierarchical, where operatives had to follow orders of the boss and his managers. This disciplined paternalist model is that of Peugeot for instance (Fridenson 1989: 53). In texts talking about the football team, Bromberger found a discourse of productivity: hard work, discipline, no discussion or questioning being accepted (Bromberger *et al.* 1995: 183).

It is worth underlining that pressure for creating a national professional league in 1932 came more from Peugeot and a few club chairmen than from overwhelming popular demand. While crowds had of course increased around certain clubs to the point of making gate receipts important in developing the club, footballers did not have a national profile as stars in the same way as other sportsmen. Between the wars the national sporting heroes were boxers, tennis players and cyclists. The result of Georges Carpentier's fight for the world heavyweight title against Dempsey in Madison Square Garden had been awaited with bated breath by thousands of Parisians outside the Press Agency offices. Just before the war, the two epic world-title battles of Marcel Cerdan (whose affair with Edith Piaf merely served to increase his celebrity) were even more eagerly followed. The President of the Republic is reported to have announced the result of the second contest during an after-dinner speech. The four musketeers of Davis Cup tennis fame (Borotra, Cochet, Brugnon and Lacoste) were important enough to have had the new Roland Garros stadium specially built to show off their world-beating skills. Tour de France cyclists and exponents of the six-day races in the Vélodrome d'hiver in Paris were heroes (the Pélissier brothers and André Leducq). Club footballers did not generally enjoy national fame, and the results of France's international football team were poor (further fuel to the modernisers' argument for professionalisation). The odd personality, inevitably an international player, gained a certain notoriety. Before and after the First World War, goalkeeper Pierre Chayriguès was the first goalkeeper to command the penalty area. Lucien Gamblin was the rock at the heart of the French defence in the first victory against England in 1921. Paul Nicholas was national captain and a prolific goal scorer in the 1920s.[1]

Among the first professional club teams, some of the most successful played in small provincial towns of less than 50,000 inhabitants (Sochaux, Sète, Antibes, Cannes). Crowds were inevitably limited. Cities like Lyon, Bordeaux and Nice did not have successful teams, or for certain periods had no professional club at all. Toulouse had a team only from 1937 onwards, with little success. Football pulled the crowds only in the north, the south-east and Paris. The south-west preferred rugby, the west cycling, and the centre was a sporting desert, report Lanfranchi and Wahl (1998). Significantly for the future, however, the four teams to attract crowds of over 10,000 for league games, l'Olympique de Marseille, le Racing Club de Paris, le Racing Club de Strasbourg and l'Olympique lillois, were the ones from major industrial conurbations (Lanfranchi and Wahl 1998).

Against the background of slow, small-scale and patchy industrialisation, there is a set of hypotheses to explain why support for football did not grow as much as in England or Scotland. The habit of travelling to away matches to support one's home club did not develop, as distances between French towns are far greater, and so more expensive than in England, and transport axes made it less easy to travel between provincial towns (all roads and railway lines led to Paris). The late start of the national league and its interruption before the end of its first decade meant that spectator habits were ill-formed and it had to start again almost from scratch after 1945. Since football developed typically in small to medium-sized towns having only one club, supported by the municipality, there was less chance of the development of local derby rivalries to increase the intensity of support. Another distinctive feature of football support was the different shape of the working week: the English Saturday afternoon at the match was a French Sunday afternoon, since the five-and-a-half day week did not establish itself in France until 1936 or even later.

Lanfranchi and Wahl (1998) also point out that the size of stadiums generally reflected this relatively modest following compared to other national leagues. In France, two of the better teams, Sète and Sochaux, played in grounds with a maximum capacity of 5,000 spectators. Elsewhere in Europe in the 1920s and 1930s huge new stadiums were being built: in England Wembley (over 100,000 capacity), in Italy, in anticipation of the 1934 World Cup, Rome, Bologna, Milan and Florence (50,000), in Spain the Neucamp in Barcelona, and in Berlin the Olympic Stadium. The only French contribution to this trend was the Stade de Colombes, north of Paris, with a capacity of 45,000, built not specifically for football but for the 1924 Olympic Games held in Paris. It none the less acted as national stadium for international football (and rugby) matches, and, significantly, for the final of the French Cup, thus giving status to this annual match and to football in general. As later (1984 and 1998), the hosting of international football tournaments in France provided opportunities for football to benefit from public authority help to improve its infrastructure. The first of these, the hosting of the World Cup in 1938, saw the capacity of Colombes increased to 60,000, and the old Parc des Princes (Paris) to 35,000. Two new stadiums of 30,000 were built in Bordeaux and Marseille, although they too were, significantly, built as multi-sport stadiums. The name of the Marseille stadium, *le Stade vélodrome*, indicated it was built to be able to host the finish of stages in the Tour de France as well as other cycle races. The stadiums in Lille, Strasbourg, Reims, Le Havre and Antibes also underwent refurbishment (Pickup 1999: 32; Sinet 2002: 63).

The nationalisation of football was not solely a function of the professional league. The French Cup, with the possibility of small teams beating the big professionals, had a similar 'magic' to the FA Cup in England. Some tiny localities have gained momentary or more lasting fame in the annals of the Cup by famous victories (or famous stumbles at the last hurdle – for instance the recent case of the semi-professionals Calais who reached the final in 2000 only to lose to a disputed penalty against cup holders Nantes). Examples of successful small industrial clubs go back to the pre-professional era. The large village side of Valentigney (Franche-Comté) reached the final of the French Cup in 1926. The majority of its 5,000 inhabitants worked in the Peugeot car factory, and all but one of their players were from the region. The following year a similarly small side, US Quevilly, sponsored by a Normandy industrialist (who imported two English stars Puddefoot and Deans) reached the final (Thibert and Rethacker 1996: 61).

Cup legends inevitably involve larger-than-life club chairmen, figures who have always loomed large in the folklore of French football. Georges Bayrou, Chairman of Mediterranean coast club FC Sète, used to stay in the dressing room for big matches, unable to watch his beloved green-and-whites. Losing Cup finalists in 1923, 1924 and 1929, when they reached the final in 1930 he decided he had to join the President of the Republic, Doumergue, in the *tribune d'honneur* at Colombes. He sat through the goalless first half with top hat firmly planted on his head, but at half-time could stand it no longer and left for the dressing room, where he took off his hat and frock coat, mopped his brow, and opened the window to listen to the 35,000 spectators outside. He heard Racing Club de Paris take the lead, and then with a minute to go he heard Sète equalise, and go on to win in extra-time. That evening in the Gare de Lyon, Paris, a ticket inspector was surprised to find in a second-class compartment, Chairman Bayrou sitting with the Cup placed lovingly on the seat opposite. He was even more surprised when Bayrou took out his wallet and paid for a separate ticket for the sacred object he had been dreaming of bringing home to Sète for the past ten years.

Football versus Rugby: Bordeaux and the Conquest of the South-west

In the nationalisation of the sport, soccer's conquest of the rugby regions in the south-west took much longer than that of industrial France. Bordeaux had had English influence through the wine trade for even longer than other ports, and Anglomania in Bordeaux in the late nineteenth century ensured that modern sports clubs were founded just as early as anywhere else in France. The Girondins de Bordeaux club dates in fact from 1881, but was not originally a football club, and it became an outdoor omnisports club in 1910. Rugby was promoted by the Bordeaux social and merchant elite who sent their sons to British public schools. This trend was helped by the existence of a local traditional version of rugby, 'barette'. From 1889 rugby was actively spread to local schools, as local tournaments were organised. The majority of south-west rugby clubs were subsequently founded as offshoots of school associations. A snowball effect, strengthened by Bordeaux winning the national rugby championship in 1904 and featuring in every final up to 1911 (losing only two), spread the trend to all sections of the population and to the surrounding towns and villages of the whole of the south-west, not an industrialised part of France, before football had a chance to compete with it.[2]

In 1920, Bordeaux, France's fourth or fifth largest city, was the only large town with no football club, but the split of rugby into amateur and professional in 1931 and the creation of a national professional soccer championship in 1932 broke down the dominance of the Coubertin ethic of sport as a game, that valued fair play and amateurism, the essential being to take part. The idea of sport as a ritual, bringing together people from the same locality or community behind a winning side, enticed the Girondins de Bordeaux to join the professional football league in 1937. The building of a magnificent new municipal stadium (now a listed building) for the 1938 World Cup, where two matches featured Brazil, went some way to setting a trend and giving the Bordeaux public a new 'lieu de culte' (shrine) and a team they could identify with in the national and international context that football was beginning to offer. The successful implantation of soccer in the south-west is such that in the 1980s, at the initiative of its ex-rugby international mayor, Jacques Chaban-Delmas, Bordeaux was to become one of the first French cities to move into the modern football business and make the club a symbol of both the city and the region on the national and international stage (Augustin 1990: 106).

Modernisation and Suburbanisation: Football's '30 Glorious Years' of Decline

After 1945 France underwent the great economic and social transformations that are commonly referred to as 'les trente glorieuses'(Fourastié 1979), thirty years of economic growth up to the period of the mid-1970s and the 'chocs pétroliers', the economic downturn associated with the sudden rise in crude oil prices. Importantly, by the 1960s and 1970s, the post-war rural exodus had finally transformed France into an urban society and this urbanisation worked against the small-town football culture that had grown up. Mignon and others explain the crisis that afflicted French football in the 1960s as a consequence of the scale of the urban change that then took place. The first-generation city dwellers of this era had not been socialised into football culture. For members of the new urban youth culture, football was old-fashioned. Pop music was a more attractive focus around which to build an identity and a lifestyle. For the adult aspiring middle classes there were newer and more family-based leisure forms to tempt them, especially television, which became a mass social phenomenon in the late 1960s and 1970s. The generalisation of car ownership offered the possibility of escaping from the cities, at least on Sundays, especially for those first-generation city dwellers who still had roots in the countryside or a former family house now used as a 'résidence secondaire'. Prestigious small-town French clubs disappeared or dropped into the second division never to come back up – for example, Sète, Alès, Roubaix-Tourcoing.

Regular weekly sports spectating had never established itself sufficiently widely in France to survive the watershed of the Second World War. Compared to English spectating habits, there is no summer equivalent of cricket. Geographically, rugby is not a national sport. Horse racing is concentrated in the Paris area and practically all betting is off-course, indeed in cafés, via the publicly run PMU. Post-war there were thousands of cafés named 'Café des sports' where enthusiasts gathered rather than on the terraces. The main spectator events are one-offs – the French Open tennis at Roland Garros (socially elitist); and motor sport: the French Formula 1 Grand Prix, the Le Mans 24-hour race, and the motor-cycle Bol d'or. The Tour de France cycle race, although it lasts three weeks, is a one-day per year outing for most followers, or even less: 'two minutes of lurid lycra', as Julian Barnes (2000) strikingly describes the experience for most roadside onlookers.

While football certainly re-established itself post-war as the major French spectator sport, it still attracted much smaller crowds than in England or Italy. Indeed the period from 1950 to 1980 was characterised by declining or stagnant attendances. From an average of 11,403 per D1 match in 1949/50, attendances fell steadily to 6,555 in the 1968/69 season, climbing to 11,301 in 1976/77, only to fall back again to 9,778 in 1984/85 (Wahl 1989: 309; Chaumier and Rocheteau 1997: 554). Attendances only returned to 1950 levels (12,000) in the 1987/88 season (Mignon 1999: 80–81). If the drop in numbers in the 1960s may be partly explained by rising standards of living that opened up access to new daytime leisure activities through the motor car, by the time football changed to evening kick-offs (on Saturdays) many potential spectators had acquired the other modern habit of staying at home in the evening to watch television.

The Special Case of Paris

Most European capital cities have long boasted major football clubs. London, Rome, and Madrid have a tradition of more than one top side. There are various reasons why Paris was never a traditional footballing city, at least until the late 1970s, and it is not a coincidence that this was the first time Paris got an elected executive mayor (Jacques Chirac). Compared to provincial teams, large-scale support for a Paris football club, such as has developed since the 1970s for Paris Saint-Germain, is unusual. Geographical mobility, the influx of more and more provincials into the capital, had over decades, even over the last two centuries, diluted any special Parisian identity. The extent of the long-standing pulling power of the capital was famously criticised by Jean-François Gravier in his book *Paris et le désert français* (1958), a call for a halt to this hyper-centralisation. As early as 1923, *Le Miroir des sports* noted the difference between the sense of identity of provincial towns as opposed to the metropolis. The newspaper claimed: 'Paris is now a concentrated version of the provinces. Paris has in this respect lost its character' (Wahl 1989: 227). Parisians with provincial roots long remained attached to their original *département*, as opposed to building up partisan support for a Parisian team, at least until the major demographic changes of the 'trente glorieuses' culminating in the mid-1970s.

Football had certainly taken root as a leisure activity in Paris in the late nineteenth century among middle-class practitioners, and the French Cup, in the days of amateurism, had been dominated in the post-First World War period by clubs from the Paris region, such as its first winners Olympique Pantin. Red Star and the Racing Club (both founder members of the professional league) were also successful teams of the pre-war period and into the 1940s, Red Star winning the French Cup four times in the 1920s and again in 1942, and Racing five times between 1936 and 1949. These successes are now but a distant memory in the Paris region. Red Star was relegated from Division 1 in 1948, reappearing between 1967 and 1973, and unexpectedly emerging from nowhere as giant-killers when reaching the semi-finals of the League Cup in 2000. Racing, after a spell in Division 2 in the 1950s, maintained their position in the top flight until the early 1960s. However, by the end of the 2000/01 season Racing was languishing in the National (Division 3) from which Red Star were relegated into the amateur ranks of the CFA (Division 4) (Labrunie 2001a). Racing still play at the famous Yves du Manoir stadium in the middle-class suburban district of Colombes. Red Star has its headquarters in the working-class town of Saint-Ouen to the north of the city of Paris, and plays almost in the shadow of the new Stade de France in Saint-Denis. Ironically there had been a brief hope in 1998 of Red Star becoming a realistic candidate to use the new national stadium as its home ground. Neither of the two clubs, from very different social milieux, were seen as representing the city of Paris. Even though based in the Paris region they were significantly identified with suburban municipalities quite distinct from Paris *intra muros*.

As we have seen, football developed most successfully in France, at least until the oil crisis and the recession of the 1970s and 1980s, around small town clubs supported by a homogeneous working-class community and sponsored by its dominant family firm and the local authority. This may help explain the fact that, until the era of football as big business, the city of Paris itself has never really had a highly successful team. Identification of the whole city of Paris with a single club has been difficult, and unlike other towns, local municipal aid had not been forthcoming until very recently (Marseille 1990: 71), since Paris (unlike all other municipalities) has only had a local government structure allowing an executive mayor since 1977, therefore no structure that allowed political capital to be made out of supporting the local club, and so no source of municipal financial help for a club. There were also difficulties to do with fan identification, as will be discussed in the next chapter.

More recent attempts either to found major clubs in the capital or to revive existing clubs have depended heavily on big business sponsorship and broadcasting rights. Indeed, as we shall see below, it is becoming the case in the current era that big clubs can now only emerge from large metropolitan areas. The founders and particularly the sponsors of the newest Parisian club, Paris Saint-Germain (PSG), realised that the city of Paris is well placed to capitalise on this, and PSG emerged as a European force out of nothing in a very short time in footballing terms.

Founded in 1970 in the small suburban town of Saint-Germain-en-Laye to the west of Paris, and admitted to Division 2, they immediately won the Division 2 championship and have played henceforward in the top division. The couturier Daniel Hechter took over in 1973 as one of the earliest of the new breed of businessmen-chairmen, but left with a life ban from football after the double-ticketing scandal of 1977 (Bourg 1986: 152). PSG was then built up in the late 1970s and 1980s by Chairman Francis Borelli and a board of other business specialists, winning the championship in 1978 in the chairman's first season, and then two French cups (1982, 1983), and another championship in 1985. But subsequent performances on the field were uneven, with a big loss of projected income when being eliminated from the European Cup in the first round in 1986 to Vitkovice, and qualifying for Europe only once more under Borelli, in 1989, again going out too early to make any money. Using the renovated Parc des Princes in the 1980s, Borelli was the first chairman to install private hospitality boxes, bringing in an income of 5 million francs in 1985 (Wahl 1989: 340). Borelli found himself under further pressure from a rival initiative in Paris from one of France's most successful businessmen.

The highly successful arms and communication company chairman Jean-Luc Lagardère, wanting to associate his Matra-Hachette-Europe 1 firm with a top sports brand, chose to try and revive the historically famous and (as he saw it) under-exploited brand of Racing Club de Paris. He was elected chairman of Racing in 1983. He spent 50 million francs in advance budget in 1984 and 1985 (twice as much as Air France's annual advertising budget) (Bourg 1986: 73–74). He was quite open about the promotional advantage he intended to achieve, saying he was not doing it simply out of a personal interest in football (ibid.: 71). In addition to the domestic promotional opportunities, he tried to use the multiracial character of the team to promote his companies in Black Africa and North Africa. Racing was promoted from D2 in 1984, immediately relegated, promoted again to D1 in 1986, changed the club name to Matra Racing in 1987, and finished seventh in D1, was relegated as Racing Paris in 1990, and re-formed as Racing FC 92 after the Matra partnership failed, and now play in front of fewer than a thousand spectators in the National (D3). The fate of PSG's ephemeral rival suggests that even a city as big as Paris cannot escape the rule that, in France, a town or city is only big enough for one football club, otherwise there is a problem of identification and support. The late 1980s and early 1990s were however not good for Paris football. Borelli left PSG with a 51 million franc deficit.

It took the beginning of the latest era in the economics of French football – as subscription television took a more dominant role in the organisation of the game – for things to start looking up for the Paris club. In the 1990s, support from the City of Paris and the television company Canal+ made PSG one of the biggest clubs in France. The commercial side of this success will be discussed in Chapter 7. However, as will be seen in Chapter 4, there is still a fragility about its identity with its fans to be overcome, even in a period when the big city clubs are starting to assert their dominance over French professional football.

The Rise of the Big City Club: Regional Capitals, International Ambitions

Alongside Paris, the 1990s saw the rise of France's regional capitals and major cities among the football elite – half a century after England and Italy. This can be seen in the clubs that have been taken over by major national and international media companies (see also Chapters 7 and 8) and in the candidacies for host city status for the 1998 World Cup finals. Within the European Single Market and with the decline of the nation-state as the key framework within which cities have to operate, it appears that major French towns are using football for promotion of local and regional identity and as an instrument for attracting inward investment.

Bordeaux

A forerunner was the city of Bordeaux, which attempted in the 1980s to re-brand itself via football. Historically, as we have seen, French football clubs have been closely tied to their locality, and indeed to their local town hall, and therefore to local politicians. Municipal subsidies were sought to counter increasing travel costs of clubs in the period following the First World War. In 1920 the town of Marseille financed the construction of a new stadium (Wahl 1989: 231), and in 1931 Saint-Etienne followed suit. By the 1980s, municipal subsidies remained on average at one-quarter of a club's income. Seen as a public service and something the town (and its local politicians) could and should take a pride in, football clubs with relatively small income through the turnstiles became very reliant on free use of the municipal stadium, or an annual grant often equalling the amount of local taxes that would have been paid by the club on its turnover. A town's aid usually had a stabilising role rather than being a driving force behind the business. But this created a dependency relationship and town halls felt they had the right to interfere in the running of clubs. Their representatives sat on the management committee in Metz, Nancy, Nice, Toulouse, Lens. Sometimes the mayor was the club chairman, as in Lens (Wahl 1989 328–329). However, in the 1980s, with the advent of new economic conditions, came a new breed of club chairman and a new relationship between club and locality, at least in some ambitious big cities such as Marseille and Bordeaux. Cities began to have ambitions to use their football team to promote their image more widely.

In the 1970s the political fortunes of the mayor of Bordeaux, former Prime Minister Jacques Chaban-Delmas, were ebbing. He had lost badly as official Gaullist candidate in the presidential elections of 1974, lost the presidency of the Greater Bordeaux council, lost the presidency of the Regional Council of Aquitaine and lost influence in the local county council (Conseil général). His need of a coup to re-establish his standing coincided with the arrival as Chairman of Girondins de Bordeaux of the ambitious Claude Bez. With the help of significant municipal aid they collaborated to turn the Girondins into a top French club, and indeed succeeded to the extent that Bordeaux qualified for Europe every year from 1981 to 1988, reached European semi-finals in 1985 and 1987, and were French champions in 1984, 1985, and 1987. Chairman Bez's success in building up the business side of the club brought greater support from the mayor, which through advances and loans helped renovate the stadium. The club was used as a unifying symbol of the whole region. To help win inward investment, the local Chamber of Commerce marketed the region by inviting decision-makers to see matches from new private hospitality boxes (Wahl 1989: 340). In 1988 the Girondins went to play exhibition matches in Los Angeles as regional standard bearer of an Aquitaine delegation attempting to sell local produce and attract investment from across the Atlantic. Mayor Chaban-Delmas claimed the promotional effects for the town were worth 25 to 50 times the original investment (Augustin 1990: 106–109). However, unexpectedly exiting the potentially lucrative European Cup in the first round in 1985/86 to Fenerbahçe (Turkey) cost them dear and began a financial destabilisation of the club. Chaban left civic office only through age and infirmity in 1995, after 48 years as mayor.

World Cup Host Towns

The 1990s saw other large towns and in particular the major cities of France take an interest in the possibilities of using football for communication purposes. The host towns of the 1998 World Cup make a useful case study to investigate this new or confirmed interest in football by the major regional capitals of France, and to see how this is transforming the economic geography of French football in the twenty-first century.

One of the issues that preoccupied all the host towns was image communication. Every large town in France now has its communications strategy and communication unit (often reporting directly to the mayor's office). Distinctive market positions are defined, corporate images are created to endow the town with a recognisable personality and these are communicated by logos and slogans. The aim is to encourage inward investment, sometimes to promote tourism (France is after all the world leader as a tourist destination annually welcoming more visitors than its own total population). Equally important aims are to involve local citizens and engage them in a common purpose (Sperling 1991: 20–21), and always, at the very least indirectly, to serve local electoral purposes by heightening the profile of the mayor and his or her team by publicising their work for the municipality to the electorate (Parker 1993b: 163). Municipalities are communicating to at least two distinct publics, therefore, one internal, one external, and are able to use football to do both.

Even medium-sized towns (under 90,000 inhabitants) spent between 150,000 and 1 million francs per year on communication in the 1990s (Alvis 1994). Much smaller towns, and more recently the new regional authorities with their own elected bodies with large powers and budgets since the decentralisation law of 1983, also rapidly followed suit (Hare 1995). Municipal public relations are often built around annual events organised by the town or with which the town is associated through sponsorship or participation. Some events have achieved national notoriety and are powerful vectors of image: whether relatively new ones such as *Francofolies*, the La Rochelle festival of popular song, or the Montpellier Classical Music Festival. News coverage in the press and on television offers much more credibility than direct advertising (Sperling 1991: 37–42). Paying for the privilege of being a *ville d'étape* in the Tour de France cycle race ensures exposure during the television sports coverage, but also guarantees media portraits of the town and its attractions and local specialities. In 1994, for example, the year of the opening of the Channel Tunnel and of the TGV Nord, Calais and Lille invested in this public relations exercise as *villes d'étape*.

Whereas television coverage of the Tour is followed much more in France than abroad, the 1998 World Cup had been (correctly) predicted to have the biggest global television audience ever, and the opportunities for self-publicity to the rest of Europe and the world for purposes of attracting inward investment was a once-only opportunity. Hosting the World Cup in the region was a way that local cities and regions could prepare the way, in partnership with big business keen to invest in major city clubs in the late 1990s, to forge a new relationship between football club and locality. Being a World Cup host city was crucial for ambitious municipalities; as the mayor of the smallest host city put it: 'In the collective memory, Montpellier will be one of the ten best known French towns in the first quarter of the twenty-first century' (Echégut 1998: 39).

Dauncey (1999) found that, to a great extent, the candidates to host matches in the World Cup of 1998 were self-selecting, given the nature of French professional football where only a restricted number of top teams attract the followings to warrant the large grounds demanded by FIFA (seating for 40,000 spectators). However, the geography of the host cities tells us something about the local politics and economic geography of French football in the late 1990s. France's hosting of the 1984 European Championships, and the infrastructure development that had then occurred, also favoured some grounds, such as the Stade de la Beaujoire in Nantes, purpose-built in 1983, which meant the updating was comparatively inexpensive. Leaving aside the two stadiums in the Paris area (the new Stade de France in the suburb of Saint-Denis, and the Parc des Princes), the provincial host cities (where 49 of the 64 matches were played) were geographically spread across the country: Bordeaux and Toulouse in the south-west, Nantes in the west, Lens in the north, Lyon and Saint-Etienne in the centre-east, and Marseille and Montpellier on the Mediterranean coast.

From amongst the initial group of candidate cities, Rouen, Lille and Nancy reluctantly withdrew because their regional authorities realised that the renovation or new stadium costs involved – even with subsidies from the State – would be too great when the clubs were not in Division 1. Geographically the north of France was covered by the choice of Lens, a successful top club for many years, and so Lille had to bow to its near neighbour, although Lille's home town club, LOSC, has since been promoted to Division 1 and indeed looks capable of establishing itself as a major force. Of France's big regional capitals with big football stadiums, Strasbourg notably excluded itself. Although in general its stadium was considered of high quality, having been much renovated for Euro 84, it could only provide 17,000 seats. The club and the city and regional authorities could not agree. The club is one of the modernisers in its organisational structures and ambitions, being owned by the French arm of the international McCormack sports management group, but the socialist mayor, Catherine Trautmann, had other priorities in a city that is both a major European capital in terms of European institutions and has major problems of delinquency and a large extreme right vote. The club had cost the city a lot of money in subsidies in previous years (not least in the 1984 European Nations Championship), and the municipality opted out of subsidy of football. This controversial refusal was none the less seen by the local political opposition as a missed opportunity (Saint-Martin 1998: 60; Scotto 1997: 29, and 1998: 25).

The final list of cities hosting matches was (for Dauncey) predictable. He argues that the historical links of French football 'to industrialisation and the demography of French towns and cities, combined with political traditions of centralism and contemporary moves towards more responsibility for the regions created a complex of forces favouring regional capitals' (Dauncey 1999: 104). The one anomaly as a host town appears to be Montpellier, so low in the urban hierarchy (twenty-fourth largest city in France), but its municipal ambitions meant it was determined to be a host city as part of its long-term strategy of self-promotion. The local city and regional authorities invested heavily in football in the 1980s and 1990s, which have seen the club rise from the lower leagues (*Division d'honneur*) to European competitions. As part of the communication exercise that was the World Cup the mayor and the president of the Regional Council undertook a regional tour as early as 1996 to publicise the city's hosting of the World Cup among the local population. They were able, before the end of 1997, to measure economic effects, in terms of jobs, with many local firms working on the renovations to the stadium, the smallest of the ten, its capacity being enlarged by 50 per cent to turn it into a 35,500 all-seater stadium. The Montpellier conurbation has grown rapidly over the past 20 years, fuelling the ambitions of its long-term mayor Georges Frêche. The general gain for Montpellier, as for other host towns, was in notoriety abroad or brand awareness.

The town of Lens is a different case. It appears very small, but is in a largish conurbation in the densely populated Lille region, and has a highly successful, long-standing Division 1 team (1997/98 champions) with the excellent facilities of the Stade Félix-Bollaert. Its support was voted the best in the country in the 1999/2000 season (*France Football*, 7 January 2000). The position of Saint-

Etienne, geographically close to Lyon and relatively low down the urban hierarchy, would normally suggest that it would lose out to its much larger neighbour; however, the unparalleled footballing tradition of Saint-Etienne and the facilities available at Stade Geoffroy-Guichard outweighed such concerns.

For the host towns and cities, the World Cup was very much about selling themselves as regional capitals to the half-a-million foreign supporters among whom were a good proportion of VIPs invited by sponsors, as well as a thousand foreign journalists and many 'deciders' from French companies (not to mention the potential visitors watching on television). The State (seeing the cities also as part of 'le produit France' in general) provided expertise and staff: the key public relations operation was organised by the host towns in collaboration with the DATAR, the regional Development Agency. One hundred and twenty foreign company directors were invited to the host towns in a highly targeted fashion. Thirty American industrialists in biotechnology were invited to Lyon; Belgian food industrialists to Bordeaux; British aeronautics and aerospace interests were present in Toulouse, to cite just three examples (Echégut 1997, 1998).

Becoming a host club for the World Cup was equally crucial for the local football club, since it was a once-only opportunity to benefit from huge State and local-authority help to improve stadium infrastructures. One might say that what was happening was public investment in clubs whose 'modernising' chairmen were aiming to privatise once the investment had been made. Total costs of improving these mostly rather old stadiums and of furnishing infrastructures around them were shared by central government, cities and regions, and did not fall onto the clubs that use them. Public input to the improvement of football's infrastructures was therefore considerable. The *collectivités locales* (city, metropolitan, departmental and regional authorities) contributed overall 1.44 billion francs (£140 million) simply to the renovation

Table 3.1 *Stadium and Infrastructure Development for the 1998 World Cup: Shared Costs (in Millions of Francs)*

Town/city	Cost of renovation	State	City	Metropolitan area	Department	Region
Nantes	42	16	17	–	5.5	4
Lyon	213	28	114	25	25	20
Marseille	355	107	188	–	30	30

Source: 'Dix villes mobilisées pour la Coupe du monde 1998', *La Gazette des communes*, 9 June 1997, quoted in Dauncey (1999: 101).

of grounds and the improvement of general urban facilities (for instance the city of Lyon built an extension of the city Metro to the Stade de Gerland). The sum disbursed by local authorities represented some two-thirds of the total costs. Taking Nantes, Lyon and Marseille as examples, going from the least to the most expensive of the old stadiums, the total costs of renovation and its sharing out between the State and different local authorities may be seen in Table 3.1.

Big Towns, Big Budgets, Big Clubs

The World Cup was a major opportunity for French cities and regions to position themselves on the national and international stage through sport. Whereas 30 years ago French football's economic geography was different, it is less and less of a surprise to see that France's seven biggest cities had Division 1 clubs in 2000/01: Paris, Lyon, Marseille, Lille, Bordeaux, Toulouse, Nantes. Toulouse were subsequently relegated, but have one of the top rugby clubs in France. Monaco exists too at this top level because it is heavily subsidised by its ruling royal family, in the same way that the biggest city clubs are sponsored by their municipalities. Rennes comes in at twenty-second rank in the biggest French towns, and has as majority shareholder one of France's richest businessmen, François Pinault, owner of the Pinault-Printemps-Redoute group, whose sponsorship allowed Rennes to spend 345 million francs in new recruits at the start of the 2000/01 season. Montpellier still manages to punch above its weight.

The other top division clubs in 2001/02 were all based in towns of 100,000 inhabitants (Metz) or less. Metz and Sedan are throwbacks to the earlier period of dominance of small to middle-sized industrial towns; Auxerre and Troyes are middle-sized market towns with strong footballing traditions, like Bastia (in Corsica). What at first sight seems the most obvious exception to the rule about French football becoming dominated by the top city clubs is recently promoted Guingamp, a small-town Breton club, founded 1912, with a stadium of 18,040 places that had never been full prior to their promotion in 2000, and which has an honourable record in professional football, having been in D1 before in the 1990s. It is not a club quite like those small-town clubs around whom the professional league was built, since it rose to prominence in recent years having taken over players from Brest when their neighbour was in financial trouble. However, Brittany is a traditional footballing area, as witnessed too by the promotion of Lorient to D1 in 2001. The public and officials of small-town clubs such as Lorient and Guingamp are not yet ready to be consigned to sporting history, as their results show, even though they are unable to generate great income from gate receipts, sponsorship, or merchandising. It was perhaps not a surprise that in 2002 both clubs were struggling against relegation, with Lorient losing out yet winning the French Cup.

   In the current situation the size of a club's budget is a major key to success. Table 3.2 shows there is a link between size of budget and size of conurbation. Guingamp, the smallest town represented during both seasons, had the lowest budget of D1 clubs in 2001/02. While Rennes and Monaco (for reasons to do with their particular individual sponsors/owners) are ranked higher in the budgetary hierarchy than their size of conurbation would warrant, it is clear that there is a relation between the size of urban population where the club plays and its financial position. Lille is an exception, being ranked much lower than its conurbation (the fourth biggest in France) would warrant. However, the 2000 season was Lille's first in the top division after three years in the second and there is evidence it is attracting more financial support through its success. Lille finished a remarkable third and qualified for the preliminary round of the 2001/02 Champions League. The financial gain this represents allowed budgetary increases that suggest the club may well survive and prosper in the

Table 3.2 *Club Budgets in 2000 and 2001, in Millions of Francs*

D1 Club 2000–01	Provisional budget 2000	League position 1999–2000	League position 2000–2001	Average gate 1999–2000	Conurbation size	Provisional budget 2001
Paris-SG	500	2	9	43,185	9,000,000	450
Lyon	400	3	2	35,449	1,260,000	500
Monaco	375	1	11	10,259	66,000	320
Marseille	280	15	15	51,686	1,100,000	320
Bordeaux	260	4	4	30,085	690,000	260
Nantes	250	12	1	28,333	500,000	400
Rennes	250	13	6	13,723	240,000	250
Toulouse	250	Promoted	16*		600,000	
Lens	230	5	14	38,805	320,000	230
St Etienne	210	6	17*	27,994	310,000	
Strasbourg	200	9	18*	19,845	390,000	
Bastia	140	10	8	6,915	45,000	140
Metz	139	11	12	19,867	100,000	130
Auxerre	130	8	13	11,950	40,000	100
Sedan	120	7	5	12,953	30,000	140
Lille	120	Promoted	3		900,000	150
Guingamp	100	Promoted	10		22,000	100
Troyes	90	14	7	14,139	60,000	110

Source: Chaumier and Rocheteau (2000, 2001).

* = Relegated

longer term. The key is that the club is in the fourth biggest city and conurbation, has received important support from the municipality in the recent past, and before the municipal elections of 2001 extracted promises of major investment in the stadium.

Lille and Lyon: Eurocities

The north of France was a hotbed of soccer in the same way as the north-east of England, with a similar industrial working-class tradition. LOSC (Lille Olympique Sporting Club), whose predecessor Olympique Lillois won the very first professional championship in 1933, was most successful in the immediate post-war years. LOSC won two championships and five French Cups between 1946 and 1955. Then, as the old heavy industries gradually saw themselves overtaken in terms of wealth and job creation, LOSC yo-yoed between Divisions 1 and 2 in the 1960s and 1970s, even going down briefly to Division 3. Since winning the Division 2 championship in 1978, LOSC has generally been seen as a natural Division 1 team, if a mediocre one. However, the catastrophic position of the club's finances in 1994 almost cost them their professional existence. The key factor then as now is the support of the local authorities. The city, which was in fact from the mid-1990s the club's major (80 per cent) shareholder, picked up huge bills to wipe out the club's deficit of 75 million francs. This did not prevent relegation to D2 in 1997. The socialist-led municipality of Lille came up with a strategy to save the club and to rid themselves of the debt by privatising the club, with a promise of major renovation of the stadium. In the summer of 1999 talks were opened with two businessmen, Luc Dayan and Francis Graille, with a view to a take-over. The attraction for the investors was the history of the club (it already had a brand), its location in a big regional capital (Lille is after all a key hub on the high-speed train lines linking Paris, London and Brussels) and the backing of the local authority and metropolitan area. The city sold its shares for 250,000 francs and gave a promise either to build a new stadium or to renovate the existing stadium from top to bottom by 1 March 2003. The buyers have invested 40 million francs in the club's budget.

The impending municipal elections meant that the timing of the plan was not accidental. The position of executive mayor in a city the size of Lille is a not inconsiderable political prize. It usually brings with it the chairmanship of the metropolitan area, great influence in the regional authority, and leadership of one of the key Socialist Party federations. It is a key springboard to national political office. Martine Aubry (who happens to come from a political family, being the daughter of Jacques Delors) gave up her post as Minister for Employment and Solidarity and effective number two to Prime Minister Jospin in 2000 in order to fight the mayoral election. Her predecessor, long-term mayor Pierre Mauroy, was a major national figure, and a former Prime Minister. The issue of what to do about the city football club was not something that could be neglected by candidates for mayor in Lille, nor shelved once elected. Before her first month was out and before the end of the already very successful football season, Mayor Aubry revealed the plan to increase the capacity of the existing stadium from 20,000 to 35,000, increasing also the number of corporate hospitality boxes, at a cost to local and regional taxpayers of 200 million francs. The metropolitan area – *la Communauté urbaine* – will finance it (Dufour 2001).

A month later, the earlier than expected success of LOSC in gaining a place in the qualifying round of the Champions League (which brought in much extra money to the club) caused a planning problem regarding the renovation of the stadium. Champions League stadiums must be all-seater and Mayor Aubry was of course determined that LOSC would not play its home games anywhere else than in Lille. However, the necessary work proved impossible and LOSC borrowed the nearby stadium of Lens.

The fact that LOSC has an opportunity to establish itself as a major force in French and European football says much about the changes in the economic geography of French football that in the last decade have seen the rise of big city clubs in regional capitals with international ambitions inside the new European Union. Despite the cost, an ambitious city like Lille cannot wash its hands of one aspect of a regional capital's assets: a professional football team with European clout. As its private buyers were aware, a club playing in a big metropolitan area is able to command larger crowds from their urban catchment area, significant municipal support, the sponsorship of major companies, bigger budgets, and thereby, in the post-Bosman era of highly mobile players more susceptible to financial inducements than to club loyalty, the likelihood of success on the pitch.

A more substantial symbol than Lille in this respect, in the sense that their success has already been confirmed over a number of years, is Olympique Lyonnais. They are a better example of the new big-city club, too, in that Lyon is not a traditional football area. Succeeding a moribund predecessor, the modern 'OL' was born in 1950 with encouragement from the city and the use of the municipal Gerland stadium. OL went on to establish a record at the time for the number of successive games in Division 1 (1953/83), and won three French cups between 1964 and 1973, with a semi-final in the European Cup Winners Cup in 1964. Despite this honourable record as a relative newcomer to the professional league, compared for example to Marseille, Lyon has not been regarded as a footballing hotbed and the club had no real footballing pedigree. They had never won the French league championship and, until 2001, their last cup dated back to 1973. Over the years, OL had had various promising teams but had been unable to keep their best players. In the last few years, however, the club from France's second city has established itself not only as an importer of international stars such as their Brazilian captain and striker, Sonny Anderson, but also as a regular competitor in European competitions, and following the French League Cup victory of 2001 they at last won the coveted League Championship trophy in 2002. Although historically Lyon has been described as a cold, bourgeois city and the Lyon public is reputedly 'difficult and demanding' (*L'Equipe électronique* dossier, 21 December 2000), for the 2001 Cup Final the team were able to bring 35,000 supporters with them to the Stade de France (*Le Monde*, 8 May 2001), and the celebrations of the Championship win brought tens of thousands of Lyonnais onto the streets.

The turn-around is such that the club is now regarded as one of the most ambitious in the league (*Le Monde*, 8 May 2001), having gone, under the chairmanship of local businessman J.-M. Aulas, from Division 2 to the Champions League and from a budget of 17 million francs (including a deficit of 10 million) to 500 million francs between 1987 and 2001. Their stadium, owned and carefully maintained by the city, is of international standard, with 43,000 seats, having been upgraded for both the European championships of 1984 and the World Cup in 1998. Their chairman does, however, feel that the future of big clubs includes either ownership or management of their stadium and in 2000 was negotiating with outgoing mayor, another former Prime Minister, Raymond Barre, a jointly funded development doubling the number of corporate hospitality boxes in the Stade Gerland (Barth 2000d). Since 1999 they are also sponsored to the tune of 100 million francs by the media company Pathé, giving them the biggest budget in the league. Nor are their ambitions restricted to buying players and success, since investment in youth coaching (they own their Youth Coaching Centre, medical centre and training grounds) has led to their under-17 and under-15 sides becoming French champions in 2000.

The emergence of OL as one of the strongest clubs in French football at the turn of the century is not accidental. Lyon has now joined other major European regional capital cities in having a successful football team to go along with other international esteem indicators. These include an international airport and other major communications links (like Lille, Lyon is a key beneficiary of the TGV high-speed train service) and internationally celebrated cultural institutions and events.

The rise of the big-city club in a regional capital reflects wider social and economic changes that Manuel Castells and Anthony Giddens relate to globalisation, where the nation-state is no longer the key site of development. Rather than undermining cities, globalisation is transforming them into vital hubs within the global economy, says Castells (1996). Building on the idea of 'global cities' (Sassen 1991), Giddens (2001: 592–595) argues that the contemporary development of the world economy has created a strategic role for major cities, which are increasingly standing apart from their surrounding region and conceiving their areas of influence as transnational, through a network of links with other equivalent cities across the continent and the world. If local and city governments are more 'agile forms for managing the global' (Borja and Castells 1997, cited in Giddens 2001: 594), partly because they enjoy legitimacy from and are closer to those they represent, they can use sport – a football club or the hosting of a major international sports event – as a force for the integration of their plural societies and for galvanising urban regeneration and social and economic change. Barcelona is a model here. In hosting the 1992 Olympics the city's assets and vision were on show to the whole world, and this generated additional enthusiasm within the city for completing its urban transformation in the strategic Barcelona 2000 plan. Lyon, like Barcelona, is part of the Eurocities movement, 50 of Europe's largest cities that came together in 1989 to work together as economic actors. Competing in Europe, then, is not just a footballing goal, it is a major part of a big city's whole economic strategy. The city of Lyon's strategic plan under its new mayor is entitled 'Lyon porte d'Europe' (Lyon Gateway to Europe). It was not out of love for football that the mayor accompanied OL to Barcelona for a Champions League match, along with 25 key Lyon businessmen, and bought pages of space in Catalan daily papers advertising the city with the slogan 'We were made for each other' (Landrin 2001). Rather, it was from a recognition of the importance of a city's football club in contributing to a city's international image and economic development.

Conclusion

When the small town club CS Sedan-Ardennes, from a rural wooded region close to the Belgian border region, found themselves at the top of the French Division 1 in November 2000, their chairman and major shareholder Pascal Urano, a local businessman, accepted that the weakness of the local economy prevented them from paying either huge transfer fees or high salaries. Nor could they afford a training pitch or youth academy, so quickly had they come back into the top division. They also had to rely, not on locally produced players, but on picking up at bargain-basement prices solid professionals who had left other clubs for a variety of reasons, such as over-staffing or personal incompatibility (Potet 2000b). The original strength of the professional league was largely built around such small or medium-sized towns and the family values of the local factory (and some of these clubs still make themselves felt in the top two divisions). None the less, in the immediate future, in the era of cross-national and even global commercialism and growing importance to clubs of international competitions, French football looks as if it will be more and more dominated by the big-city clubs. In both cases, the past and the present, the support of the local town hall is crucial. There was a symbiosis that was initially dependent on a set of values that was to do with political self-interest certainly, but in the name of local democracy and a sense of public service. Today the interests of the big-city club and its locality are equally part of a mutual dependence, but with a shared desire to count much more widely than at the local or indeed the national level. These are now secondary to competing in Europe.

The French clubs with the biggest budgets are now from the major conurbations. They are the ones that are most consistently successful. The odd one out is Monaco, but its royal family has similar regional and international ambitions and resources to the elected mayors of Paris, Lyon, Marseille, Bordeaux, and Nantes, to which elite list one may be able to add Lille who are set to challenge Lens for the football leadership of the northern metropolitan area. These half-dozen cities are attractive to major commercial sponsors with similar global ambitions, whereas a club from a small town is no longer attractive or able to muster similar resources, whether from local crowd support or sponsorship. Sedan (founded in 1919) has never won the French League Championship, but has two French cups to its name – from a previous era, 1956 and 1961. In 2001, in their second season back in the top division, they finished an extremely creditable fifth and qualified for the UEFA Cup. The difference is that Lyon has by 2002 qualified three times running for the more lucrative Champions League. Lille, in finishing third in 2001, also qualifying for the Champions League, established a base camp that can be used by the city in its bid to become recognised as a major European regional capital. Their weakness is that, unlike Lyon, they did not have the resources to prevent the loss of key players to top English clubs in the close season of 2002.

Notes

1. For information on players of this early period, see 'Le roman de l'équipe de France (1904–1975)', *France Football* special issue, 25 December 2001.
2. See Augustin (1990) for the history of football in the south-west, and Dine (2001) for a discussion of the relationship between rugby and the south-west of France.

4

Fans: a Sociology of French Club Football

The lack of spectators and therefore of income has been a recurrent structural weakness in French football at club level. Sports spectating has never been a key feature of French social fabric in the same way as it has in Britain, at least not on such a mass scale. Football has long been the major spectator sport, but it has attracted far smaller crowds than in England or Italy. Since the French World Cup victory, however, publicity has been given to an extraordinary increase in crowds, although in fact the spectators have been coming back gradually over the whole of the 1990s – to the extent that numbers in French Division 1 stadiums are now almost comparable with other major European footballing countries – which it had never before been possible to claim.

Whereas 1997 (i.e. pre-World Cup) figures were, with the exception of PSG and Marseille, more akin to non-Premier league gates in England (Chaumier and Rocheteau 1997: 554–555), now crowds have significantly improved. Table 4.1 records a historic high for almost every club. The season 1999/2000 saw for the first time in French football history the average crowds for all D1 matches break the symbolic 20,000 barrier, the average being 22,324 for the season's 306 league matches (Chaumier and Rocheteau 2000: 309). The major clubs now compare with their English equivalents, with Marseille averaging over 50,000, PSG and Lens just over and just below 40,000 respectively, Lyon around 35,000, and Nantes and Bordeaux hovering around 30,000. However, what is interesting in the figures for Olympique de Marseille, as undoubtedly the best-supported club in the league, is that they attracted so much support even when finishing so low in the championship. Some explanations for OM's level of support will be explored later in the chapter. Meanwhile, smaller clubs have been looking optimistically to the future. In the close season of 2000, the stadiums of Rennes, Metz and Lille were all improved, Sedan moved to a new stadium in 2001, and Lille's stadium is due for a complete upgrade by 2003.

The oddity of the league in terms of attendances is AS Monaco, who play before very small gates in their 20,000 capacity stadium, which has not been full since a UEFA Cup quarter-final against Roma in 1992. The travelling

Table 4.1 Division 1 Home Attendances (1999/2000), in Order of Best Supported Club to Least Best; plus Average Attendances 2000/01 and 2001/02.

Club	League position	Average crowd	Percentage of capacity	Highest gate	Highest against	Lowest gate	Average 2000/01	Average 2001/02
Marseille	15	51,918	89.9	56,898	St Etienne	47,859	50,755	50,072
Paris S-G	2	43,185	89.0	44,784	OM	40,698	42,759	41,400
Lens	5	38,805	91.7	40,485	Strasbourg	33,103	39,638	37,336
Lyon	3	35,456	84.4	40,080	Sedan	27,917	34,565	34,838
Bordeaux	4	30,084	86.1	32,656	OM	24,542	29,363	27,870
St Etienne	6	28,052	77.9	35,095	Lyon	18,769	26,495	
Nantes	12	28,051	71.9	35,853	OM	22,669	32,058	33,368
Metz	11	19,868	77.0	25,648	OM	15,043	18,388	17,876
Strasbourg	9	19,852	48.6	35,946	OM	10,166	13,831	
Troyes	14	14,139	94.3	17,334	PSG	10,705	14,940	13,926
Montpellier	18	13,956	39.3	27,960	OM	9,228		13,861
Rennes	13	13,723	62.4	22,072	OM	9,873	19,457	17,854
Sedan	7	12,953	76.2	17,113	Metz	9,161	14,294	16,587
Le Havre	17	12,323	68.5	16,319	Monaco	9,141		
Auxerre	8	11,954	52.0	20,983	OM	7,701	10,513	12,138
Nancy	16	10,373	64.8	15,760	OM	7,308		
Monaco	1	10,026	55.7	14,915	PSG	5,810	9,071	8,564
Bastia	10	6,926	68.7	9,835	PSG	5,056	7,358	7,210

Sources: Chaumier and Rocheteau (2000: 507); LNF Infos, 35 (2001: 4) and 45 (2002: 8).

support from Italy that helped fill Monaco's Stade Louis-II a decade ago, has no equivalent in the French League, with the possible exception of Marseille. It is significant that nine of the 17 other clubs in the 1999/2000 championship achieved their highest gate when OM were the visitors, and three others against PSG, a number of whose supporters also regularly travel. A third club with significant travelling support is Saint-Etienne, whose historic rivalry with OM ensured the highest gate of the season in Marseille's Stade vélodrome. The latter's 60,000 capacity has, however, not been fully used since the World Cup – the league record being 57,603 against PSG in an end of season game in 1998. Relegation to D2 meant a drop in average crowds at Saint-Etienne from 26,495 (2000/01) to 15,873 (2001/02) (by far the highest in Division 2).

What is causing some optimism for future consolidation is that the upward trend is not attributable solely to the 1998 World Cup factor, but is a longer-term phenomenon. Table 4.2 shows that D1 attendances have more than tripled since the low point of the 1960s and, more importantly, have almost doubled in the most recent ten years of growth. They seem however to have peaked.

Table 4.2 *Average Division 1 Attendances since the Second World War*

Season	Average French D1 crowds
1949/50	11,403
1958/59	8,710
1968/69	6,555
1976/77	11,301
1984/85	9,780
1993/94	13,024
1994/95	13,277
1995/96	13,233
1996/97	14,212
1997/98	16,572
1998/99	19,807
1999/2000	22,324
2000/01	22,960
2001/02	21,737

Sources: Chaumier and Rocheteau (1997: 554, and 2000: 507); Wahl (1989: 309); *L'Equipe* web; LNF website [http://www.lnf.asso.fr/] 21/5/01; *LNF Infos*, 35 (2001: 4) and 45 (2002: 8–9).

One factor in the increases is that pricing of seats is not prohibitive, especially season tickets, and, in part thanks to renovation of stadiums as part of the hosting of the 1998 World Cup, there is still room for further increases. Season ticket sales ('abonnements'), for many clubs a relatively new phenomenon, more than doubled between 1997/98 and 2001/02. They appear relatively cheap compared to English equivalents. The cheapest season-ticket seats in 2002 (via supporters clubs) cost the equivalent of £50 in little Guingamp, £65 in Marseille, and Lyon, £70 in Bordeaux, and £150 in Paris. The most expensive season tickets cost about £1,000 in Paris, £700 in Marseille, £650 in Lyon and £550 in Bordeaux (*Le Parisien*, 3 August 2002: 14). Increased live television coverage since the mid-1980s (on subscription TV) seems not to have encouraged spectators to stay at home – quite the contrary.

Local Fan Culture: Interest, Passion or Militancy?

The sporting public has always felt a strong sense of identity with, and indeed ownership of, their local and national teams since the advent of the professional era. In the pre-professional era the attachment of local publics to the local club was actively encouraged by paternalistic employers, in so far as it might be a way of structuring the lives of their workforce. The sport's values fitted the needs of a big factory. Recent studies of fans (Broussard 1990; Wahl 1989) have stressed the emotional investment in supporting their team, not to mention the investment of time and money in travelling to matches, such that issues of identity and status are bound up with manifestations of so-called football hooliganism. However, Patrick Mignon (1998: 181), one of the French football sociologists most familiar with the British football context, prefers to talk of lack of passion as characteristic of French football supporters. France (at least until very recently) had no football fan culture. Writing in 1997 he put the number of French Ultras at 50,000 as opposed to 200,000 in Italy. The term 'Ultra' has been borrowed from Italian football culture to describe the 'real fan', usually young members of a supporters club. Only a minority of the most fervent supporters used to come to matches wearing the team's colours. He saw a link between this lack of passion for football and the lack of interest shown in it by national politicians or by intellectual elites, who traditionally looked down on it as a pointless activity. A recent manifestation of this attitude that provoked some interest was an article by Robert Redeker, on the editorial board of the influential left-wing journal *Les Temps modernes*, in which he argued that France's growing obsession with sport was destroying political life in France. He argued that the impact of sport has been totalitarian, impoverishing the lives and intelligence of millions of men; that sport (and football of course is the main culprit) has destroyed a real community united in the form of a political community and replaced it by an ersatz, phoney community united by sport. He condemns the star system of sportsmen, its corruption and drug taking and its adoption of the commercial values of big business. He draws a parallel with Marx's description of religion as 'opium of the people', saying that sport is worse. He admits to being unable to understand why the French public does not find professional sport 'unutterably boring' (Jeffries 2001: 21).

How do we explain this traditional lack of passion for football? It has always, since its beginnings in the late nineteenth century, been in competition with other sports, whether it be initially gymnastics and cycling or rugby, especially in certain regions such as the south-west. Cycling in the shape of the Tour de France bestrode the century in the French imagination, and since the 1960s onwards the Five Nations rugby tournament and the Roland-Garros tennis championship have interested all social classes in France. More recently, in the 1970s and 1980s, basketball, volleyball and handball have established followings in small towns and in the suburbs of the three metropolises. Alongside this change, newer participatory and individualistic sports such as 'la randonnée' (hiking or walking), jogging, swimming and the west-coast sports and their offshoots such as various forms of 'glisse' (covering surfing, new snow sports, and rollerblading) are threatening the traditional 'English' sports. Mignon quotes a figure of three-quarters of the population in 1985 who declared they undertook some form of sport or physical exercise, compared to a quarter in 1967. This had risen to 83 per cent of 15- to 75-year-olds in a survey of 2000 (Mignon and Truchot 2001). This growth of individualistic and less institutionalised sport may be interpreted as a change in values within French society, and a form of modernisation, divesting themselves of local attachments, and cultivating a greater distance from partisan passions within sport. From this perspective, the spectator becomes more of a Baudelairian 'flâneur', interested certainly, but maintaining a degree of ironic detachment and distrust of passionate involvements. Surveys showed that while football crowds were fairly young, the working classes (white collar and blue collar) made up a good half of fans in the stadium. However, overall the crowd was socially very heterogeneous, and representative of French society as a whole, with the exception of the under-representation of the highly educated from within the upper middle classes. There were variations according to whether the club came from a heavily industrial town or from Paris, where white-collar fans were more numerous (Mignon 1998: 186–189).

This social heterogeneity cannot on its own explain the lack of passion for football in France. Mignon's thesis is that whereas in Britain, until recently at least, football support was traditionally very much the expression of a class culture and supporters formed a more homogeneous community, in France football supporting was secondary to other more important attachments and divisions that defined identity. The nineteenth-century struggle between the Church and State and its associated ideological rivalries divided football. So too, later, did the Labour movement's opposition to football organised around the factory and the revolutionary left's subsequent criticism of the professionalisation of the sport. The French Labour movement (whether socialist or communist) did not favour the growth of a separate working-class culture, but sought to promote access to a more universal culture as part of its emancipation. British class divisions were more rigid in the key period of the growth of football culture – between the wars and up to the 1960s – and this tradition lives on in the stadium (or did at least until the 1990s). In France the promotion of the Republican ideal through the school system from the late nineteenth century onwards has created a dominant value that views society as a sum of autonomous individuals, who cannot be reduced to groups defined primarily either by their social class, region, sex, age or ethnic background – censuses in France cannot for example ask questions about racial or ethnic origin. French football support has therefore to situate itself in a public space defined by this tension between community and society. Being a fan means declaring a group identity, but in a context where forms of collective action have always been seen as part of a struggle for the right to belong to the *national community of citizens* as a whole. The argument, after Ehrenberg, that the attraction and impact of football is linked to the struggle for equality and social mobility (the level playing-field of sport being a metaphor for the Republic), means that in a country such as France where the egalitarian movement has found expression in a social struggle (the Labour movement) but also a political struggle (the Republican movement) for access to citizenship and not for the right to live according to one's own rules in one's own community, it is understandable that private passions such as football supporting have been accorded a secondary position. Football support has consequently been in a fragile position in the context of other competing leisure interests. Whereas Mignon sees the British and German models of football fandom as based on community identity (i.e. class identity as much as local identity), the French model, he hypothesises, might be based on an activism or militancy model ('mobilisation'): a club, just like a political party, needs to convince its supporters that what it is offering is worth investing time and effort in; and there needs to be more than a single reason to join: to be together with like-minded people (sociability), certainly, but also to see a high-quality spectacle, that projects a meaning beyond itself, that is offering some symbolic value (Mignon 1998: 195–199).

The lowest point in football support in France was the late 1960s, which corresponds to a period of great social change and great socio-political mobilisation. Henri Mendras (1988: 20) chooses 1965 rather than 1968 as the date marking the break between tradition and modernity in France. It saw the start of modern mass commercialisation and mass consumption (France's first supermarket), mass higher education and the inevitability of the university crisis (Nanterre University opened), mass access to literature through increasing levels of education (expansion of the 'livre de poche'), mass television (as ownership of sets rose), personality politics (the first directly elected French President), the beginning of the drop in the birth rate, and an increase in women's employment. The drop in numbers of football fans in the 1960s may also be partly explained by new leisure activities. At a more profound level, the great social institutions that had socialised the French for decades had entered a period of crisis, from the Catholic Church to the education system, from the orthodox political parties to the Army (conscription for service in the war of decolonisation in Algeria rendered national service ideologically suspect). Pop culture was becoming the dominant part of mass culture, being at one and the same time a key element of mass consumption and a site of counter-culture in which to protest against the massification of culture and society. In this context football had little symbolic meaning to offer. 'Modern' life in the shape of Anglo-American pop music, mass consumerism, mass ownership of cars, television, the cinema, restaurants, on the one hand, and more active engagement with alternative culture or 'gauchisme', on the other, left football looking old-fashioned to some, male chauvinistic to others. To the more politically militant it could be regarded as the opium of the people, distracting from revolutionary consciousness. Stadiums were particularly empty in 1968, except on the occasions when they were full to bursting point with political protesters, such as the famous Charléty stadium meeting in May 1968.

Mignon's view (1998: 199–200) of football fandom as a form of militancy rather than an expression of community can also be used to explain a particularly French phenomenon in football support of the modern era: the Ultras, who stage-manage their engagement with the world of football in their noisy and colourful spectacles on the terraces, and who have thereby reinvented French traditions of football support. As a by-product, for a while at least, they also invented a particular French type of football violence that appears to have different roots and different aims to British 'football hooliganism'.

However, before moving to a consideration of the new supporter phenomenon in the major clubs of today, any history of French fandom would need to start with the saga of 'les Verts', AS Saint-Etienne, that was crucial in the rebuilding of interest in football from its low point in the 1960s. Since the Second World War, only a few club teams have established strong local and national followings and international reputations: Reims was one in the 1950s, followed by Saint-

Etienne in the 1970s. In the 1980s and 1990s, despite incursions by Monaco, Nantes, Bordeaux and Auxerre, the domestic scene has been dominated by the rivalry of big-city clubs Olympique de Marseille (OM) and Paris Saint-Germain (PSG), both of whom have tasted national and European success, and European-level followings as well as spectator violence. These two clubs, plus Racing Club de Lens, are the only ones that have fanatical supporters such as English clubs take for granted, and they will be examined below.

The Green Cauldron gives Birth to 'le 12e Homme'

For more than a decade from the middle 1960s to the late 1970s, French football was dominated by 'les Verts', the Greens from Saint-Etienne, who won seven championships out of ten between 1967 and 1976, and five French Cups between 1968 and 1977, finding themselves in a European competition in every season bar three from 1967 to 1983. The unfashionable little industrial town in the Forez region was, metaphorically at least, dominated by the Geoffroy-Guichard stadium, that came to be called 'le chaudron vert', the green cauldron, such was the heat generated by their supporters – not only in matches against their key rival Olympique de Marseille but especially during their progress in the European competitions of the 1970s. Just as Anfield built up a reputation for invincibility that affected teams visiting Liverpool, so did Geoffroy-Guichard for European visitors to deepest France. Saint-Etienne was an attacking team, their star players had charisma: the Revelli brothers, Jean-Michel Larqué the organiser, and striker Rocheteau, with a perm to put even the 1970s Keegan in the shade. Their European matches were often very closely contested, with results in doubt, which heightened the tension and the noise in the stadium. In the European Cup, 1975 saw the Greens' progress halted at the semi-final stage by Beckenbauer's Bayern Munich, the eventual winners. But the match that stays in the memory of the sporting public is the quarter final against Dynamo Kiev in 1976. Having lost the first (away) leg 2–0, Saint-Etienne snatched a nail-biting victory in the return home leg 3–0 after extra time. Defeat in the final against Bayern (again) at Hampden Park, Glasgow, by a single goal confirms, for Wahl, 'the national public's attachment to losing heroes courageously resisting inhuman adversaries' (Wahl 1989: 315). In 1977 they lost in the quarter-finals, again to the eventual winners, this time Keegan's Liverpool, who scored the winner late in the game at Anfield. Some Liverpool supporters look back on this game as a high point in their European saga, defeating the then favourites for the cup, with the noisy and colourful support of the Kop.

The support given by the Saint-Etienne public gave birth to the notion of the extra player, 'le 12e homme', 'the twelfth man' helping the team to success.

Since the Second World War, only a few French club teams have established national followings. If Reims were the first in the 1950s, then Saint-Etienne were certainly the second, significantly aided by television coverage of their European matches. While a national following for a club team on live television was new, so too was the supporter phenomenon in the stadium. What we now may too easily take for granted in terms of noise and colour was uncommon at the time. Saint-Etienne supporters in their masses, adopting English fan cultures, dressed in the club colours of green and white, waving scarves and banners, sang and chanted their support throughout the matches. The European influence of Liverpool fans' travels, following their team into Europe, should not be underestimated in the creation of a new fan culture by imitation, in France and other countries. It was the British model of support that was the major influence available to Saint-Etienne, who adopted it all the more easily since the Geoffroy-Guichard stadium was built on British lines and the town and its supporters fitted the industrial working-class model of British football. Saint-Etienne's visit to Anfield in 1977 and Liverpool's victorious European Cup Final in Paris in 1981 were important landmarks. However, the Greens very first European Cup match was at another home of British football fervour, Ibrox Park, against Glasgow Rangers in the 1957/58 season. They visited Celtic Park in 1968/69, Ibrox again in 1975/76 (and won). The 1970s were a time when British and Italian fan cultures were in advance of the more sedate Germans, as confirmed by interviews with Liverpool players of the time ('When Liverpool ruled the world', 15 May 2001, BBC1). Saint-Etienne's travels were the vehicle for importation into France of the more colourful, noisier and, in the 1980s, the more violent aspects of British fan culture.

Since then, while AS Saint-Etienne have gone through various ups-and-downs of relegation and promotion, sometimes associated with financial or transfer scandals, the tradition of fervent support has continued. Geoffroy-Guichard is, in the minds of opposing supporters, a 'lieu de mémoire', a place to respect and to show one's mettle.

Ultras: Support, Involvement and Identity

In the middle 1980s the new spectator phenomenon became more organised, and more violent, with English and Italian influences, as French clubs played more often in Europe and travel became easier and cheaper. Mignon (1998: 212) reports that 'Kops' initially typified northern clubs, with a quieter and more community atmosphere, whereas southern stadiums had more organised groups of 'Ultras', who imitated the Italian type of terrace spectacle. The Italian style has gradually come to dominate French stadiums. In most club stadiums, the favoured position for the young Ultras, as at Anfield, is behind the goal, in the *virages* or ends. A characteristic of the new French supporters is their organisation into 'associations', or supporters clubs, whose members make up more than 20 per cent of total fans. A key point to stress in terms of differences between French supporters associations and English supporters clubs is their relationship with the football club. Mignon's concept of activism or militancy as the model for French supporters is useful here.

Some supporters associations are highly integrated to the club. Their members participate as unpaid volunteers (*bénévoles*) in tasks such as stewarding, selling drinks and sandwiches and other merchandise on behalf of the football club. While remaining legally separate from the club in terms of their constitutional existence, some 'official' supporters associations earn a percentage of the sales of the merchandise and are effectively subsidised by the football club – this helps pay for travel to away games for example. Some associations raise a significant amount of money for the club. The official supporters associations are usually quite distinct however from the groups of Ultras who put on the *animations* or *tifos* in their ends.

The new supporters associations of the 1980s and indeed today, are much more independent of the football club, sometimes produce their own fanzine, and are much more militant and critical of club policy (see pp. 73–77 *re* Marseille). These associations can be subsidised by the football club to help organise the terrace spectacle – buying a huge flag for example – and may be allowed storage space at the stadium. Under Tapie's chairmanship at Marseille large supporters associations gained the right to sell season tickets cheaply to their members. Mignon's analysis of the different types of association is that some seek to increase their influence and presence by sheer weight of numbers; others define themselves as avant-gardist or an elite of the most faithful followers of a team, apt to turn on the fair-weather supporters with the equivalent of 'Where-were-you-when-we-were-shit?' chants. At the extreme end of the Ultra phenomenon are groups who refuse all contact with the football club hierarchy, and who may refer to themselves as 'casuals' or 'hools', adopting an English vocabulary and attitude to support as confrontation, either with police or with other supporter groups. Some are openly neo-fascist and xenophobic. Mignon (1998: 221) claims there are also one or two who are ideologically of the extreme-left. This ideological orientation will be explored further *re* Olympique de Marseille (pp. 74–75) and Paris Saint-Germain (pp. 80–89).

Some football clubs such as Lens have adopted a paternalistic attitude towards the 'official' supporters clubs in an attempt to exercise some control over the image of the club. Broussard (1990: 208) describes French club hierarchies' lack of understanding of the football supporter in the 1980s and their suspicion of the Ultra movement. Writing in *Génération supporter* (1990), he claimed only two or three French clubs had fanatical supporters such as English clubs take for granted: Paris Saint-Germain, Olympique de Marseille, and perhaps Girondins de Bordeaux. Looking back to the 1990s the 'sang et or' of Lens would have to be added to such a list.

Racing Club de Lens

When, in May 1998, Racing Club de Lens won the French championship for the first and so far only time, with an 87th minute goal at Auxerre, not only were there 5,000 fans waiting at the Lille airport to welcome home the players and officials at 1.30 a.m., but by the time the team reached Stade Bollaert, at 3 a.m., the stadium was three-quarters full with 30,000 home fans singing the *Marseillaise* and waving red-and-gold scarves to acclaim the arrival of the trophy and the *Sang et Or* (Ramella and Touboul 1998: 3). In terms of overall numbers, Lens can now count on the third highest average home crowd (38,800 in 2000/01) behind OM and PSG, which means an average 91.7 per cent of seats filled in the stadium (Chaumier and Rocheteau 2000: 507). In a *France Football* survey (published 7 January 2000), Lens fans were the most satisfied of any with their stadium facilities and entertainment value. They were also voted the best fans in France, the most passionate, with the best singing. Whereas most French clubs built up a tradition for their young fans to gather in the *virages* behind the goals, the Lens public's favoured position was in the stands, and young and adult fans mixed, all dressed in their blood-red and gold colours. They reportedly used to share their half-time chips and beer with opposing supporters, except with the local rivals Lille and Paris (Mignon 1998: 213). Friendly visitors were more likely to be those from similarly proletarian towns such as Saint-Etienne or Le Havre.

In explaining the particularities of the Lens fans, Marie-Pierre Toulet (2000) found that while the Lens club has cultivated cheap ticket prices, there was also a culture of control in the relationship of the club to the supporters associations. There are concessions to allow families to attend: more than 1,500 ticket holders are children, and 15 per cent are women. Although the directors acknowledge the important role of corporate sponsorship, the club endeavours not to penalise the bulk of working-class fans and so has a policy of affordable entry. Half of Lens supporters come from modest backgrounds or are unemployed. Tickets are easily available locally, for example through seven Auchan hypermarket stores in the region. The 1998/99 campaign increased attendance, with new deals for the under-16s who benefited from special reductions: 400 francs per season (20 francs per match). Season ticket holders have priority seats for European and national cups with certain seats costing only 10 francs (Toulet 2000: 38–39).

Their northern fan base in an old mining area is reminiscent of those of Newcastle or Sunderland. An important symbol for many fans is the miner's lamp on the head. Their down-to-earth passion has led some commentators to conclude that the Blood and Gold supporters are the most 'British' of all French fans. Indeed the club stadium looks more like the square English ground as opposed to traditional French curved omnisport grounds. Club Chairman Gervais Martel recognises the heart of the club is 'populaire', close to the 'peuple', but is attempting to extend the club's popularity to the whole region Nord-Pas-de-Calais and further afield. Their official supporters club has subscribers scattered through regional branches all over France: Aisne, Pas-de-Calais, Oise, Somme, Seine-et-Marne in the north of France, and even in the Puy-de-Dôme in the centre, the Bouches-du-Rhône and the Drôme in the south-east. Fans are encouraged to use the club's well-developed Internet site to keep in contact with the club. (ibid.: 38–40)

The other side of the coin is that in 1991, following recommendations by the League management committee, Lens grouped all its supporters associations under a new entity, *Supp'R'Lens*. The club's declared aim in setting up this official supporters club was to promote and reinforce local attachment to the club: 'The mission of these sections is to make Racing Club de Lens and its colours more widely known, that is to get people talking about the club . . . positively. Lens supporters, apart from their reputation for loyalty and sportsmanship, therefore offer through their associations a dynamic image which can only benefit the club' (Demazière *et al.* 1998: 232). Toulet concluded (2000: 40–41) that this strategy was part of a wider process, initiated by Martel, aimed at transforming the club's structures by increasing contacts with local firms and developing merchandising. In the era of football-business, *Supp'R'Lens* has become both a PR tool and an instrument of control. The club has expectations of its official supporters. Annual meetings between club officials and supporters reinforce the message that the supporters are ambassadors of the club and of the town. With its 6,500 affiliated supporters and 65 sections spread over eight departments and five regions, *Supp'R'Lens* is hegemonic.

However, as elsewhere, in the 1990s Ultras groups emerged, more militant and determined to remain independent of the club authorities. They are highly visible in the stadium, organising the visual spectacle. Most of them are students and have adopted the Ultra culture from Italy or England. The main ones being *Red Tigers* (200–250 members), *North's warriors* (100–150 members). These groups reject the traditional image of the Lens supporters voted as the best public in France. By doing this, as well as asserting their independence from the club, they go against a system of values that is at the heart of local football support in Lens: the inheritance of the mining communities with strong values of community and solidarity and local pride (Demazière *et al.* 1998: 234).

Despite the existence of these independent fan groups, the Lens model of support is none the less the more traditional model. *Supp'R'Lens* is closely controlled by the club, and has been seen as a reflection of the paternalism of the Nord-Pas-de-Calais's old social democratic tradition. What Lens is not doing and cannot afford to do, is to gentrify their approach to fans at the risk of losing their traditional fan base.

Olympique de Marseille (OM)

The second city of France is much more a part of Mediterranean and Latin culture, with a linguistic as well as cultural history opposing it to the north of France, and a reputation for an explosive and exuberant temperament. The best study is Bromberger's work on football supporter ethnography, based on an analysis of Marseille in comparison to the Italian cities of Naples and Turin. He found the local context was highly determining as regards supporter culture and identity (Bromberger *et al.* 1995: 72–73).

Marseille has cultivated an identity as a rebellious city ('frondeuse'), and over the centuries this reputation has provoked either fear or amused condescension in the rest of France. Janus-like, it has been portrayed in literature and film as a cosmopolitan city with a reputation for organised crime, lack of law and order, and a murky political history, at the same time as resembling the set of a comic opera, peopled by tall-tale-telling lovers of *pastis*, carefree and uneducated perhaps but with the gift of the gab. Over time, various episodes have created a consciousness of being the nation's scapegoat. In the 1914–18 war the Marseillais were stigmatised as being unpatriotic. Between the two world wars the city was portrayed as the French Chicago, the Mafia capital of France. This negative image of the town worsened with the serious structural crisis following France's decolonisation and the consequent decline in the activity of the Marseille port, hitherto fully employed in trade with the French North African empire and beyond. Previously the link between the North and the South, it had lost both by the 1970s. There followed de-industrialisation, poor urban planning, depopulation, and recession.

In the local passion for the city's football team is this bitterness about its history and wounded local pride, directed against the rest of France, but particularly against the capital city Paris, representing power, as opposed to the apparent powerlessness of the Marseillais. So any major victory of OM is seen as ostentatious revenge on fate and a legitimate reversal of the course of history. Any setback such as a refereeing error awakens a sense of injustice and evidence of a plot brewed by an arrogant capital. For Bromberger *et al.* (1995: 73) the dominant form of the local culture as represented in the local fan culture is that of victimisation. Humiliation is a word that still comes to the lips of fans in response to defeats they can attribute to poor management or here-today-gone-tomorrow directors (see reports by *Le Monde* following the 5-1 defeat by Saint-Etienne in December 1999 – Barth 2000a). This is not restricted to the poorer classes, Bromberger observes, since OM's supporters come from all social classes (Bromberger *et al.* 1995: 74). As a fan explained: 'The stadium has taken the place of the local area. It is where people meet each other, where the labourer rubs shoulders with the lawyer, where people fall in love, and where a silly little bugger will be accepted as a silly little bugger and not be rejected' (Barth 2000a).

In the 1980s, for economically hard-hit Marseillais, the football club became a life-belt to cling on to, a community offering mutual support. A number of young Ultras created an atmosphere that new OM chairman Bernard Tapie recognised as important for the whole of the football public of the city. The Ultras had 1,200 members in 1990, a place in the stadium to store their gear (flags, drums, etc.), a van, various products to sell (T-shirts, stickers, scarves, and so on), but they remained fairly independent of the club, that at different times had been suspicious of them and felt they detracted from the image of Marseille. The relations between club (directors, manager, and players) and supporters is historically different to that in England or Italy where the players, whether winning or losing, will go and applaud their fans at the end of the match. For supporters who have made the effort and expense to go to an away match, this is seen as a recompense for their loyalty and their sacrifice. Until recently this has been rare in France, where there has been no real encouragement by the clubs for players to get involved in the community by visiting hospitals, youth clubs, supporters club, etc., and where there is a huge gap between players and spectators. In Britain players are more likely to come from the same milieu as the fans and often have stood on the terraces that they now play in front of. Chris Waddle was one such: a supporter of Sunderland as a lad, who, when he came to Marseille, was much appreciated for his attitude towards the fans. Other French players had little idea what it was like to be a supporter. Brought up in the isolation of a youth coaching centre, they had lost contact with the day-to-day realities of fandom.

This growing gap is a key factor in the process of marginalisation of groups of young fans in the 1980s. Some adopted attitudes associated with the extreme-right party, the Front national. Having grown in support from nowhere after the recession of the early to mid-1980s, by 1989 the FN was getting 15 per cent of votes in local elections in the Marseille area, and racist taunts from the terraces to visiting black players developed at about this time (Broussard 1990: 192). The terraces were reflecting the atmosphere of the region. More recently, by the year 2000 most members of supporters clubs declared themselves 'a-political', yet against the Front national. A majority of them indeed are of immigrant extraction. A leader of one such association (*Marseille trop puissant*) attended meetings of *Ras l'front*, a militant anti-racist organisation (Barth 2000a). *Le Monde* claimed that no OM fans were now supporters of the Front national (Samson 2000).

Whether winning or losing, but particularly losing, football has reinforced Marseille fans' sense of local identity that Bromberger defines as paranoia wider than the local football culture and typical of the whole city, a population feeling unjustly under attack from the outside, creating a propensity to regroup behind its own colours and look after its own. In 1993/94 this 'syndrome of exclusion' (Bromberger *et al.* 1995: 74) was reawakened, after several years of success, through conflict with the national football authorities over the 'affaire Tapie'. Revelations of match-rigging and corruption brought the enforced relegation of OM to Division 2. Fans again exhibited a persecution complex, against the media and against fans of other clubs. The Ultras often feel they are not understood by their club, and that they are the only ones carrying the flame, drawing strength from this isolation. As with Saint-Etienne, Marseille fans have claimed their aims are 'not to kill, but to support OM and to take responsibility for the spectacle', along the lines of Italian supporters (Broussard 1990: 189).

Their militancy and latent violence was particularly apparent in the 1999/ 2000 season: the club had sold their captain Laurent Blanc in the close season, and during a particularly poor spell of results demonstrations by fans led to a meeting between players and fans organised by club officials in an attempt to calm the situation. However, the meeting turned into a confrontation, verbal and physical. Fans attacked two players' (expensive) cars and manhandled players and officials, who were clearly intimidated (Barth 2000a). At the end of the season their new captain Robert Pires left for Arsenal. In the 2000/01 season pressure from the fans on the chairman Robert Louis-Dreyfus was instrumental in the controversial return of Bernard Tapie as director of football.

Marseille would seem to be the club where relations between supporters clubs and the football club are the most complex – not only because of the particular culture of the city, but also because of certain concessions made to them by Tapie in an attempt to encourage support. The result of this has been the creation of vested interests that divide the club and supporters associations. In the 1980s the club gave concessions to the biggest associations of Ultras to sell OM merchandise and season tickets to their members. In the 1999/2000 season, for example, the associations were able to cream off 100 francs for every 600-franc (£60) season ticket they sold. The sums involved are not inconsiderable, since four major supporters associations have about 5,000 members each. They are thought to control 28,000 season tickets, giving them a turnover of 2.8 million francs (£280,000). This financial income has over the years helped the Ultras supporters associations to grow and to organise themselves into powerful pressure groups. Two of these, called 'les Ultras' and 'les Yankees', have set up limited companies to sell merchandise such as scarves and T-shirts. Whilst Tapie tolerated this economic activity as the price of their support – and indeed it may be argued they repaid it when fan pressure made the club bring him back in 2001 – the club directors have appeared more and more irritated by it in recent years. The club chairman up to 1999, Jean-Michel Roussier, attempted to regain control of the database of the associations' several thousand season ticket holders' names and addresses with a view to using it for direct selling of merchandise on behalf of the club. A struggle to regain full control of season ticket sales is also a latent issue. Demonstrations by fans preceded Roussier's replacement in April 1999 by Yves Marchand, the director-general of Adidas-France, appointed by Robert Louis-Dreyfus, who, as owner of Adidas, had bought the club in 1996. Poor results and more fan demonstrations in 1999 through 2001 led to changes of manager and to Louis-Dreyfus taking personal executive control of the club.

Apart from the long-standing local cultural explanation (civic pride and/ or humiliation being closely linked to the success or failure of the football club) and the issue of vested interests on the part of certain local associations, a wider explanation of the current battle for power is to see it as a battle of values, with fans using the same militant tactics as used by the steelworkers of the north of France or other professional groups in the defence of their jobs and their community. The club is certainly a community for the more militant young fans. A membership leaflet describing what the Ultras association offers says: 'This is where you can talk about what OM and the Ultras are doing, get involved in the group by bringing new ideas or helping prepare the [terrace] spectacle. Various activities are available: [French] bowls, card games, bar football games, table tennis, darts, pool' (Barth 2000a). Fans often criticise the business values of the club: 'For [the club directors], the best team in the world is not the one with the most championships but the one selling the most shirts' (ibid.). There may be a lack of coherence in the expressions of fans' anger (wanting the club to buy the best players, wanting Tapie back, and rejecting business values), but Marseille fans are rejecting the take-over of 'their' football club by outside commercial interests, the transformation of the people's game into a global business. And the different supporters associations do not find it easy to work with the club. *Le Monde* quotes one association leader as saying: 'This club has been carried by us and our parents, we have worked for it, we have made it known world wide, and now we are being dispossessed by financiers' (ibid.). This has resonances of any number of industrial disputes (more likely to be called 'social' disputes in France) to save factories, jobs and communities, as the French economy adapts to global forces. The vocabulary of the Marseille fan is more parochial and less political than that used by those attacking McDonald's and the global commercial values it seems to represent, but the tone is similarly militant and angry. Supporters associations have had difficulties in working together at national level, and so far no equivalent of José Bové, the leader of the *Confédération paysanne*, has emerged to give them an articulate national focus such as he has created by linking in the public mind 'la malbouffe' (poor-quality industrially produced food) with a whole economic system and globalisation. Food is still more central to French culture than is football.

Ultras and Soccer Violence

Violence between French fans is a relatively small-scale activity compared to England and may have been exacerbated by lack of police experience in controlling it. French police have not developed the habit of accompanying visiting fans to and from the ground to ensure security. Police authorities, particularly in some towns such as Saint-Etienne, were used to relying on repressive rather than preventative measures, and were also reticent about taking down fencing in stadiums for the World Cup.

In his analysis of British 'supporters and hooligans', Patrick Mignon (1990) points the way to understanding certain differences in the phenomenon of 'football violence' between France and Britain. He uses Ehrenberg's analysis of hooliganism as being a way of getting noticed, as opposed to the ordinary supporter remaining invisible and anonymous. The ones see themselves as participants in the spectacle, the others merely spectators. 'Keeping up appearances' has become democratised through its expression in football grounds. Mignon situates the phenomenon in the global context of an individualistic society having lost its accepted markers of social position and identity. At a time when the whole of our culture exalts individual achievement through personal effort rather than collective action, fans from the bottom of the social scale with no prospects through school or job manufacture an identity by displacing attention from the pitch to the terraces, and thus emerging from anonymity. As with the punk movement, they manage literally to make a spectacle of themselves. They have taken over the symbols and the space provided by the modern football game in their bid to be noticed at all costs. Football gives them a rare occasion to confirm they exist. Appearance is everything, and usually it is only the *appearance* of violence, rather than the reality, that they threaten, as Broussard found.

While the above is common to both British and French expressions of soccer 'hooliganism', there are differences that emerge from the different social, cultural and economic history and geography of the two countries. Mignon claims British class barriers have lasted longer than in France and that the chances of social mobility for the British unskilled or semi-skilled industrial worker are less than the French. Hooliganism is therefore a logical solution in an unreasonable situation, whereby part of the working class is using traditional forms of collective solidarity to produce individualistic strategies allowing them to become somebody. Other differences include the reduced scale of spectators in French stadiums, the relative lack of local rivalries in France, including religious ones – no towns have two big clubs, not even Paris – and the deterrent effect of the longer distances to travel to away matches in France. Whereas the British five-and-a-half day week allowed football, on a Saturday afternoon, to be lived as an expression of a working-class community whose name and honour the team was defending, the lack of a free Saturday afternoon for decades in France, combined with the smaller scale of industrial towns, did not favour a parallel evolution with its attendant passionate rivalries. More general regional and north-south rivalries are lesser in France, Mignon claims. It is true that the main opposition is between Paris and the provinces, which explains why the problem of hooliganism as confrontation between rival fans has concentrated around Paris Saint-Germain as the club everybody loves to hate.

The Invention of a Footballing Tradition: PSG and its Fans

Parisian partisanship in football is new. In 1923 *Le Miroir des sports* was already arguing that geographical mobility had diluted any special Parisian identity to explain the lack of partisan support for a Parisian team (Wahl 1989: 227). Patrick Mignon, who has directed the most sociological research on Parisian supporters, argues that to understand how modern football support in the Paris region is different to elsewhere one needs to look at how, since the 1970s, there has been a conscious effort to create a new club, PSG, a new public and a local identity. This involved the invention of a tradition and the creation of a community of fans more or less from scratch (Mignon 1998: 225–226). What football traditions there had been in Paris had been broken when Racing Club de Paris had gone down to Division 2 in 1964, and then into Division 3. Daniel Hechter's Paris Saint-Germain tried to fill the void in the middle 1970s. As a relatively new club, having been founded in 1970, PSG was looking to create a loyal following. The innovation for Paris of an executive mayor elected by universal suffrage in 1977 and the city's interest in the club in the form of subsidies and then the arrival of the television company Canal+ as major shareholder in 1991 made PSG important to stakeholders of far greater financial and political weight than a few thousand supporters. But supporters were needed. In 1979, the new chairman Francis Borelli played a key role in encouraging the formation of a group of young fans that came to be known as the Boulogne Kop, by offering ten matches for 10 francs to under-16s at the Parc des Princes.

The club also subsidised travel to away matches and lent premises for storage of drums and flags.

By the 1980s these fans had taken on a punk fashion and then became skinheads in imitation of fans of English clubs (whose scarves they wore), and turned to fairly run-of-the-mill violence against visiting supporters. Footballing success came to PSG in 1982 and 1983 with French Cup wins, then the League title in 1985/86, and frequent participation in European competitions; but good seasons could easily be followed by poor ones. From 1985 the PSG fans organised themselves on Italian lines, into supporters associations, by organising travel to away games and pre-match 'entertainment' (smoke bombs, giant flags), and selling T-shirts and other items with their logos on them. They remained independent of the official supporters clubs that were subsidised by the club, and all-told numbered 300–400 fans in the late 1980s.

The 1990s saw PSG become one of the most successful clubs in France if not *the* most successful, winning the Championship in 1994, three French Cups (1993, 1995, 1998), two League Cups (1995, 1998), and the second European Competition won by a French club, the European Cup Winners' Cup in 1997. Success allowed numbers of spectators to grow, as seen in Table 4.3.

In terms of spectator numbers in the 1990s, PSG has consistently attracted the highest crowds in the league – except for the exceptional seasons of OM

Table 4.3 *Average Home Crowds : Paris Saint-Germain (1975/2002)*

Season	Average crowd
1975/76	17,250
1981/82	24,000
1984/85	16,254
1985/86	24,571
1990/91	14,465
1991/92	26,600
1996/97	35,582
1997/98	36,664
1998/99	40,910
1999/2000	43,185
2000/01	42,759
2001/02	41,400

Sources: Mignon (1998: 29); Chaumier and Rocheteau (1997, 1999, 2000); *L'Equipe* web; *LNF Infos*, 45 (2002: 8–9).

since 1999/2000. Crowds in the Parc des Princes have begun to resemble those of other major European cities in terms of size (almost), in numbers of supporters associations, in manifestations of hooliganism (in the 1980s), and in their association with the extreme right, in a section of the Kop de Boulogne. In the early 1990s, Mignon's surveys showed that the fans were 90 per cent male, coming from the whole of the Paris region (20–30 per cent from the city of Paris *intra muros*), and were fairly representative of the social classes of the area – that is, far more white-collar working class than blue-collar. Fans were young: 41 per cent under 24 and 64 per cent under 35. The public included fans representing the different waves of immigration into France (Portuguese, black African, French West Indian, North African Jews). Underrepresented were women (as elsewhere) and fans of North African Arab extraction. There were also a few showbiz personalities. Figures from 1996 for the *virages*, where the most committed supporters, including the Ultras, congregate, show 91.5 per cent male, 8.5 per cent female: mostly from the poor suburbs and less than a quarter from the city of Paris, 54 per cent between 15 and 24, and 36.5 per cent between 25 and 34 years old. One-third were students; about half were in regular work. There were differences between the Boulogne end and the Auteuil end: the Boulogne Kop was a bit older and less studenty, and very white – the Boulogne end is where the extreme right-wing elements have traditionally congregated, whereas the Ultras in the cheaper Auteuil end attract some fans of black African or Maghrebi extraction. Those who have been arrested for 'football hooliganism' are often from a higher social class background than other categories of delinquent (Mignon 1998: 226–231).

If, as Mignon has revealed, the crowds are now in some sense representative of the social mix of Paris and its region, what identity if any has been created around the new club, and has it changed over the years? The supporters associations have names that often give them an identification with Paris (*Lutèce Falco* – after the Roman name for Paris; *Gavroches* – after a famous literary character, the heroic Paris street urchin from Victor Hugo's *Les Misérables*; *les Titifosi* – a play on words, combining the Italian *tifosi* (fans) and *titi*, another name for a young Parisian urchin. The *Boulogne Boys* and the *Supras Auteuil* are references not so much to the two local Parisian *quartiers* around the stadium, but to the two opposite *virages* where the groups congregate, plus a reference to the English or Italian supporter traditions they identify with. Other names also refer to this foreign tradition with some reference to Paris or sometimes not at all, as if the support for the local team was less important than being part of a wider tradition. *Crazy Gang Génération Parisienne* seems to refer to Wimbledon FC, whereas *Titans* may be an Italian reference. *Tigris Mystic* is less clear. However, the colours they all wear are the club colours of red and blue (the colours too of the city's coat of arms). In interviews in the 1980s, Broussard reports, fans referred to their local chauvinism, claiming to defend the capital against the provinces. Among their chants is 'Si t'es fier d'être parisien, frappe dans tes mains' ('If you're proud you are Parisian, clap your hands'). This is not unexpected to a British audience, and seems to be a direct translation of chants expressing local identity heard in English grounds.

Whereas it could be said that, before and during the 30 glorious years of growth following the war and liberation, Paris was a concentrated version of the provinces, urban growth since the oil crises of the 1970s and recessions of the 1980s have been such that, as Mignon (1998: 237) puts it, Parisians are more and more Parisian and more and more suburban. Paris no longer has the monopoly of being the only big urban metropolis in France, and the term *banlieue* in France does not mean a middle-class suburb of detached houses nor solely ghettos of high-rise flats. The whole of the Paris region is now far more important than Paris *intra muros* in terms of numbers, and is socially mixed, even if over a million people travel into Paris every day to work. The football team can in the modern period be seen as representing a new bigger Paris, the *Paris region* that is open to people of all origins and backgrounds. Proud of Paris identity does not necessarily mean, therefore, pride in some older view of what the city of Paris represents as administrative, economic and cultural capital of the nation. Indeed the original young working-class or lower-middle-class supporters, students and the unemployed occupied the Boulogne end, claims Mignon (1998: 238), as a protest against the bourgeois Paris that they saw in the area around the Parc des Princes – Boulogne and Auteuil are very expensive, upper-middle-class areas. The early club chairman Daniel Hechter set the tone for the officials of the club, as Broussard (1990: 174–175) reports. When the couturier-chairman and his directors turned up at home matches or arrived in the provinces, they would inevitably be dressed in the latest high fashion (seen as 'des fringues de pédé' – 'poncy gear' – by opposing fans).

Seen from the provinces, this sense of Parisian distinctiveness is easily understood as provoking hostility. The club from the capital has always been disliked in the provinces, as too wealthy, too self-confident, in short too Parisian. This Paris–provinces rivalry in football merely extends the common notion of the whole of French wealth and power being concentrated in the capital, turning the provinces into an economic and cultural desert. The concept of Paris as opposed to the desert that was the rest of France is a part of everyday mythology, mental processes and resentments, which the 1983 decentralisation and regionalisation reforms have not yet broken down. Supporting the only Division 1 side based in Paris, the small numbers of PSG supporters who travelled to the provinces quite naturally took this Paris–provinces dichotomy as defining their identity and their superiority, and indeed provincial resentments forced it upon them. They would call Lille fans drunkards, or Auxerre followers peasants, reserving their most abusive insults for the Marseille supporters.

If identity *vis-à-vis* the provinces was a given, identity of fans within the Paris region needed to be invented. In these terms, the appropriation of a territory in the stadium can be interpreted as an affirmation of an identity by the dis-affected youth of the poor *banlieues*. In contemporary France the term *banlieues* is generally qualified by 'pauvres' or 'chaudes' (i.e. poor and liable to degenerate into urban violence), and more particularly it is a euphemism for predominantly second- and third-generation immigrant districts, suffering more than other districts from social exclusion. While they are not entirely ghettos, they do contain a high proportion of population descended from black and North African Arab immigration. An alternative term with similar connotations is 'cités' (estates). The initial creation of the Boulogne Kop seems to have come about for some fans as a prolongation of street rivalries between 'white' 'French' youths and 'black' and 'beur' sons of immigrants. Sometimes, Mignon found, these white youths, whether from working-class or more middle-class backgrounds, were experiencing downward social mobility or felt threatened at least by loss of status. They also felt threatened by or were jealous of the apparently freer and more macho lifestyle of immigrant youths in their gangs, which seemed like communities that gave them strength. A skinhead style was adopted by this group of disaffected young white suburbanites and their coming together in the Boulogne Kop in the 1970s and 1980s was an expression of their insecure identity, and an attempt to define their own group identity in contradistinction to what appeared to them to be strong communities representing the 'other'. Explained in terms of centre against periphery, they were claiming the centre against the ethnic other who had, in their minds at least, taken over the periphery in the form of the *banlieues*.

A large section of the Boulogne Kop was formed, therefore, according to the logic that they were claiming one territory against another territory, and creating a place where like-minded people could come together. This was easily exploited politically by the nationalist extreme-right. The popularisation in France of the British punk and skinhead culture from 1978 to 1981 (itself associated with football hooliganism) gave an easy model to follow. There were examples of violence against visiting supporters. The skinheads, fewer than a hundred, gained notoriety on the occasion of a friendly international in Paris between France and England (29 February 1984). The resulting press coverage gave PSG fans a reputation for violence. There was damage to other stadiums in August 1985 and links with racism and neo-nazism at the time when the Front national was beginning to gain a following. The Socialist government seemed to have failed to deliver in the same way as the orthodox right-wing governments had failed to deliver in the 1970s. Unemployment was soaring and the fabric of urban life was degenerating in the early 1980s. Mignon explains modern racism within this context as the response of people wishing to protect their status in society and prevent their way of life from being degraded; or as the response of the already marginalised or those excluded from mainstream society who see racial difference as both the cause of their misfortune and the distance they need to keep in order to maintain their own identity. It is one effect of a feeling of the loss of control over the conditions of their own way of life and the feeling that the powers that be were far removed from the day-to-day concrete problems of life. The presence of foreigners in other teams was, for them, proof of the country's decadence and an easy target for abuse, although black players wearing PSG colours were usually well supported (Mignon 1998: 238–240).

A recrudescence of violence happened on 18 October 1989 at a European Cup match against Juventus. A group calling themselves the Pitbull Kop, publishing a fanzine with the title *Pour le prix d'une bière*, were featured in a TV programme *Ciel mon mardi* (Christophe de Chavanne) in March 1990. Advocating football violence, they called themselves 'les hooligans du PSG'. The skinhead sections seemed to be using football as a recruiting ground for extreme-right-wing ideas (Broussard 1990).

The reputation of the Boulogne Kop for racism and violence, along with the situation of the Parc des Princes in its bourgeois district, Mignon argues (1998: 249–250), long prevented the region as a whole from fully identifying with PSG. It strengthened the idea that there was a clear division between the city of Paris and the *banlieues*, a divorce inside the Paris region between the city centre and the surrounding areas, that PSG was a club for those people who kept their distance from 'les jeunes des cités' (kids from the estates), from the new France of the *banlieues*. Equally, it spread the idea that the youth of the 'cités' were not welcome there and did not feel comfortable there. Choosing PSG was choosing the centre over the periphery. Seen from the poor estates, the club seemed either bourgeois or neo-fascist.

The Re-invention of PSG's Identity

The more political side of the Boulogne Kop began to lose its monopoly of Ultra support when other associations more focused on footballing issues were founded, such as les Gavroches in 1985 and later the supporters clubs congregating at the Auteuil end, which, Mignon recounts (1998: 254), were formed as a refusal of the definitions of fandom imposed by skinheads, casuals or the extreme right. These more independent supporters associations, independent of the ideological bent of the original Ultras and more independent of the club, began in the early 1990s to break the identification of the club with hooligans and racists. They adopted the Italian model of support rather than the British one. If the hooliganism aspect was now out of date, the other aspect of British football support did not really fit the social situation of the Paris fans either. The British model was of a working-class community coming together with its rituals, its particular route, on foot, to the stadium, the pubs on the way to the ground and on the way back, sharing a beer, the physical closeness of the terraces, the chants and songs, all too exotic for Paris. Too working class and not reflective or intellectual enough, too based in social class and not enough on political militancy, argues Mignon (1998: 255). Knowing the chants and songs, which are less spontaneous than they appear, also depends on long tradition and familiarity. In Paris, supporters set out from too far away, were too few, and had not been socialised into a traditional football culture by earlier generations. Their fan culture fitted the Italian model better, with its stress on organisation, pre-planning and spectacle.

From the mid-1980s onwards, but particularly in the 1990s, the influence of the Italian model had begun to be felt. It is highly organised, through hier-archically structured associations based on militant political groups. Activities in the stadium are planned in great detail, and use various accessories such as megaphones, huge banners to unfurl, and confetti. Their objective is to organise a *tifo*, a particularly Latin form of entertainment, with a number of *animateurs* whose role is to conduct the chanting and singing and generally to stoke up an atmosphere of support for the home team. The Auteuil end, much more under Italian rather than English influence than the Boulogne end, is nowadays full of 5,000 well-drilled young fans with scarves and professionally printed banners identifying the different organised groups. Two or three conductors, each with their own supporting drummers, on semi-permanent podiums, one with a portable PA system, initiate and co-ordinate the chanting – which to English ears is pretty unimaginative, lacking the wit of Anfield or the passion of St James' Park. But the *spectacle* is the thing. The pre-planning and stage directions of the *animateurs* make up for the lack of 'spontaneous' fan culture stemming from a long tradition. A visit to a PSG home game has a different feel to an English match. The Parc des Princes, with the typical oval *virages* of French omnisport stadiums, and a narrow moat, keeps the crowd further from the pitch than most big English grounds, and absorbs the noise. Only a few visiting fans might be there – very few clubs have more than a couple of hundred fans who travel to away games, which also removes a focus for atmosphere. The ends attract the young members of official and unofficial supporters clubs, who gather in the stadium much earlier than would be expected in an English game in order to organise the *tifo*. The fairly full lateral stands barely take up any of the chants and the whole affair is relatively passionless. A few screwed-up programmes may get thrown at a linesman for a close off-side decision against the home side, but the pitch is too far away for them to reach their target, and the police have frisked the fans as they go in to relieve them of any bottles or other potential offensive weapons. The Boulogne end seems quieter than Auteuil, but still has a reputation for booing visiting black players. The extreme-right gunman arrested on 14 July 2002 for attempting to shoot President Chirac was described as an avid supporter of PSG, a member of the Boulogne Kop, having been a local election candidate representing the MNR, a break-away party from the FN (*Guardian*, 16 July 2002: 9).

Mignon concluded in 1998 by asking whether the topophilic challenges inherent in creating PSG had been successful. Certainly the club now has carved its place in football history; it is linked to a particular territory, its stadium, and enjoys the emotional attachment of its fans. In the current state of the relations of television and football, this is not as simple as it used to be, and this will be returned to in Chapter 7. There is a certain fragility and certain contradictions about the relationship of PSG with its supporters, and indeed its stadium. In 1999 the club owners were tempted to start again in the new Stade de France, the national stadium built in the poor northern *banlieue* of Saint-Denis. Government was keen since it would have found a tenant to make up the income that for the time being requires a large State subsidy. It holds 80,000 spectators rather than the 50,000 of the Parc. It would be a very prestigious home for a club. There was the danger too that the old Division 3 club based near Saint-Denis, Red Star, would manage to raise their budget and ambitions sufficiently to adopt it as their home and in the long run create a more credible competitor than PSG for the *banlieue* identity. The immediate community around the Parc des Princes has never become attached to the club, but changing stadium and habits would be risky in terms of the relationship that has been built up with the PSG fans, even though, in various ways, as Mignon says (1998: 259), many Paris fans come to the Parc and to PSG 'faute de mieux' ('because they have nothing better to do').

Against this background of depoliticisation of Parisian fans and their gradual achievement of representativeness of the greater Paris region and its social mix, a major policy decision by the club in the year 2000 suggested that the club was finally prepared officially to divest itself of its old bourgeois and Ville-de-Paris image and to promote itself as the club of the 'banlieues' and the 'cités'. The attempt to renew PSG's success in 2000/01 that went along with various changes of club directors and managers saw the huge investment in the transfer fee (218 million francs) for Nicolas Anelka. As the club put it: 'Nicolas is the leader of a global project for Paris and its region' (Barth 2000c). His arrival from Real Madrid followed those of Stéphane Dalmat and Peter Luccin, both under-21 internationals from Marseille, and Sylvain Distin, a former PSG apprentice, from Gueugnon. All three, like Anelka, were young, gifted and black. They joined other young black players who had come through PSG's youth academy at the same time as Anelka. It was the re-signing of the latter that was accompanied by declarations from the club about the concept of creating a club to represent the *banlieues* and the 'young' of the Paris region *cités*. The re-signing later in the season, from Newcastle, of another former PSG apprentice from the Parisian suburbs, Didier Domi, was justified in the same way. *France Football* quotes a club official as calling the *banlieue* idea a strong emotional signal to a large section of the population of the Paris region that the club was not excluding or forgetting its 'children' (8 May 2001: 24).

The buying of Anelka was certainly a media coup and stimulated great interest and initially huge sales of season tickets and replica shirts. In terms of re-branding, if there had been a feeling that PSG had hitherto been seen as too bourgeois by some parts of the population of young Paris football fans, then this move was an interesting attempt to change that image and to appeal to a similar audience that the television channel, Canal+, the owner of PSG, was also trying to target: for instance the young *beur* comic, Jamel Debbouze, had also been recruited by Canal+. *France Football* suggests that this move towards recruiting high-profile young players with whom the *banlieues* can identify may have been premeditated by the club's owners without due regard for the footballing balance within the club (8 May 2001: 24). True or not, the young team, under the pressure of the high expectations created, started well (top of the league in October and qualifying for the second phase of the Champions League), but in the end failed to match the success of the previous season, and slipped to mid-way in the French championship, the poorest result for some time – this despite the appointment as coach in mid-season of Luis Fernandez. His appointment was also a 'return to his roots'. Fernandez, the son of poor Spanish immigrants, had been a PSG player and hero in the 1980s, before managing them to their only European success in the mid-1990s. He had left his Spanish club Bilbao at the end of his contract in the summer of 2000 and had become a paid consultant for Canal+'s football coverage. The suspicion was that the TV channel was simply waiting for a convenient moment to impose him on the club.

The attempt to re-brand the club and match a segment of the Paris region audience with the signing of certain types of player had further (unforeseen?) consequences. Fernandez and many of the players did not get on: Fernandez could not command automatic respect from his players – they were too young to remember his exploits as a PSG player. There was, in addition to this generational problem, a religious and social divide. Jean-Philippe Bouchard (2001) contrasts the mentality of the *banlieues* where the present-day Parisian players grew up as having nothing in common with the poor suburbs of Les Minguettes where in the 1970s Fernandez benefited from a climate of social inclusion and advancement. The economic crises of the 1980s taught his successors to be individualistic and egotistical. In the 1990s, Islam, the religion of those of North African and Sub-Saharan African immigrant extraction, has also developed in the *banlieues*, and PSG youth teams, recruited from the *banlieues*, have a majority of Islamic players. Their training has to take account of this and adapt for example to the fasting of Ramadan. At least three professionals including (reputedly) Anelka converted to Islam. French young players, after the Bosman ruling, are also more likely to see their footballing future with a prestigious club abroad and therefore less likely to be as loyal to the PSG jersey as Fernandez might wish. Officials say there are clans within the club rather than a single community spirit. The players also refused to wear club blazers, arguing they could not possibly wear PSG badges to go out on the town (Bouchard 2001: 28).

The unrest within the club and its lack of success has been mirrored in the stadium amongst the fans. Fans from the Boulogne end had tried to storm the presidential box in February 2001 after a 4–0 home defeat to Auxerre. A seat had been thrown down on a Marseille fan in October 2000, putting him in a coma. The most serious incident was during a European match against the Turkish side Galatasaray in April 2001. Violent incidents with various offensive weapons that must have been smuggled in earlier, with the complicity of stewards (*bénévoles*), had led to the match being interrupted for almost half-an-hour and police being called (too late) into the stadium. The incidents were overtly racist in nature, some of the authors of the violence admitted trying to 'casser du Turc' (Turk-bashing). The incidents may not have been unconnected with the deaths of two Leeds fans in Turkey the year before, in view of the links between the Boulogne end and English fans. UEFA imposed a fine of over 4 million francs on the club, plus a requirement to play its next three European 'home' games at a neutral ground at least 300 km from Paris. The club is now reinforcing the barriers to prevent movement between different parts of the ground, adding many more security cameras, and preventing objects being passed into the ground through external railings. One of the biggest and oldest supporters associations, the Boulogne Boys, has broken off all relations with the club and 'declared war' on the club chairman (Bouchard and Harscoët 2001).

The complicated relationship between PSG and its fans looks set to continue. Are we seeing the start of a new stage in the invention of a footballing tradition in Paris, an overt club policy that identifies PSG and its team with the new

France of the *banlieues*, trying to capitalise – a little late – on the wave of euphoria for the rainbow French nation that the national team has come to symbolise? Will this entail an eventual move to the Stade de France situated in a more appropriate part of the Paris region and forever associated with the 1998 World Cup victory? Is it the fear of this that is reactivating the violence of those elements within its fans for whom PSG gave an identity which precisely rejected the new *banlieues* and their 'black, blanc, beur' mix? A discontented member of the Boulogne Boys made explicit certain fans' opposition to this change of direction by the club, implicitly rejecting the import of players representing the black *banlieues*, when *Le Parisien* newspaper gave column inches to interviews with fans towards the end of the 2000/01 season. Olivier is quoted as saying: 'It is true we support PSG while at the same time carrying on a struggle against the club. Anelka, Luccin and some other young players should not be here. They have not understood that they had responsibilities. They are destroying the image of Paris' (Bruna 2001: 3). Luccin, Distin and Anelka all left the club at the start of or during the 2001/02 season.

Conclusion

Seen from the perspective of the 1960s or even the 1980s, the size of attendances at French Division 1 matches at the turn of the twenty-first century is surprising. More than twice as many people attend matches than in the 1980s and more than three times as many as in the 1960s. All-time records were regularly broken after the World Cup victory. But crowds had been improving even before 1998. A judicious and cheap season ticket policy was a factor. There was plenty of room for more people following improvements to grounds in preparation for the World Cup, and most grounds are still rarely completely full. However, an average of 50,000 at Marseille or over 40,00 at PSG compares reasonably well with other European cities. There are huge differences, however, in gates between the best and least well supported clubs, and still a suspicion of fragility about the depth of commitment.

The lack of traditional passion for football in France may be put down partly to a late start for professionalism, that had to begin again from scratch following the Second World War. This, plus the late industrialisation and urbanisation of France which happened really in the 30 years up to the oil crises of the mid-1970s, meant there was no traditional working-class supporter culture established into which to socialise the next generation of fans. By the 1960s a new more affluent lifestyle and new more modern leisure activities made football old-fashioned. Where recognisably modern forms of support developed was in Saint-Etienne in the 1970s, precisely in an old industrial working-class town that was starting to suffer the consequences of economic downturn that was to decimate the European coal and steel industries. European Cup travel allowed them to adopt styles of fandom they saw in Liverpool and Glasgow and to express an identity that was strengthened by their sense of an old industrial community losing its place in the modern world under pressure of impending or actual restructuring of the national economy. Similar remarks could be made about Lens support in the 1990s. In the case of Marseille, where passionate support does exist, it was the loss of Empire across the Mediterranean and beyond and its consequences for the local economy, based as it was on its trading links to the south and the Far-East, that gave Marseillais a sense of resentment against the rest of France – that OM's defeats and victories alike fuelled to stoke up a strong supporter identity. The uneasy relationship between the OM supporters associations and the club is but an extreme example of a developing phenomenon in France.

While English influences were important and are still evident in stadiums, the Italian influence has become stronger. The Ultra phenomenon, fandom as militancy, opting for a freely chosen identity rather than an inherited one, fitted the French situation. Television in particular gave an opportunity for fans to become visible, whether through English-style 'hooliganism' or spectacular Italian-style terrace displays. This post-modern interpretation fits PSG fans in particular. The city of Paris had always lacked an identity other than being a microcosm of provincial France, and until the mid-1970s it had lacked the political will (and the local political structures) to support a big club. Once PSG had been established as a brand new club, fans and traditions of support had to be invented from nothing. Initially, a dominant identity that emerged among the Ultras was of a young white backlash against unemployment and disintegration of the social fabric of the Paris region. This expressed itself by the occupation of a part of the Parc des Princes stadium (representing the centre) against the periphery of black and Arab *banlieues*, the scapegoats for their sense of frustration. At the dawn of a new century the club adopted a new branding strategy. It tried to re-invent an identity and appeal to the wider Paris region by promoting players from the deprived *banlieues*, like Nicolas Anelka, even if they had to buy him back expensively from abroad. At the time of writing it is too early to say whether this strategy will work in the long term, except that the policy's figurehead, Anelka, has not settled – again – and has been sold on at a big loss.

5

Coaches: Building the Successes of French Teams

Seeing the two English teams walking out to compete in the 2001 FA Cup Final in the Millennium Stadium in Cardiff rather than at Wembley raised, for some, the issue of the inability of government and sporting authorities to agree on building a national stadium; but many viewers could not fail to be struck by another novelty: two French managers leading out the teams. Did this signify that British coaching had fallen behind continental practices? Gérard Houllier led out the eventual winners Liverpool, and Arsène Wenger (who has since won his second League and Cup double) headed an Arsenal team that also contained five French players. The same season, a third French coach, Jean Tigana, brought Fulham into the top flight as champions of Nationwide Division 1. Behind the successes of individual French coaches abroad is a national French system that is recognised as a model for the future of national coaching elsewhere in the world. A *Guardian* journalist's comment is typical: 'Now France is quite simply the world-wide example for the production of young footballers' (Williams 2000b). The English FA now has a National Technical Director – the very post is an imitation of the French system and its first holder, Howard Wilkinson, a friend of Gérard Houllier who had such an influence when he established the functions of the French equivalent. A national Centre of Excellence is also to be set up by the English FA on French lines. Whatever French professional clubs' structural weaknesses in the 1980s and 1990s, it is now generally recognised that it is sporting development policies, particularly regarding coaching, that have allowed France to produce such successful teams and impressive individual players in the 1990s, after minimal sporting success in international or European club football in earlier years.

French Coaching Policy and Structures

The coaching systems and strategy adopted by French football fit into a wider national sports policy for the development of elite sport. They are regulated and part-funded by the State and local authorities, even in the case of a professional sport like football.

The French Model of Development of Elite Sportsmen and Women

The development of football and of elite sport in general in France can be traced back to State intervention and long-term strategic planning, which gained urgency following the national humiliation represented by the country's poor showing at the Rome Olympic Games of 1960, the first major international competition under de Gaulle's presidency (see Dine 1997b, 1998b). De Gaulle conceived of sport as one strand of his broader national project to restore the nation's grandeur, and commissioned the Joxe-Herzog plan in the 1960s, which initiated a major programme of capital investment in the nation's sports facilities, with particular emphasis on achieving success in international competition. Over the years the importance attached to sport within government has increased from sport being represented, when de Gaulle first became President, by a High Commissioner, then, in 1963 a Junior Minister, and for two years by a full minister. After de Gaulle the position was generally at Junior Minister level, until 1991. Since then, with one brief interlude, a full cabinet place has been occupied by the Ministre de la Jeunesse et des Sports (Ministre des Sports from 2002).

Government strategy for sport included, in 1975, the establishment of the State-funded Institut national du sport et de l'éducation physique (INSEP), a combined national sports research and training centre. A fundamental part of the Institut was the establishment of the special status of the 'sportif de haut niveau', elite sportsmen and women who are housed and trained within the INSEP at the State's expense. In 1997 there were 5,500 sportsmen and women with this status. It allows them to get sponsorship from public service organisations such as the Post Office, France Telecom, or a municipality such as the City of Paris, which can give them a job with special hours of work to facilitate training and competition. This is under the supervision of the Ministry, which provides some 50 million francs for it (*La Poste* 1997). Although this status tended not to affect professional football as directly as it did athletics, judo, swimming, gymnastics and other Olympic sports, a model and a tone were created, and the football authorities, in collaboration with the State, gradually took this on board. Changes within education took France in a similar direction: since the 1950s all candidates for the school-leaving examination, the *baccalauréat*, have to take a sport and PE test, and from 1984 this test counted for 8 per cent of the overall result. Since 1992 this has been doubled, and is an incentive for youth participation in sport and physical education.

Of Western European countries, as seen in Chapter 2, France has the strongest State intervention in sport. High public expenditure on sport is one thing, but the key element of the French model of development of elite sport is what it is spent on. Top of the list is the organisation of coaching, with close collaboration between the State and the different sports federations. The French Sports Ministry employs 7,000 officials, 95 per cent of whom work in the regions (Callède 2000: 163). This includes 1,700 specialist coaches and sports development staff whom the State seconds to sports *fédérations*. An important category of civil servant (*fonctionnaire*) was created by the State in the 1950s: the *directeur technique national* (DTN – national technical director) whose mission was to work with a sport's governing body to develop their particular sport. This was initially aimed at Olympic sports, but was later extended to professional sports including football (Mignon 2000: 237). Since 1985 there are over a hundred *Centres permanents d'entraînement et de formation* (CPEF) at national, regional and local level, usually in establishments run by the Ministry. Miège (1993: 72) reported that they were used by 2,800 sportsmen and women. He also reports that by 1993 specialist Sports Medicine centres were run by local authorities and the State, for example in the INSEP for elite sports people. The State built a lot of sports facilities between 1962 and 1975, and still builds national facilities, although local ones are the responsibility of the local authorities (ibid.: 72–73).

The whole system of coaching, from school level through grass-roots amateur to professional level, from mass participation to elite sport, is very 'joined-up' and coherent. As in other fields of education and training (for example via the selective *grandes écoles* system), there is an unapologetic policy of democratic selection and training of an elite. An important part of this is the encouragement of mass participation and therefore equality of opportunity, so that chances of succeeding in the competition to become part of the elite are fair. This legitimises the creation and training of an elite and State spending on it. The State ensures fairness by a highly regulated system. In football the responsibility for the development of this elite is shared between the State and the French Football Federation. First of all the sport of football itself has been organised into a single hierarchical pyramid, from small amateur grass-roots clubs to the elite of Division 1 and the international side. There is also obvious progression through the different age groups, who eventually grow into the adult ('senior') level through two-year steps. In theory, it is possible for a team in the lowest district division to rise through promotion to the regional and national divisions, and for a player starting off in a small amateur club to emerge through the ranks, benefit from coaching centres and become part of the professional elite. (See Appendix for football's league structures.)

French National Football Coaching Strategy

The football coaching system operates on a similar pyramidal structure to that of the leagues, with the elite system very much attached to the grass-roots system.

This is reflected in the FFF's published mission statement regarding its coaching structures: its three aims are (1) to develop football as a mass game, (2) to develop an elite of top players, and (3) to train coaches and sports officials (Thomas *et al.* 1991: 86). At the top of the pyramid is the National Technical Director of Coaching, the DTN, who, in concert with the Federation's president and management committee, sets policy at the strategic level in four-year plans. Under his authority are eight national coaches, each in charge of a different level national team and each with particular responsibilities for co-ordinating a specific aspect of either player coaching or the training of coaches at different levels. Below them are 27 Regional Coaching Advisers (*conseiller technique régional* – CTR), and a further 80 Département[1] [County] Coaching Advisers (*conseiller technique départemental* – CTD) working with the regional and district leagues respectively. Most of these are paid by the State – somewhat fewer in recent years, but the FFF has been able to fund their own CTRs and CTDs to fill gaps (Miège 1993: 71; FFF website June 2001; Thomas *et al.* 1991: 90–95).

The post of DTN is a highly prized and high-profile position. Gérard Houllier took on the job in 1990. He was replaced by World Cup winning coach Aimé Jacquet in 1998. It is quite the opposite of a sinecure and the DTN's priorities were described in 2001 by Jacquet's number two as: (1) setting targets for increasing numbers of registered players at grass-roots level; (2) developing elite players through youth training schemes and in collaboration with professional clubs; (3) (described as the most important) training coaches (*éducateurs*) at every level; and (4) promoting underdeveloped or new forms of football, such as women's football and *Futsal* (indoor five-a-side football) (Morlans 2001).

The DTN staff firmly believe that the key to their success is both the training of coaches and a youth coaching policy, the first being just as important as the other:

> One of the major reasons for the success of French football in the last thirty years is its having been able to push forward concurrently the training of coaches and the training of players. In concrete terms, by the establishment of training centres for players and the creation of a coaching and management diploma. (Morlans 2001)

The CTRs and CTDs put this coaching policy into action on the ground. They train 17,000–19,000 *éducateurs* per year, a figure they still regard as insufficient for the 20,000 French amateur clubs (which run several teams each). At grass-roots level these coaches organise competitions, identify young talent for further training, and run training courses for young coaches and organisers. In 1990 it was estimated that France had about 9,000 qualified *éducateurs*, mainly unpaid volunteers running small amateur clubs. The term *éducateur* is not a neutral one. It carries within it the status long attached to the teaching profession, which since the educational reforms of the 1880s has carried with it a notion of Republican mission, and a wider view of the function of a youth coach than simply passing on skills. In order to select an elite of players there has to be a massive input at grass-roots level, which in a country with a Republican ethic also means providing appropriate training to widen access. This is the role of the CTR and CTD: 'As regards mass participation, a major activity has been the development of local competitions and of organised football from beginners to the end of primary school age' (Morlans 2001).

In the district leagues, the CTD has three functions: (1) *animateur* (organiser/developer): liaising with schools and amateur clubs to encourage competitions and generally encourage mass participation; (2) *entraîneur-sélectionneur* (trainer and selector): scouting for the best young talent, selecting, coaching and managing the representative teams for his county (*sélection départementale*) ; (3) *formateur* (trainer or instructor): training coaches at all levels and all ages within his area (again regarded as the most important of his tasks, since it is the FFF's priority). Between 100 and 200 *éducateurs* are trained per year in each district, and they are subsequently followed up through up-dating of skills (Pion 2001).

The DTN's deputy, Jean-Pierre Morlans, co-ordinates the training of the country's *entraîneurs* (managers), the rank above the *éducateurs*. *Entraîneur* is the term used to describe the qualified, paid coach working with teams from the Regional Division d'Honneur upwards. Morlans is very conscious of the huge evolution of their role in recent years, but already sees the day when the 300–400 French *entraîneurs* will need to have even greater skills. The more sophisticated training programmes will consequently need to include, according to Morlans, further differentiation of levels and objectives of the job of *entraîneur*, basing the qualification on real knowledge of the job on the ground backed up by theoretical knowledge, and not the other way round.

This comment raises the issue of the extent to which the French model is based on a unique set of State-backed and Federation-backed coaching qualifications, including written as well as practical tests that must be studied for and passed before a coach or manager can be authorised to work at a given level. Gérard Houllier, as DTN, added the more practical Federal diplomas. Table 5.1 sets out the range of official French coaching qualifications, from lowest to highest. The DTN sets the tone and the standards for these qualifications. The lowest level above requires a three-day training course, at district or regional level, the second 25–30 hours of training at weekends or evenings. The second-level diploma to become an *initiateur* requires attendance at a six-day course ending in written tests covering football, fitness training,

Table 5.1 *Official French Coaching Qualifications (State or FFF)*

Title of qualification	State or FFF	Description
Le diplôme de jeune animateur	Federal	A youth leader certificate: to help young young people fulfil responsibilities of captain, referee, coach, or official for youth teams.
Le certificat d'animateur-accompagnateur de football	Federal	Certifies training for responsibility for a local youth team: managing, refereeing, advising.
Le diplôme d'initiateur 1er degré	Federal	First-level coaching certificate to deliver introductory football initiation to 6–11-year-olds.
Le diplôme d'initiateur 2ème degré	Federal	Second-level coaching certificate to deliver football pre-training to 12–15-year-olds.
Le diplôme d'animateur seniors	Federal	Certifies training to manage junior and adult amateur teams at district level.
Le brevet d'Etat d'éducateur sportif 1er degré (BEES 1), or Brevet d'Etat de Moniteur de Football	State	First-level State coaching certificate qualifying the holder to work in a paid capacity for adult amateur teams at regional or district level, below Regional Division d'Honneur. Lower levels of qualification (see above) give dispensation from part of the examination.
Le brevet d'Etat d'éducateur sportif 2ème degré (BEES 2 spécifique)	State	After two years of coaching at BEES 1 level, the holder can enter for this second-level State coaching and managerial qualification, with special option in football.
Le diplôme d'entraîneur de football (DEF)	Federal	Needs BEES 2, with special option in football, to enter for this Federal qualification to coach at Division d'Honneur and Championnat de France amateur levels.

Table 5.1 *Official French Coaching Qualifications (State or FFF) (continued)*

Title of qualification	State or FFF	Description
Le brevet d'Etat d'éducateur sportif 3ème degré (BEES 3)	State	General State coaching and managerial qualification after four years of coaching at BEES 2 level.
Le certificat fédéral d'entraîneur de centre de formation	Federal	Qualifies holder to manage a Youth Training Academy. They must hold a DEF and have played football at national Division 4 (CFA) level or above.
Le diplôme d'entraîneur professionnel de football (DEPF)	Federal	Must hold DEF to undertake this training. Qualifies holder to manage and coach professional clubs.
Status of 'maître-entraîneur'	Federal	An honorary title given by the FFF to coaches with ten years' outstanding experience at the top level
Filière sportifs de haut niveau	State	Officially recognised elite sportsmen and women (international level) may enter for BEES qualifications by an accelerated route; continuous assessment by attending special training sessions.

Sources: FFF web site: http://www.fff.fr/; Thomas *et al.* (1991).

the laws of the game, and associated regulations; and practical tests in teaching skills and technical football skills. The first-level State exam, the Brevet d'éducateur (without which it is illegal since the law of 1984 to coach or teach sport for money) includes, for instance, a compulsory first-aid and life-saving certificate, knowledge of technical skills, the humanities, the spirit of the game, human biology, teaching skills, institutions and management of a training institution (Thomas *et al.* 1991: 92–94). Assuming the earlier FFF certificates have already been done, the training period lasts for 250 hours. Just as a teaching certificate for a school requires a period of teaching practice, this certificate has a practical 160 hours of supervised coaching practice.

The DEF level of qualification requires a two-week training course (practical and theoretical) covering written and oral exams in human biology, the humanities, law, and social science as related to sport. It is followed by a season's supervised coaching in a club and a further week's course organised by the local CTR. To become a coach/manager of a professional club requires first of all to have gained the DEF diploma with a mark of at least 14/20 in the football-specific elements, to have followed six three-day training courses (on fitness training, skills and tactics, communication skills, psychology and man management, business management and administration, and video skills). The very French nature of the qualifications does not mean the system is very inward looking: the training deliberately includes the study of football beyond the French borders. A compulsory element in the training is English as a foreign language, and if all the above exams are passed, there follows a compulsory full week's work placement in a professional club abroad, with a written report and an oral report to be given before an audience of fellow candidates. The placement is another Houllier innovation.

Not only are the standards of training of coaches very closely specified and controlled jointly by the State and the FFF, but also, once in post in an FFF club, practising coaches have to conform to quality control demands and regular updating of skills under the aegis of an FFF national committee, the Commission centrale du Statut des Educateurs. The official job specification of football coach under French employment legislation runs to 14 pages of A4 paper (as printed from the FFF website). This *statut des éducateurs de football* requires in the first month of a coach's contract that he sends to this Committee a copy of his club's weekly training schedule for the year, plus twice-yearly reports on his activities. Failure to do this can lead to fines and even suspension. Coaches holding the State *brevet* qualification are also required to engage in activities to cascade their skills down to lower-level coaches by putting on training days locally. They themselves must attend an annual seminar run by national coaches to update their skills. The cascading of knowledge and the continuity of the coaching system from one generation to the next may be illustrated by the case of Yannick Stopyra, who was trained by Pierre Tournier at the Sochaux *Centre de formation*, and who, after a successful playing career has become the Director of the Lorraine regional *Centre de préformation* (Tournier and Rethacker 1999: 114).

Clubs too are required to play their part in spreading coaching expertise by facilitating their players' attendance at coaching training on request. Any qualified coach who has not exercised the profession for five years has to retrain before becoming employable again. In recognition of the full-time nature of the position of *entraîneur*, players are not allowed to act as player-manager in the top four divisions. If, in the name of continuous quality management, there are these constraints on coaches, then this employment legislation also prevents clubs from employing people in coaching positions who are not qualified. (This can also be construed from outside as protectionist.) Clubs can be fined or even have points deducted if they do not employ properly qualified coaches for the level in which they play. To facilitate their job, depending on their level, coaches have free entry to matches either in their regional league or, for DEPFs, in the national professional league. The jobs are pensionable and minimum rates of pay are set down nationally in a collective bargaining agreement between the coaches' representatives, the FFF and the LNF. The professionalism of the function of coach is thus taken very seriously and defined as such by both the State and football authorities.

If, thanks to top-down, highly centralised coaching models, the skills training of French players has improved, to the point that players like Zidane and Henry have few equals, one aspect of the French preparation that has been recognised as falling short is physical fitness. DTN Gérard Houllier picked this up in 1997 after the under-20s World Championship, where France lost in the quarter-finals to Uruguay (on penalties). In his report he says: 'In terms of athleticism, we only just came through, whereas others coped easily. That confirms that our 18–21 year olds do not play enough, or do not train enough' (Tournier and Rethacker 1999: 141). Ironically, as Aimé Jacquet noted in 1998, after many French internationals had been lured abroad, for Zidane the physical work done in Italy allowed him to play a whole match at top pace, which gave him great confidence. Two daily training periods of three hours in early season, plus weight training, had been very hard for him initially, but he had gritted his teeth. The ex-Monaco coach Pierre Tournier comments that the French internationals playing in Italy would probably not have accepted the same work regime or the same discipline in French clubs (ibid.: 142).

Youth Training and *Centres de Formation*

Alongside the training of coaches and the system of coaching qualifications under the aegis of the DTN, the other key element in the success of French football since the 1970s is the coaching of players from an early age, and in particular the creation of the *Centres de formation*, the youth academies.

La Préformation

Football, alongside other sports in France, has a strongly developed national and regional structure for finding and coaching talented youngsters. The CTDs are key figures in the scouting and selection process that takes a number of youngsters into *préformation* (pre-training); that is, special coaching in football academies or in sports sections of certain secondary schools. In fact coaching and scouting for talent begins now even earlier than secondary school age, and outside the school system. Registration with amateur clubs, coaching and organised football games begin at the so-called initiation phase (6–11-year-olds

with 5-a-side or 7-a-side games, before the pre-training phase (12–15 years).
The universality of the early organisation of children's sport in France is shown
by the existence of distinct names for the different age groups for participants
(across all sports): Débutants (6–8), Poussins (8–9), Benjamins (10–11), Minimes
(12–13), Cadets (14–15), and Juniors (16–18). The *préformation* period
corresponds conveniently to the age-range of the early secondary school, the
collège, which takes pupils at 11 or sometimes 10, for four years of study, before
they move on to the *lycée*, the upper secondary school, for three years' study
towards the *baccalauréat*. As we have seen above, qualifications for *éducateurs*
generally include modules on coaching to this age group. There are 71 special
Sport-études sections in French *collèges*. Additionally, agreements with 600 schools
allow combined football coaching and schooling for 11,000 pupils (figures for
the year 2000). François Blaquart, as the assistant DTN responsible for co-
ordinating and planning *préformation*, which includes the training of special
coaches of course, works on both mass participation and elite selection in this
age group (see Thomas *et al.* 1991: 71–86).

In terms of the production of an elite at this level, the FFF has opened seven
regional centres of excellence, called *Centres de préformation*. The first of these,
founded in 1990, is the Institut National du Football housed in the National
Centre of Excellence at Clairefontaine. The adoption of *préformation* as official
policy was enthusiastically pushed by Gérard Houllier as DTN in the 1990s.
He stopped the 15–18 years *formation* at the INF to devote all its efforts to
13–15-year-olds. He added regional centres from 1994.[2] He saw them as the
next step in improving French youth training. These now set the standards,
claims Blaquart (2001), in terms of ethos, pedagogy and general education,
pointing out that the emphasis is not on producing footballing performance
at any price, but on the individual child's personal development. Graduates
of these *Centres de préformation* go on, at the next stage, in the 16–18 age group,
to opportunities in *Centres de formation* in professional clubs (see pp. 102–105)
or in 27 *Sports-études* sections in *lycées* (including one in Martinique).

Scouting and selection of prospective elite players begin at 12 years of age
in each *département*. At age 14, the regional inter-district league competitions
allow the best players to represent their *département* in an Easter cup competition.
After other representative matches and trials, by August, the best 25 players
are called into an under-15 national squad. The DTN justifies this strategy
of national youth teams in terms of it offering 'an excellent complement to the
activities of *préformation*. Selection for international matches gives the youngsters
an international culture regarding tactics and irreplaceable experience of the
highest level of football' (Morlans 2001).

L'Institut National du Football (INF)

Within the context of the national strategy for improving technical skills in sport, the French Football Federation created a National Football Institute near Vichy in 1972 to coach an elite of young players, when a National Technical Director of Coaching for football (Georges Boulogne) was first appointed (Tournier and Rethacker 1999: 26). In 1976 the President of the FFF, Fernand Sastre, took the decision to develop a purpose-built Centre Technique National du Football to house the INF and to prepare all national teams. A site was chosen and bought in 1982 at Clairefontaine-en-Yvelines, 50 km to the south-west of Paris. It started functioning in January 1988. Its national importance was recognised by an official opening by President Mitterrand in June of that year. The mission statement of French Football's National Skills Centre has five elements:

1. Elite football: to act as a training centre for the national teams, and to house an elite of young male and female footballers in a period of youth training.
2. Training and up-skilling of football coaches and managers; acting as an examination centre for State and FFF qualifications.
3. Research into skills and sports medicine, which includes an audiovisual centre and sports medicine centre
4. As *la maison du football*, the home of French football, to play host to French and foreign clubs wishing to use its facilities; to put on seminars for officials of the French regional and district leagues; to host meetings of French referees; to host sports medicine conferences.
5. To host meetings, seminars and conferences for private sponsors.

Within the Clairefontaine complex, now called Le Centre technique national Fernand-Sastre, the Institut National du Football fulfils the youth training function (for boys), alongside its more recent equivalent for girls, the Centre national de formation et d'entraînement (CNFE). Like the other regional *Centres de préformation* the INF operates as a boarding school, bringing together 24 of the best young players of a given age group (at 13 years old) for three years. They train for about two and a half hours once a day, after school in nearby Rambouillet, where they attend from 8.30 a.m. to 3 p.m. They go home to their families (and local clubs) at weekends, except in their third year when they represent the INF in a local league. Practically all boarding expenses are paid by the FFF and the French Football League, except for school lunches, school books, and weekend travel to and from home (Bourcier *et al.* 2001: 14–16; FFF web site; see also Holt 2001).

Figures from the Clairefontaine centre are quoted by the FFF website as showing that the concentration of coaching activities on *préformation* has been successful. The justification they give is that 95 per cent of pupils go on to a club's *Centre de formation* at 16 years old. More than 50 of them have been selected for the national team of their age group (but this could be a self-fulfilling prophecy). Fifteen of them, however, have gone on to play for the French European Cup winning teams at the under-18 level in 1997, 1998 and 2000. More than 30 have signed professional forms. They include Thierry Henry (Arsenal), Nicolas Anelka (Manchester City), Louis Saha (Fulham), Philippe Christanval (Barcelona) and William Gallas (Chelsea).

Youth Coaching in Professional Clubs

Alongside the national system run by the Federation, since 1974 all French professional league clubs have also been obliged by the FFF and the League to run *Centres de formation* for apprentices. Eric Cantona and Basile Boli, for example, emerged from the Auxerre club by this route, as did Deschamps, Desailly and Karembeu from Nantes, Zidane and Vieira from Cannes, Thuram, Petit, Trezeguet and Henry[3] from Monaco. Every member of the World Cup winning squad came through a national or club *Centre de formation* (Tournier and Rethacker 1999: 161). The majority of players making up both the 1995 and 2001 Nantes championship winning teams were developed though their own youth scheme. Indeed, in 2001 22 out of their squad of 27 had come through the own *Centre de formation*, often regarded as the most successful French youth academy. But French youth training, such as it was at club level, has produced results from earlier days: the Saint-Etienne European Cup Final side of 1976 contained nine home-produced players and two foreign imports (Mignon 2000: 238). Arguably the origins of a youth policy go back to 1949 and FC Sochaux. The club used the Peugeot car distribution network to recruit 18-year-old talent nationally and bring them to Sochaux to form the 'Lionceaux' (lion cubs) in the hope of becoming professionals (Tournier and Rethacker 1999: 24).

From the 1974/75 season the professional League encouraged clubs to set up academies. A number invested in facilities, equipment and appropriately qualified staff (BEES 2). From the 1976/77 season a centre became an obligation for Division 1 clubs, although residential facilities varied enormously from club to club (ibid.: 32). One issue today is the tension between school work and football training. In the 1970s recruits were aged 17–19 and so did not have to attend school, but a qualification called Certificat d'Aptitude Professionnelle des métiers du football gave an opportunity for subsidy, and centres put on classes in accountancy, administration, maths, French, anatomy and English. In the mid-1980s, through parental pressure, as recruitment got younger and younger, a full parallel school curriculum came in (ibid.: 119). As the Mission Sastre declared in 1989: 'The aim of the training is first of all to prepare the profession of footballer while not neglecting general education' (ibid.: 100). Since the 1990s, and the acceptance of the idea of *préformation*, recruitment of 13-year-olds means one of the main changes has been the reduction of the number of hours training – initially the DTN demanded 20–25 hours per week. With experience, this came down gradually to 15 hours, and with the appearance of a more complete school programme, the weekly norms were 12–15 hours in 1999 (ibid.: 71–72).

Just as the coaching qualifications are highly regulated, so too are the *Centres de formation* in clubs. A centre has to apply for official approval annually, and is assessed on the quality of its resources (physical and human) and its results. Centres are awarded a classification that fixes among other standards a maximum number of trainees, and the amount of aid it will receive from the League (ibid.: 38–39; Faure and Suaud 1994b: 17).

One of the more detailed published accounts of a professional club's youth coaching programme is to be found in Tournier and Rethacker (1999: 71–108), based on Pierre Tournier's own practice as head of the youth academies of Sochaux (1974 to 1982) and Monaco (1982 to 1993). Youth coaching has concentrated on skills, tactical sense, and fitness development. He recalls how Platini had left the job as national team manager in 1992 complaining that the graduates of the French youth academies were not sufficiently good in ball skills. Tournier claims that the solution has been the earlier start represented by *préformation* (Tournier and Rethacker 1999: 85). Sports science has been extensively used to measure and improve fitness and athleticism, and also ball skills (bio-mechanics of movement) (see Mandard and Zilbertin 2000). In comparing the Liverpool FC academy to youth training in France, Grégory Vignal picked out the level of French technical training as being better, not questions of mentality, structures or facilities (Rivoire and Ortelli 2002: 24). The dimension of 'le mental', mental attitude and strength of character, was what Michel Hidalgo deplored in French club teams competing in Europe. Tournier describes how to inculcate initiative, personal responsibility, will to work, self-confidence, and competitive spirit during training (Tournier and Rethacker 1999: 98–99).

Tournier's assessment of the most successful club training schemes in terms of producing professional players is, uncontroversially, to put Nantes clearly at the top of the list, followed by Auxerre. Faure and Suaud (1994b: 17–18) cite figures from the 1980s which show Nantes, Auxerre and Sochaux as the top youth academies. Nantes, with a series of outstanding directors of youth coaching (Arribas, Suaudeau, and Denoueix), have constantly cultivated their own 'pass-and-move' style of play that pervades the club, whereas Auxerre, under the long-term influence of Guy Roux, have their own man-to-man marking style of 4–3–3, mixing home-produced players with experienced buys from other clubs for his first team. PSG and Marseille, on the other hand, certainly in the 1980s, traditionally relied more on a star system and buying in established first-team players, using the income from their large crowds. They invested the minimum required of them by the Charte du football of 1973 in the obligatory *Centre de formation*. Faure and Suaud (1994b: 17) show that they, and Monaco too, in the 1980s, were not giving their home-produced talent opportunities. Their trainees often leave the club, like Anelka (Tournier and Rethacker 1999: 104–106). This was what PSG seemed to be trying to change in 2000 (see Chapter 4). In the Tapie years OM were between 31st and 22nd in the official classification of centres and since then still seem to be looking for a 'quick fix' (Faure and Suaud 1994b: 17).

The Example of FC Nantes

Looking at youth training on the ground, with the Nantes club as an example, we find a very systematic approach to youth recruitment policy. Nantes prefer to take in young players at age 13, but do so up to 16. They recruit within a 200 km radius for 13-year-olds, and nation-wide for the rest. Three times a year, for each age category, they organise training days in what they call their subsidiary clubs in different parts of the country, such as Saint-Maur, near Paris, and Albi in the south-west, as well as locally. They also have agreements with African clubs.

In 2001 they had 22 trainees in their academy at *préformation* level (13–15 years), and 48 in *formation* (16–18). They run four teams in local competitions: one at under-15 level, another at under-17 level, a third in the regional Division d'Honneur, and one in the Championnat de France Amateur. Their youngsters alternate school (27 hours per week) and football training (10–11 hours). In the first year, the football training concentrates on ball skills; the hard physical work and muscle building comes later. The centre has three grass pitches, and one synthetic, and five coaches (including a specialist goalkeeping coach). The pupils have an school exam success rate of 88–90 per cent.

In terms of football outcomes, on average three out of ten youths sign a professional contract, and 80 per cent of the squad has been trained at the club. Others go to other Breton clubs. They claim to be particularly keen to ensure that the ones who are less successful on the footballing side leave the academy with a good educational record (Bourcier *et al.* 2001: 20–21).

The survey by Bourcier *et al.* (2001: 18–21) suggests that Nantes is not untypical. In 2000/01 16 out of 18 Division 1 clubs ran approved *Centres de formation*, whereas Sedan and Troyes, recently promoted, had been given official dispensation. Sixteen out of 20 Division 2 clubs had *Centres de formation*. About half of Division 1 academies now take their youths in at age 14–15, two or three at 13, the others at 16–17 years. Lyon claims the ones who succeed after starting training after 15 are the exception.

Auxerre has some 'satellite clubs' in France; Bordeaux has a link with Casablanca (Algeria); Lens has links with clubs mainly in the north of France; Lille operates partnerships with 30 clubs from the Paris region to Belgium; Marseille looks only in the south-east and abroad; PSG concentrates on the Paris region.

Few clubs recruit more than ten youth players per year, often less. Numbers in residence in youth academies vary widely: Lens and Monaco about 50, Bordeaux 42, Auxerre has 35, little Guingamp 22, the same as Marseille. In the bigger cities, understandably, there appear to be more non-resident youth players on the club's books. Practically every centre echoes Nantes's concentration on individual skills before physical/athletic development. Most centres mention physiotherapists and doctors on their staff, with on average at least one coach per 10–11 players.

Auxerre claims to have the most home-produced players on their professional books among D1 teams. Most agree that three or four players signing professional forms per year is not uncommon and is a good result. A number of centre directors mentioned the importance of personal development of the youngsters or the family atmosphere of the club as a plus. The Lens academy director best echoed official FFF policy:

> Lens means values, the stadium, the crowd, the jersey. It's also a philosophy regarding the youngsters. Training a kid is 25% about football, 75% about his life. Our aim is for him to succeed in life, for him to achieve fulfilment. We take an interest above all in the individual, and in the individual you'll find the player. (Bourcier *et al.* 2001: 19)

The beneficial effects of five years of French professional youth training are well known in Italy, where many clubs have bought products of French academies. The Juventus manager Lippi has been reported as saying that 'the good thing about buying a French player is a good education, a good attitude, very professional, very focused and tactically fully aware. He knows all the systems' (Hopkins and Williams 2001: 189).

While the success of French youth policy is not in doubt, there are still those players who come into the game late from outside the system. The 2000/01 players' Player of the Year Eric Carrière played for Nantes, but had not emerged from the conventional youth system. Small and slight for his age – in 2001 aged 28 he was still only 1.73m in height and weighed 61 kilos – he had been refused entry to a school *Sports-études* section and had played amateur football up to the age of 22, when he was spotted by Nantes playing in a Championnat national (Division 3) side, Muret. Leaving his higher education studies, he signed apprentice forms (*stagiaire*), and joined the Nantes *Centre de formation* as an over-age player. Going from three training sessions per week, to one or two every day took a toll on his body, until he decided to employ a personal physio and a specialist adviser to help him analyse his play on video. He played two games for the first team in 1996/97, and has not looked back since, winning his first international cap as play-maker in 2001 in the Confederation Cup tournament, and steering his new club Lyon to the championship in 2002 (Revault d'Alonnes 2001a).

New Coaches for Old: from Batteux to Houllier and Wenger

The terminology of football coaching and management is not interchangeable between France and Britain, although it may be converging as international exchanges and globalisation move on apace, and club structures become more alike – in the elite clubs at least. Football management culture has long been different on opposite sides of the Channel. There has of course also been evolution of the reality behind the terminology in both cultures. The average post-war English 'manager' always employed a track-suited 'trainer' to put the players through their paces on the manager's behalf on training days and to wield a 'magic sponge' on match days, commonly an ex-player. The third person running the club was the Club Secretary. This was the model set in the 1920s and 1930s by the success of Herbert Chapman, aided by his trainer Tom Whittaker. They set the standards for what was the new model: the manager thinking creatively about tactics, and the trainer working on individual players' fitness (Giulianotti 1999: 130–131; Walvin 1994: 137–138). Equally important was their example in setting the managers free of the Board of Directors. It was to be followed by the managers of the 1950s like Stan Cullis and the first 'track-suited' manager, Matt Busby (Russell 1997: 127), who dominated their clubs and were in charge of the office and administrative sides of the club as well as tactics and team selection, even if they did not publicly berate any director unwise enough to interfere, as Brian Clough was later prone to do. Managerial autonomy was slower to come to some clubs: the Newcastle United Board still chose the team well into the 1950s (ibid.: 90). There were one or two clubs where this alternative model had remained even more firmly in place: the club dominated by an old-style chairman, such as Burnley's Bob Lord, who was the spokesperson to the press and who interfered in team matters. However, this model of relationship between Board and manager remained a minority one.

The Liverpool 'boot-room' model of a managerial team with a number of coaches under a dominant 'manager', that Bill Shankly had so intuitively begun in the 1960s, is a development of the manager–coach pairing. Writing as recently as 1996 about managers' 'right-hand-men' no less a judge than Hugh McIlvanney (1996: 319) concluded: 'Perhaps managers will soon need more than an assistant. Maybe they will need professional support from above as well as below.' From the perspective of the first couple of years of the twenty-first century, this remark already seems very dated, such has been the effect of Houllier and Wenger. Many major clubs have indeed followed this direction: in addition to large coaching staffs below, there is considerable expertise above: a chief executive here or a vice-chairman there who takes full responsibility for transfer and salary negotiations, while leaving the 'club manager' to make all footballing decisions. However, as clubs have become plcs, tensions can emerge between the Board of Directors and the manager particularly in terms of buying and selling and therefore about issues of footballing strategy.

In France, despite the odd exception, there is no equivalent of the traditional British model of an autonomous 'manager' dominating the club, setting the tone, and making all the decisions, footballing or otherwise, thus creating a club in his own image like a Busby or a Clough. The dominant figure within French club football, the person who has been most likely to mould the club in his own image, and sometimes for his own ulterior (extra-footballing) purposes, has been the chairman ('président'). In the public eye, when we look for the major public figures of the post-war club game (not including players), club figureheads have most often been chairmen, like Roger Rocher (Saint-Etienne), Bernard Tapie (OM), or, today, Jean-Michel Aulas (Lyon) (see Chapter 8). Since the dawn of French professionalism, businessmen-chairmen like Jean-Pierre Peugeot have been the driving forces in clubs. In this model of club management, the key dialectical relationship between *président* and *entraîneur* (literally 'trainer') has meant that the role of the team manager/trainer/coach has traditionally been more constrained and more narrowly defined than in Britain. It was summed up at the start of the 2001/02 season by the Lyon manager Jacques Santini, who had not appreciated the lack of consultation before his chairman had sold a player to Fulham: 'Tensions? No, he's the chairman, I'm just a manager*[entraîneur]*, who should confine himself to on-the-field matters' (Labrunie 2001b).

The terminology reflects the cultural differences. When the FFF and State diplomas were set up to dignify the status of the French coaching and managerial staff, the terms chosen to describe their functions, as we have seen above, were 'éducateur' and 'entraîneur'. The word 'entraîneur' is the default term, used by pre-teenage children in the lowliest amateur club to describe the man who looks after their team to the 'manager' of a professional team as expressed in the name of the official qualification 'diplôme d'entraîneur professionnel de football'. A variation on this, especially at national level is 'entraîneur-sélectionneur', which refers back implicitly to a time when the coach was not the selector of the team. There is therefore within the French term a notion that the function is not autonomous, that there is implicitly some other authority to whom the 'trainer' reports, that it is a service position. The term does not have the status that the notion of 'manager' has acquired in the English-speaking world, consolidated through the importance of business values that have been more pervasive in British football and British society in general. In a sense, French football never completely professionalised and has never really accepted business values. The word *éducateur*, which, in another context, is used to refer to a 'social worker', has much wider connotations than simply passing on technical skills. There is unavoidably a notion of being responsible for the social aspects of personal development, which ties in with some of the values of public service that we have come across earlier in the voluntary and public sector involvement in mass and elite sport. More informally, the word *formateur* is also in use, in particular to describe the function of coaches working in youth coaching. The word is much more value free than *éducateur*, but not quite as neutral as 'instructor'. Finally, with the increasing frequency of international travel, and the influence of American English via media coverage of basketball for example, the *franglais* term 'coach' can be heard as the mode of address of players to manager.

Even if the French club manager has generally never had the same autonomy that many English managers enjoy and indeed take for granted, the role of the *entraîneur* has evolved. The number-two to Jacquet as DTN, charged by the FFF with overseeing the training of coaches, Jean-Pierre Morlans, describes how the role and image of the club manager has changed since the 1970s:

The role and image of the manager have evolved considerably. Thirty years ago, people had in mind a man with a bag of balls over his shoulder. Twenty years ago, as people became conscious of the physiological aspect of training, they imagined a man with a stopwatch in his hand, allowing him to measure effort and recovery times. Today, this image is largely out-of-date. His role is much wider and goes beyond the purely sporting dimension. The manager must also be a psychologist, a good communicator, able to teach and have a preventative role. He has become a powerful figure within the club, but is not really recognised as such in France. (Morlans 2001)

Looking at the key figures who, since the war, have established the French model of coaching and management at club level, there is a clear genealogical tree of successful managers and coaches, leading indeed directly to the French

World Cup win and beyond. The spiritual father of the profession (to quote *France Football*, 26 December 2000: 44–45) is generally recognised as Albert Batteux, who coached the two most successful teams of the 1950s and 1960s: Reims and Saint-Etienne. He also coached the French World Cup side that finished third in 1958. His assistant in Sweden with the national team was Jean Snella, who managed Saint-Etienne in the period before his friend Batteux arrived. Snella himself won three championships as manager of 'les Verts'. Robert Herbin was a key player under these two managers, and he succeeded Batteux to manage Saint-Etienne to four more league titles, three French cups and the famous European Cup sagas. Another key Saint-Etienne player who was at the club under all three of the aforementioned mentors was Aimé Jacquet. While managing Bordeaux, Jacquet went on to coach two players later to become successful managers, Tigana and Giresse. The former Lyon coach and new national team manager, Jacques Santini, also overlapped with Jacquet as a player at Saint-Etienne, and coached them from 1992–94. Personal influence, sometimes reciprocal, seems to have been important in passing on values and practices. Batteux is at the start of another genealogical branch of coaching success in so far one of his players at Reims was Michel Hidalgo, who went on to be France's most successful national manager (until Jacquet) by reaching the semi-finals of the World Cup in 1982 and then winning the European Nations Cup in 1984. Of the current generation of managers, Giresse, Tigana, and Luis Fernandez (the first Frenchman to manage a club to European success) all played many times under Hidalgo.

The other key genealogical line starts in Nantes with José Arribas who established the Nantes one-touch, pass-and-move football and the most famous French youth academy. The Nantes tradition was carried on by Jean-Claude ('Coco') Suaudeau, who in turn passed the reins to Raynald Denoueix (1997). Suaudeau had joined Nantes as an apprentice in Arribas's first year as manager (1960). By 1973 he was coaching the juniors to victory in the Gambardella Cup, and took over the senior team in 1981, at which point Denoueix became Director of the Youth Academy. This continuity and overlap of personnel is generally credited as the reason why Nantes has maintained the same style and values that are so recognisable (Faure and Suaud 1994b: 11–12, and 1999: 149–189). Nantes was the only club to challenge Saint-Etienne in their heyday, winning six titles between 1965 and 1983; and have been one of the most successful sides of the last decade (titles in 1995 and 2001). The influence of Nantes on French management is indicated by the fact that, in the 2001/02 season, there were five managers of Division 1 clubs who had spent significant parts of their playing careers at Nantes: Denoueix and Angel Marcos (Lorient) under Arribas, and Vahid Halilhodzic (LOSC), Guy Lacombe (Guingamp) and

Didier Deschamps (Monaco) under Suaudeau. Of these five only Deschamps did not win a Championship in the famous yellow shirt. Before becoming a European Cup Winner with Marseille and Juventus and a World Cup winning captain, he spent five years in the Nantes youth academy. He is spoken of as a possible future national team manager, and has acknowledged the Nantes influence on his managerial approach (Brochen 2001b: 6). One other significant manager to emerge from the Nantes school was Henri Michel, who played under Arribas and Suaudeau (as captain from 1971), went on to be assistant to Hidalgo as national team manager (1982–84), succeeded him (1984–88), and spent four years as DTN before managing the national teams of Cameroon, Saudi Arabia, Morocco and United Arab Emirates.[4] A final coach who cannot be ignored and who is out of no mould other than his own is Guy Roux, the only club manager to appear regularly on the French TV satirical puppet show *Les Guignols de l'info*, and who has single-handedly made Auxerre into a major force.

In a poll of 'experts' in 2000, *France Football* awarded trophies for the best French managers of the century, including club and country. The top ten names, in order, were: Jacquet, Batteux, Hidalgo, Wenger, Roux, Arribas, Snella, Suaudeau, Fernandez and Herbin.

Albert Batteux: the Father of Modern French Coaching

Batteux has the best club record in French football history in terms of championship wins, with Reims and Saint-Etienne (eight, including three league-and-cup doubles). As manager of both Reims and the French national team, Batteux based his teams' style on attack and individual skill. He was an excellent communicator, charismatic, a wonderful teller of stories. As a motivator he was precise in his choice of words, never violent or vexatious. His team talks would last two hours on the evening before a match, analysing players' strengths and weaknesses. He fitted his tactics to his players rather than the opposite. Kopa said of him: 'With Monsieur Batteux the player was king, his talent could be expressed without reservation' (Larcher 2000). A good judge of a player, he recruited some excellent players from other clubs: Piantoni from Nancy, Fontaine from Nice. Late in his career, when he joined the Nancy board, he is credited with preventing a skinny young Michel Platini from being sent home from the youth academy for poor academic results (Larcher 2000). His international team were called 'les Brésiliens de l'Europe'. To hone his players' skills and speed, he invented practices such as three-against-three on a basketball court where, to score, the ball had to hit the net post. He is thought to have invented football tennis. To develop attacking play he encouraged defenders to think about quick counterattacks; for example, goalkeepers were asked look for opportunities to throw quick balls out to the side to begin attacks, which was a new tactic. He was also ahead of his time in using a specialist fitness coach. His influence on successive managers is not in doubt (Larcher 2000; Penverne 2000).

The New Generation

Having traced the genealogical lines of development of the traditional coaching model of the French club manager, we can now look at how the profession is changing. Bordeaux's 1999 championship winning *entraîneur* Elie Baup confirms the view that in French clubs the model is not one of managerial autonomy – although he has strong views about the direction in which the job has to evolve. He would like to extend his field of action as a manager, to feel properly in charge of the entire 'technical' sector of the club:

> The whole sporting side must belong to the manager [*l'entraîneur*]. Everything has become hyper professional in French clubs. We have [coaching] staff, video, medical structures. Inside that, the manager is the conductor of the orchestra. He is the boss of the club. It is the manager who makes choices, and if he gets it wrong, then he dies with his ideas. (*France Football*, 2856, 2 January 2001: 8)

The journalist calls this vision as that of a 'manager à l'anglaise'. This concurs with Morlans' view at the DTN, who cites the French managers operating in England as the models:

> I think this evolution will take us to a more global function including the management of financial and administrative issues along the lines of the general manager embodied by Arsène Wenger, Gérard Houillier or Jean Tigana. This is why we have to be more effective in this area. (Morlans 2001)

The model for French clubs has clearly become the one personified by French coaches abroad, among whom the ground-breaker was Arsène Wenger.

Arsène Wenger

Wenger is certainly an innovator and a precursor, and from an early age was always interested in living abroad (ITV1 interview 12 May 2001). Houllier has said it would have been more difficult for him to come to Liverpool, but for Wenger's example. Through his articulate analyses in television interviews, as much as by his team's rapid success, Wenger is, as Paul Weaver has written (2001), 'the man who, more than any other, has popularised the notion of foreign coaches in British football'. He also had the courage to work in a culture as different as Japan's. He is highly respected in France, as shown by his rating in the *France Football* millennial survey (26 December 2000: 34), where he was voted fourth best French manager of the century. He won the French championship once, early in his seven-year stint at Monaco, and then his team was fairly consistently runner-up, before dipping in form. For a time it looked as if a similar story was unfolding in England, where Arsenal won the double in his first year in charge, and qualified for the Champions League consistently, but coming second ever after in the domestic league – until Arsenal won the League and Cup double again in 2002. He felt he stayed a year too long at Monaco, where he was sacked in the last year of his contract after earlier being begged to stay on, for which he turned down Bayern Munich (Lawrence 2000a). So far he gives every indication of wanting to stay long enough at Arsenal to make a real difference. He was rumoured to have turned down the chance to manage the French national side in 2002.

He is sometimes called 'the professor', not just because of his glasses – he is obviously an educated man, who speaks several languages. He also takes for granted the lessons of sports science when it comes to fitness, diet and lifestyle. He introduced modern stretching exercises and vitamin supplements. Steve Bould reckoned it added two years to his career (Lawrence 2000b: 208). The laddish drinking culture of English football has been seriously dented by Wenger's arrival – his captain did after all prolong his career by admitting he had become an alcoholic and sought successful treatment. 'Diet is for sportsmen what petrol is for a car. If you put the wrong petrol in a car it does not work as well as it could. If you put the wrong diet into a body it does not work well' (Humphries 2001). Steak and toast followed by rice pudding for the pre-match lunch – Jim Smith's recollections of his diet as a player – or beer, sausages and going home from the pub 'legless' after the match (Harry Redknapp) – were definitely not on the menu at Highbury. Tales of smoking and hard drinking by relegated Manchester City players in 2001 (Taylor 2001) will only confirm the sense of the new culture that Wenger has initiated, and underline his strength of purpose.

Wenger is a self-confessed football addict and workaholic – he took a week's holiday in summer 2000, one more week than he normally takes, according to Amy Lawrence (2000a). He watches a TV (or video) match every night via a large satellite dish in his back garden, in order to keep abreast of potential opponents, players to buy, or just to keep up with tactical developments. Just like his admirer Elie Baup (Bordeaux), who had gone to Rome as part of his managerial training and constantly does his scouting by video (Machenaud 1999), Wenger's football world is global.

His teams, as Ian Ridley (1999) has said, are a 'mixture of style and steel, graft and grace' (Vieira and Henry). He has relied heavily on French players, apart from his English defence, but has been criticised for being too prudent in spending. He argues there is something more to football than money: 'It's team spirit, collective quality, work on the field, giving a chance to young players' (Lawrence 2000a), which of course is what the Bosman exodus has forced upon French football as a whole since the late 1990s.

Gérard Houllier

Hopkins and Williams (2001: 183), in their insightful analysis of an interview with Gérard Houllier that shows the depth and subtlety of his thinking about football, nicely call him 'both a technocrat and a humanist'. By humanist they do not simply mean that he may occasionally quote Proust and Milan Kundera in his team talks (Whittell 2001), but that his analysis of the game is set within an ethical perspective and a broad vision of sport as intimately linked to its social and economic surroundings. Ross (1999) reports him as justifying on ethical grounds the commitment and work rate he demands of players: 'Players have responsibilities, because, whether they like it or not, they are public figures. The players have to be aware that the people who come to the ground spend fortunes in relation to what they earn on a weekly basis.' Humanist too in the sense that, from his early contact with Liverpool as a student of English, researching his Masters dissertation in the deprived suburbs of Toxteth, in his French language classroom, and on the Kop, he developed an understanding of and an admiration for the 'structure of feeling' of the Liverpool people, and the part that the football club played in their sense of identity, their 'imaginaire' (Hopkins and Williams 2001: 174). As manager of Liverpool he has attempted to connect with that spirit and place it at the core of the club's values. He cannot, for example, conceive of picking a team that does not have a 'heart' of Liverpool-born players, let alone no Englishman, as Chelsea did under Vialli. He has noticed too that football is played differently from town to town. It has got something to do with 'the way of living, the culture, the history'. 'Football is more than just eleven players, it's an environment, it's a context, and they [the Liverpool fans] have had so much more of the good football practice in the successful years that you could not break away from that' (ibid.: 187). Hence he has to play a passing game, modified only by wanting to educate his players to 'pass forward' more.

More than the style of play, he had to change the player culture. He believes in the all-round education and culture of the products of the French youth system that he did so much to shape as DTN: good decision-makers, flexible and intelligent on the field. He believes that the improvement of football skills needs to go along with a player's all-round education and culture. What he found at Liverpool was the dominant English player culture, which lacked discipline and modern professionalism: 'laddish' behaviour and mentalities, drinking, a particular 'code of masculinity', an anti-intellectual 'thug culture', and chauvinistic insularity, that has been analysed in various academic studies.[5] English training has too often produced players who require direction and supervision, and so lack flexibility, and who act irresponsibly on and off the field. Houllier quickly got rid of those whom he saw as impervious to change and resistant to his authority.

What he admired about English football was its 'culture of effort', its work ethic, which the Liverpool crowd always expects, and which often goes hand-in-hand with team spirit. This does not exclude a scientific approach to preparation. Hopkins and Williams (2001: 182) neatly sum up the 'new scientism' imported from the Continent into British football and that Houllier represents so well: 'greater club "professionalism", a more holistic view of player development and education; the need for rigorous control of player diets; a place in the game for top-class medical back-up; and careful psychological, and well as physical, player preparation for matches'. When Roy Evans left the club soon after Houllier's arrival, this marked the end of the 'boot-room' era, reliant on passing down received wisdom and Shankly's intuitive methods. A back-room team still exists, but it is more numerous and more specialist, and Houllier takes every opportunity to give them credit. He dedicated the 2001 UEFA Cup victory to his staff (*France Football*, 18 May 2001: 23), the 'team behind the team', typically containing both some of his own men (like Patrice Bergues, with whom he worked at Lens and at the DTN) and some long-term Liverpool servants (assistant Phil Thompson, coach Sammy Lee, director of the Youth Academy Steve Heighway).[6]

His book on coaching and management (*Entraîneur: Compétence et passion*, 1993, jointly authored with J. Crevoisier, who joined the Liverpool staff in 2001) is well regarded. Not that Houllier ever thinks he has all the answers; on the contrary. A key aspect of his approach is a constant calling into question what he is doing: 'If you don't question and try to update your methods you will be left behind . . . you have to be adventurous . . . that's how you progress.' This is another aspect of the learning culture that he sees at the core of modern football. Perhaps he owes much of this to his father, who, involved in the amateur game successively as player, coach, and club official, gave his son a passion for the game, but refused to let him become a professional footballer, insisting he train to be a teacher (Hopkins and Williams 2001: 175).

In the 2001/02 season he almost learned too directly the effects of taking his commitment to Liverpool football to the point where it became more important than life and death (to misquote his famous predecessor Bill Shankly). Overwork caused a life-threatening illness from which he recovered remarkably quickly in view of its gravity. The way his technical staff were able to carry on in his four-month absence is perhaps the greatest tribute to the impact he has made at Anfield. The emotional reaction of the fans to his unexpected return to the dug-out in an important Champions League quarter-final is evidence not only of how much he is now loved by them, but also of his sense of timing, since his presence heightened the atmosphere generated by the crowd, which at Anfield, as he well knew, has been so important, especially in key games.

The Coach as National Hero: Aimé Jacquet

It was with the arrival of professionalism that the FFF set up an administrative department to help the selection committee liaise in picking the national team, and only in 1964 did the committee give way to a single selector-manager. The position was made a full-time one in the 1964/65 season. Previously, selection and coaching functions were, as in the Batteux era, kept separate. From the 1970s onwards the national technical director was a support to or sometimes the same person as the national team manager. The team manager, usually with outstanding coaching credentials, has sometimes emerged from the DTN staff or gone back to the position of DTN. The modern *entraîneurs-selectionneurs* have not lasted long in the post if results have not gone their way. So far, only the two most successful have been able to resign with heads held high, after major victories: Hidalgo and Jacquet. They feature in prominent position in the pantheon of French coaches. Were they just lucky enough to have a generation of great players at their disposal, or did they contribute something that turned a squad into a winning team? Hidalgo certainly had the incomparable Platini, with Giresse, Tigana, and Fernandez making up the midfield diamond. Jacquet had a solid defence built around Blanc and Desailly, a tactically astute captain and leader in Deschamps, and the outstanding player of his generation in Zidane. Hidalgo is remembered fondly and with pride, but Jacquet reached an altogether different level of hero worship.

The warmth emanating from what seemed like the whole of the French nation towards national team manager Aimé Jacquet from the point when France reached the final of the 1998 World Cup at least equalled the admiration even for Zidane, and arguably surpassed it. This was partly because Jacquet was suddenly perceived as having been unfairly criticised for two years by the footballing press (see McKeever 1999), indeed ridiculed by the sports daily *L'Equipe* for his apparently old-fashioned and uninspiring approach – unfairly since the victory seemed to have come about less because of outstanding individual performances and more because of teamwork. Having stuck to his tactics and choices, he suddenly found himself a hero of the national press, which presented him more and more as a representative of the values of French tradition – in counterpoint to the adoption of Zidane as symbol of new attitudes to the nation and to integration (see Dauncey and Hare 2000). Almost without exception, the rest of the national press suddenly saw in Jacquet a tragic misunderstood hero. *Le Monde* and other dailies and weeklies produced glowing profiles of Jacquet before and after the final (Chemin *et al.* 1998).

Having been mocked for his provincial accent and inarticulacy in front of the TV cameras, for his refusal to play the communication game, and for generally being unfashionable, Jacquet now stood for virtues of hard work, modesty, humility, respect, honesty, rigour, simplicity, authenticity, competence, professionalism: all that was good in French tradition. His approach to football had worked: methodical, protecting his players, building teamwork, unselfishness, valuing character, effort as much as talent, getting a result rather than being flashy. He came to represent all those unpaid volunteers who coach young children in the smallest amateur clubs. The term that best described him, for *Le Monde*, was not coach, or trainer, or manager, but *éducateur*. Indeed the *éducateurs'* role was compared to that of the 'hussars of the republic' in the late nineteenth century and the early twentieth, the lay primary school teachers of the first universal free and secular State school system: transmitting Republican values to the youth of France, promoting a meritocracy, and creating the national unity that in recent decades has been eroded.

Despite the criticism that had been heaped upon him, Jacquet's track record had none the less been irreproachable, whether as a player or a club manager. The former skilled factory worker had been a key part of the Saint-Etienne midfield, winning two cup-winners medals and five championships between 1964 and 1970. As a manager he won three championships and two French cups with Bordeaux and a place in Europe every year, before being sacked by chairman Claude Bez for being 'too straight'. As national manager, for some he symbolised a new era of French football, the opposite of the Tapie years when lucre and glitz were everything. The symbolism extended to the idea that the team he had created had become an analogy of the way forward for a nation in decline. For having inspired a multiracial team, in France's image, to all pull together successfully in the national interest, Jacquet was presented as incarnating the three integrative forces of old: not only the Republican school teacher, but the other mainstays of pre-war France, the provincial priest, and the factory worker that he had in fact been before becoming a professional footballer. If the Republic was once again threatened in its cohesion and fraternity, in its troubled *banlieues*, much of the French press saw Jacquet's 'traditional values' and self-belief as the answer.[7]

Conclusion

In the mid-1980s and the Platini era, when French football began to get a taste of success after ten years of youth training schemes, three-quarters or even four-fifths of professional footballers in the French Division 1 had learned their trade in a *Centre de formation* (Tournier and Rethacker 1999: 128). The figures are not going down. The footballing success of France, in moving from a world ranking of fifteenth to first in the 25 years of the youth training in the INF and in clubs' centres, cannot entirely be put down to coincidence. In the 1990s a key development was the national and regional youth training centres for 13–15-year-olds, set up by Gérard Houllier as DTN, where a good general education is combined with training to become a professional footballer. This contrasts with the situation in Britain, as interpreted by Richard Holt, where there is no equivalent way into professional sport while maintaining one's general education and leaving open the possibility of entering higher education. He claims that the problem with English professional football is not so much a general lack of players, but the confining of recruitment to a shrinking working class, through the belief among the expanding middle class that their children can only maintain their social status through educational achievement, whereas entering a professional football career requires exclusive commitment to it at the age of 16 or earlier at the price of dropping GCSE and A-level study (Holt 1994: 39–40).

Alongside the importance of the French youth coaching system, other associated factors cannot be ignored, however: the interest and support of the State under governments of various political colours, the systematic training of coaches, a highly centralised system of qualifications obligatory for coaches and managers to be able to practise professionally, a regular desire on the part of the FFF to improve the system, concentration as much on spreading interest in football among the nation's youth as on selecting and developing an elite – all have played their part. Along with French youth training methods that have improved skills there has been the fortuitous final touch of rigorous foreign (particularly Italian) character building and fitness training for the many French internationals who played abroad. The contribution of outstanding individuals such as Gérard Houllier and Aimé Jacquet cannot be underestimated. Nor should it be forgotten that their contributions have been facilitated by the French system rather than being hindered by it.

The meanings associated in the press with Jacquet as a national symbol show how important is the figure of the *éducateur* in France and the values that are invested in it. They reveal too how much football has become a part of the wider social and cultural context of France in recent years. But they reveal something deeper about French society too, in as much as they do not equate to the commonly understood metaphor of the World Cup as acceptance of modernisation, of a new France comfortable with its definitive multiracial identity, as symbolised by the multicoloured national team winning for France.

The two metaphors are in conflict or at least in counterpoint. They represent two different understandings of French identity: the one the values of modernisation and the new France, and the other the values of French tradition, the old France, before large-scale immigration (or at least before black and Arab/ Muslim immigration), and before the second industrial revolution and the modern deprived city suburbs, before mass unemployment. Jacquet is used as a means of looking back proudly to French traditions and continuity. But the euphoria of the victory celebrations conveniently obscured these different visions of France. A reminder of their continuing actuality came in the abandoned France–Algeria match of October 2001. These issues will be explored in Chapter 6 through a study of players and national identity.

Notes

1. The *département* is, since Napoleonic times, the basic administrative division of the French State. Metropolitan France is divided into 96 *départements*, plus five more overseas. Since the 1970s a larger unit, the *région*, has been superimposed on the *départements*. Metropolitan France has 22 administrative *régions*.

2. In addition to the INF at Clairefontaine the centres are: 1994/95 Vichy, and Tours (moved to Châteauroux in 1997); 1995/96 Castelmaurou in the Midi-Pyrénées; 1996/97 Liévin in the Nord-Pas-de-Calais; 1997/98 Madine in Lorraine, and Ploufragan in Brittany. Other centres are in the pipeline.

3. Thierry Henry was in *préformation* at the INF before joining the *Centre de formation* in Monaco.

4. For article on French coaches in Africa see 'L'Afrique des coaches français', *France Football*, 2881 (26 June 2001: 36–38).

5. Hopkins and Williams (2001: 177–178) cite Wagg (1984); Williams and Taylor (1994); Williams (2000a), who also cites John Cartwright on the 'thug culture'.

6. See the *Independent* (19 May 2001: 30), for a formal photograph of all ten technical staff surrounding trophies and manager.

7. See Colombani (1998), and also Haget (1998), Chemin *et al.* (1998), Benamou (1998), Bozonnet (1998).

6

Players as Heroes: 'les Bleus', and National Identity

France has always been an importer and an exporter of players at club level. Players like the Englishman Glenn Hoddle (Monaco), the Yugoslav Josip Skoblar (Marseille), and the Brazilian Rai (PSG) have over the years been adopted as heroes by French clubs, helping open up French football to foreign influences and new ideas. Since the mid-1990s in particular, when most of their international side have been playing in other European leagues, the French press and television have also taken a strong interest in football abroad by focusing on the exploits of their own nationals. Whereas the aura of club heroes has remained at a relatively local level, the French players who have become legends and national heroes are those who have made their names representing the national team, often of foreign extraction themselves: the Kopas, the Platinis and the Zidanes. The national team's relation to national identity became an important social phenomenon at the time of the 1998 World Cup victory, when the multiracial team was turned, perhaps only briefly, but certainly memorably, into a symbol of the new France, a winning France, a multiethnic Republic at peace with itself.

Footballers as National Heroes: from Kopa to Platini

Football and National Identity

Unlike, say, Uruguay (see Giulianotti 2000), France's formation as a modern nation-state was a century too early for football to have been a tool for forging an initial shared national identity. This was achieved, in the face of major ideological conflict throughout the nineteenth century, through strengthening the *ancien régime*'s already centralised administration; the imposition by Napoleon of a judicial system, the Civil Code; and the spread of the standard French language replacing provincial dialects, a process completed by the innovation in the 1880s of a free, universal and secular primary school system promoting Republican values of individual freedom, the equality of every citizen, and social solidarity. The growing transport infrastructure following the building of a national rail network in the nineteenth century (itself helping the development of a national press), three military invasions (1870, 1914, 1940), and in particular the social and regional mixing in the 1914–18 trenches, helped unite the country and gain a sense of itself as a nation around the idea of the 'one and indivisible Republic'.

National consciousness and identity is not, however, a once-and-for-all acquisition within a society. Writers such as Philip Schlesinger (1991), Stuart Hall (1992), Chris Barker (1997) and others have argued, after Anderson (1983: 15–16), that the nation is an 'imagined community', that national cultural identity is constructed and reproduced by narratives of the nation, by stories, images, symbols and rituals that represent shared meanings of nationhood; that collective identity is always provisional and has to be continually reinforced; that it is via the newspapers and radio and television news especially that people are encouraged to imagine such events occurring simultaneously; and that national culture must be linked to shared consciousness of events that matter. This does not mean that national identity is at the forefront of most people's minds for most of the time. As Giddens has pointed out (1985), identity and meaningful experience are much more likely to arise in the realms of the private spheres of family, friends, and sexual relationships, and, one might add, in the work place. It is probably true that the routine of daily life is only occasionally interrupted by shared consciousness of events of national importance, but the key collective rituals that impinge on national cultural identity include important political events, such as presidential elections, serious disasters, national commemorations, State funerals . . . or major sporting events. Anderson's notions of the simultaneous moment and the imagined community have often been applied to sporting events, for example by Vidacs (2000) *à propos* of the modern Cameroon nation: a people's sense of belonging to a community can be cemented by imagining the nation while watching a televised transmission of an important football match, whether the result is victory or defeat.

National Consciousness and Football Myth

When football achieves national popularity it can contribute significantly to the formation of these narratives of collective national identity. In international football competitions, such as the World Cup or the European Nations Cup, it is teams representing nations that are pitted against each other and such structures have ways of imposing themselves on the popular imagination. Two important aspects of the impact of the 1998 World Cup victory was that the matches were played in France and many people went to stadiums before the matches even without tickets, just to be part of the atmosphere though remaining outside, and then went back to city centres to watch the match in the open on big screens. Thousands of people were thus able to participate collectively in these simultaneous moments, making the imagined community all the easier to conjure up in the mind's eye. A similar identification with a team as the nation's representative can happen at club level in a competition such as the European Champions Cup, where the nation's champion is pitted against the champions of other nations.

It is possible to trace a historical line of key moments when the French nation's interest was focused on football as a purveyor of narratives and images of national significance, even if the line is at times a broken one. A major early event was the national team's first victory over England in 1921, on the anniversary of Napoleon's death, regarded at the time as a historic victory, even if it was only the England amateur international side. The growing number of international matches, and the hosting of the World Cup in 1938, helped create a shared sense of national identity in supporting the country, especially since the different federations had settled their differences in 1919 in the wake of the political Sacred Union entered into for the purposes of national defence in 1914. The problem was that France was not notably successful in international football encounters.

The symbiotic relationship of football and nation was recognised early when the French Cup Final was quickly invested with a significance as a national annual ritual by the official presence of the President of the Republic to meet the teams and present the cup. The other symbiotic relationship, between football and the press, allowed newspapers, before the Second World War, to create a star system to exploit interest in the game through narratives of the exploits of a number of national heroes and characters in French soccer. Although this began in earnest in the 1950s with the popularity of radio and the increasing number of magazines with photos (Wahl 1989: 287), there were earlier stars. One indisputable hero before and after the First World War was perhaps the only famous goalkeeper in French history (before Barthez), Pierre Chayriguès, playing for Red Star with a personality to match his huge frame. He was the first goalkeeper to come off his line, commanding his penalty area. He was reputed to claim enormous expenses payments and medical bills in the days before professionalism was legal and shamateurism was consequently growing. On at least one occasion he arrived at the FFFA headquarters on crutches, leaving with a large cheque in his pocket . . . without his crutches (Thibert and Rethacker 1996: 65). Despite his size, this picture of Chayriguès fits the common national stereotype of the wily little French individualist putting one over on those in authority, a recognisable character from Maupassant's short stories to the cartoon characters in the Astérix cartoon stories. The older Chayriguès was an Astérix in the body of Obélix.

Kopa and a First Taste of International Success

The main successes of French club and national sides coincided with the beginnings and later the high points of the era of national terrestrial television, when a fully national audience could watch certain games simultaneously. *L'Equipe*, along the same lines as its organisation of and coverage of the Tour de France cycle race, also made the most of the European Cup that it had originated to stimulate interest in club football and thereby sell papers. It was in the 1950s, with the innovation of European club competitions and France's unexpectedly good performance in the World Cup, that national interest was aroused in football as a vector of national values. In the very first season of the European Cup, 1955/56, the French public was increasingly interested to follow the progress of Stade de Reims, playing all their home matches in Paris to allow bigger gates (Wahl 1989: 315). Reims dominated French football in the 1950s with six French championships in 12 years from 1949. With their star forward Raymond Kopa, they fell 4–3 at the final European hurdle in Paris to Real Madrid, who were to go on to win the trophy for five consecutive years. Reims reached the final again in 1959, but this time Kopa was gaining his third winner's medal playing alongside the legendary Di Stefano of Real. As with Platini in Italy in the 1980s, and Cantona, Henry and Vieira in England in the 1990s and beyond, the exploits abroad of a French star were also a matter of keen interest in France, and often of pride. The weekly televised football highlights programme will always devote some time to French stars abroad, as does the sporting press.

In the meantime, in 1958, the national interest created around the top French club side was capitalised on by the national team (which included six of Kopa's former Reims team-mates). France finished third in the World Cup in Sweden, with Kopa creating many of Just Fontaine's 13 goals in six matches in the course of the finals, a record unlikely to be beaten in today's more defensive game. Radio coverage by Europe No.1 (Bourg 1986: 128) was the live link with the French public, and the commentator underlined the national import of the event by greeting each of France's two goals in the semi-final with a chauvinistic 'Vive la France'. In the days before substitutes for injured players, centre-half Jonquet became a virtual passenger; France could not overcome the odds and an unknown seventeen-year-old Brazilian called Pele scored a hat-trick. Kopa was awarded the Player of the Tournament trophy by FIFA (equal first with the Brazilian Didi). What he valued more, however, was the 1958 European Player of the Year trophy, the *Ballon d'Or*, awarded by *France Football* – the only one he did not sell off in 2001 (*France Football*, 27 March 1980).

Kopa was undeniably the player of his generation, and was at the end of the twentieth century remembered as one of the top three French players of all time

(*France Football*, 26 December 2000). Smaller than average for a footballer, above all he was a technically brilliant dribbler, playing either on the right-wing or inside forward, with a short-passing game and a eye for the defence-splitting pass. He came from one of the working-class French immigrant communities – Polish in his case – in northern France (Noeux-les-Mines). His style was controversial. The Communist press stressed playing for enjoyment, whereas the more conservative sports press, such as Hanot in *France Football*, criticised this 'romantic approach' that was not effective enough in defence. As Lanfranchi and Wahl (1996: 116) point out in their article on Kopa, he polarised two opposing approaches to the game. The French Left stressed the beauty of the game, its enjoyment, and entertainment value, as opposed to the idea that winning was everything. Wider social and political values were at stake in the debate about whether the Kopa and Reims style was French or not. For the Communists, football was an expression of social harmony through leisure activity, and should not be turned into a business activity that imitated factory discipline. For the right, the new France needed to be modernised and made effective and efficient by adopting the values of contemporary (capitalist) economic life.

Kopa also became a symbol of social advancement through hard work, and appeared to be motivated by a strong desire to be fully accepted into French mainstream society. Having been unable to play for the French national youth team because he was Polish, he applied for French citizenship at the age of twenty-one, changed his name from Kopaszewski, and was proud to do his military service, as well as to 'defend the French colours' in his sporting capacity. Lanfranchi and Wahl tell us that Kopa never tried to keep in touch with his Polish roots. He denied he could speak the language of his parents (1996: 117). Naturally brilliant at the game, he was often quoted as stressing the hard work needed to reach the top: 'If I had been born into a wealthy family, there would never have been a Raymond Kopa. Without the mine, I'd have been a good player. Nothing more. But there was the mine. My name was Kopaszewski and to get out I had nothing but football' (ibid. 1996: 118). As his biographers say, by stressing this aspect of his success, he became a force for order and harmony, the image that the right-wing press had created of him (ibid.: 118–119). His one major stand against the social *status quo* was his rebellion against the professional footballers' contract for life and the retain-and-transfer system, which he regarded as a form of labour slavery.

Platini: France versus Germany . . . again

A feeling grew that the meaning of international football competition in terms of national identity was that France may play well but were always destined to heroic defeat – the Astérix complex. This fits the major trauma of the French national football consciousness of the 1980s, the era bestrode by Michel Platini. Two-thirds of the national television audience sat entranced by the interminably unfolding drama of Seville 1982. In progressing to the semi-finals of the World Cup with attacking panache that won them support from all around the world from lovers of the beautiful game, the French team under the inspired captaincy of Platini prepared to meet West Germany. For many viewers France versus Germany had an adversarial history: three successive invasions of French soil in 1870, 1914, 1940 – a history the commentators did not need to recall. Saint-Etienne had twice fallen to a German team in their failure to win the European Cup. There had more recently of course been the de Gaulle–Adenauer national reconciliation and the Giscard–Schmidt axis at the head of the European Community. But another France–Germany clash provided opportunities to stir up atavistic bitterness.

The most powerful images that remain in the mind are of the infamous turning point of the match: in the fiftieth minute, one goal each: the German goalkeeper Schumacher rushing to the edge of his penalty area and crashing into Battiston, as he chases a through ball; the shocked concern of captain Platini as he puts out a hand towards the shoulder of his unconscious team-mate who is lying motionless on the stretcher. No goal, and the Dutch referee awards no penalty, no sending off, no foul even. Schumacher was quoted afterwards as more or less admitting to a 'professional foul': 'Football has changed a lot in fifteen years. Before, perhaps, the clash with Battiston wouldn't have happened. But today you are always playing at the limit. Football is also a business; players are extremely tensed up' (Bourg 1986: 171–172).

The French continued to attack relentlessly, Rocheteau had a goal disallowed, Amoros hit the bar in the ninetieth minute, but, with no more goals, the match went into extra time. Within ten minutes Trésor, then Giresse put France 3–1 ahead. However, a tiring French team conceded a goal before the turn round and then an equaliser in the 108th minute, but extra time finished with the sides still level. In the penalty shoot-out, each side converted four out of the first five penalties. In the sudden death phase, Bossis missed, Hrubesch scored. It made draining viewing and left a sense of injustice that the best team had not won, again (see Baddiel 2000). In the memory of one of the most famous TV sports journalists, Georges de Caunes, the Battiston–Schumacher incident revived in men of his generation emotions felt during the Second World War (Lecoq 1997: 132). A whole nation experienced together the catharsis of shared disappointment for their tragic national heroes. Manager Hidalgo remained generous and dignified in defeat, and he and his players immediately entered the pantheon of valiant French sporting heroes – defeated ones, like Racinian heroes from the French classical stage, unable to sustain the unequal struggle against the inevitable course of destiny. When a few days later Germany lost to Italy in the final, *France Football* headlined: 'Justice est faite' [Justice has been done].

Victory two years later in the European Nation's Cup at the Parc des Princes for Platini's heroes, the first French victory in a major international tournament, was constantly replayed on television. Fans celebrated deliriously in the streets of a Paris temporarily diverted from worry over unemployment and socialist economic policy. Hidalgo became a national hero. Platini was depicted as a national treasure, 'Platinix le goalois', top scorer with nine goals in the tournament, a legend in France and a legend in Italy. He could never have imagined the manner in which he would win his European Champions cup medal at Heysel the following year, against Liverpool, as the final was played after 38 Italian supporters had been crushed to death on the terraces. Losing in the semi-final to Germany in the next World Cup in Guadalajara in 1986, seemed in comparison with the previous events an anticlimax, but nicely fitting the thesis of inevitable and courageous defeats for 'les petits Français'.

France Football elected Platini as the French Player of the Century. By the time he retired in 1987 aged 31 Platini had won everything except the World Cup. In France he won the French Cup with Nancy (1978), the Championship with Saint-Etienne (1981), with Juventus the Italian Cup (1983), two Italian championships (1984 and 1986), the European Cup Winners Cup and European Super Cup (1984), the European Champions Cup (1985). He was three times both top scorer in Italy and European Footballer of the Year (1983–85). He scored 41 goals in 72 matches for France, out of 353 career goals. He made the number 10 national jersey his own, ever after to be the iconic French shirt that is passed on to the key player in the national team. His vision, his eye for goal, his determination and his expertise with free-kicks, a modern skill he was perhaps the first to master, will always be remembered. His career as manager of the national team was, in comparison with his playing career, a disappointment for the French public who put enormous pressure on Platini to succeed: failure to qualify for the 1990 World Cup was, however, followed by qualification for the European Nations Cup in 1992. He preferred to leave this high pressure post and became co-president of the Organising Committee of the 1998 World Cup, having gained a reputation as a successful businessman from his later years as a player. His ambitions have not stopped, since he is seeking to establish a career within the FFF and FIFA as an international football administrator, having been an unofficial running-mate and high-profile supporter of Sepp Blatter, elected FIFA President in 1998. He is (in 2002) a vice-president of the FFF and a member of UEFA's and FIFA's executive committees.

Unlikely Heroes and Villains: Milla, Waddle, Cantona and Ginola

French football heroes have generally been those who have excelled for the national team. In their different eras Kopa and Platini were the focus of football's national audience and of national pride – particularly when playing for France, but also when excelling in club football abroad. Picking out a few other individual heroes to compete with the greats is invidious and controversial. It should be said, of course, that Kopa never forgot to mention the debt he owed to his colleagues Piantoni and Fontaine, and chose Larbi Ben Barek as second only to Platini as the French all-time great. Platini's success for France is also often bracketed with the midfield contributions of Tigana, Giresse and Fernandez. The undoubted star of the next generation of internationals was the striker Jean-Pierre Papin, author of 30 goals in 54 appearances for the national team. And who to leave out of a list of the heroes of the 1998 squad? Not captain Deschamps, nor the back line of Thuram, Desailly, Blanc, and Lizarazu. Nor Henry and Vieira from the generation that left its stamp on the 2000 victory.

At French club level the all-time highest scorer in the French league is Bernard Lacombe, whose total of 255 goals for Lyon (from 1970 to 1987) looks hard to beat in post-Bosman times. Yet he never came close, in a single season, to the Yugoslav Josip Skoblar's 44 goals for Marseille (1970/71). Will Monaco goalkeeper Jean-Luc Ettori's 602 games in Division 1 (from 1975 to 1994) ever be beaten, or, as an outfield player Alain Giresse's 519 matches for the same club, Bordeaux (from 1970 to 1988)? How could the Uruguayan Enzo Francescoli be forgotten at Marseille when Zidane named his son after his hero? Although they have wider reputations, for better or worse, the following four players, two imports and two exports, had played memorably in France. They offer different insights into French club football through the ways they managed to flourish there or not.

Roger Milla – African Player of the Century

A player who should have been a hero at French club level but who wasn't quite is Roger Milla. Cameroon is known to many as a country solely because of Roger Milla's exploits in the 1990 World Cup. The 38-year-old's stylish goals that took the *Indomitable Lions* so close to the semi-finals were celebrated with sways of the hips around the corner flag in improvised *makossa* rhythm, a televisual image that went around the world. Improbably reaching the quarter-finals, they lost only after extra-time to England. By then Milla had become a household name as a twinkle-toed goalscorer while somewhat overweight and obviously not match-fit and in the twilight of his career.

Born in 1952 he became African player of the year in 1975 and 1976 with Yaoundé's Tonnerre, before leaving for a decade with French clubs in order to become a full professional. However, he never quite fulfilled his potential and felt exploited. Arriving in the northern town of Valenciennes in 1977 he found his contract and living conditions did not live up to the promises made, and felt discriminated against because of his black skin (Ramsey 2000: 180). After two years he left for Monaco and warmer climes, but was used mainly as a substitute, scoring a number of goals. One more year and he travelled further south to Bastia, led the attack and scored more goals, including the winning goal in the French Cup. In 1982 he moved on again to Saint-Etienne who had been relegated to Division 2, and he helped them back to Division 1 with 22 goals. Meanwhile he steered the Cameroon Lions to the final of the African Nations Cup and won the Player of the Tournament trophy. Still feeling exploited, he moved on to Montpellier in 1986 for three years and helped them gain promotion. Here is where he was happiest, under the wing of chairman Louis Nicollin, whom he claims was the only club chairman who did not 'rip him off' (Ramsey 2000: 181). Then, in semi-retirement on the island of Réunion, when Cameroon reached the World Cup Finals in Italy, out of the blue he was recalled to the national team and became a legend. He has since been voted African player of the century and Cameroon the African team of the century. Many other black African players have followed in his footsteps to France, some, like Basile Boli at Marseille, succeeding and some experiencing similar or worse frustrations than Milla. Few have had his talent. (See Ramsay 2000, and Tshitenge 1998.)

Chris Waddle – 'the worst sight in football'

The enduring standing of Chris Waddle in Marseille may be hard to take in for the more insular of English football fans, but Olivia Blair may be guilty only of mild hyperbole when she says that 'Magic' Waddle, as the fans called him, was as integral to the OM of the early 1990s as fish to the local *bouillabaisse* (Blair 2000: 159). His unique skills (rather than his scruffy appearance and mullet haircut) were summed up by Alan Hansen: 'For a defender, Chris running at you is the worst sight in football' (Ball and Shaw 1996: 47). Bought by Bernard Tapie in 1989, Waddle the entertainer found in the Stade vélodrome a stage and an audience as passionate as his original Tyneside fans, and perhaps more appreciative of his skill on the ball. Some young fans even adopted his haircut as well as buying replica shirts. Harder training made him fitter (eventually) than he had been at Spurs and he was given the freedom to operate wide behind the lone striker Jean-Pierre Papin, with no midfield covering duties. With OM, Waddle won three championships, and reached the French Cup Final and a European Cup Final and semi-final – all in three seasons.

After a difficult start, Waddle recalls he began to feel at home when he scored against PSG with an extravagant back-heel. Christian Bromberger identifies the moment when the OM crowd really took the Englishman to their hearts, not only for his style and his recognition of the fans' importance – they certainly appreciated his willingness to sign autographs and to salute them at the end of matches – but also for his choice of game in which to shine. For the Marseillais, the local rival city is Bordeaux. In footballing terms, too, reports Bromberger, the Girondins and OM are sworn enemies since incidents in 1987. One of the Marseille fans' favourite chants is an insult to their the Girondin rivals: 'Bordelais, j'ai niqué ta mère / Sur la Cane . . ., Cane . . ., Canebière' (Bromberger *et al.* 1995: 79–80). They seem to have little in common as towns. Bordeaux has had a right-wing municipality since the war. Marseille had in the 1980s a long-standing left-wing mayor, Socialist minister Gaston Defferre. The Bordeaux chairman Claude Bez, having inherited his business from his father, was seen as being born into money and right-wing. The OM Chairman Bernard Tapie, on the other hand, was a self-made man, on the political left, with the same irascible volubility as the locals (if in a more standard French accent). It was against this background, in April 1990, that the Englishman Waddle endeared himself forever to the Marseillais public during the crucial, end-of-season home derby against Bordeaux. Before the game OM were second in the League behind Bordeaux, and the title hung on the result. After 52 minutes of a rough and tense match Waddle broke the deadlock by scoring direct from a free-kick, thus earning his nickname 'Magic Waddle'. He also scored the second goal, in the last minute, ensuring OM were practically certain to win the championship. He claims in his autobiography that his popularity remained such that he received a louder welcome back from the crowd at Papin's testimonial than even JPP himself (Blair 2000: 165). His other enduringly memorable contribution (for the fans at least) was his winning goal in the quarter-finals of the European Cup in 1991 against the reigning champions AC Milan, when OM came of age in Europe. Waddle himself recounts how he had been so physically manhandled by Paolo Maldini that he ended up in hospital for two days with concussion and remembered nothing of his instinctive volley (Ambrosiano 2002b: 101).

Eric Cantona – Still Chasing Rimbauds[1]

Just as the English do not really appreciate the impact made by Waddle in France, the French too may not really understand the stature attained by Cantona within the English game. Not that he did not show in French club football flashes of the talent that became the player's stock-in-trade in the red of Manchester United, but that he seemed incapable of controlling his temper and remaining on good terms with his various clubs and his team-mates. A memorable TV image is of Cantona angrily throwing away his muddy Marseille shirt in 1989 as he walked out on yet another club. He does not figure in the French team of the century selected by the premier football annual (Chaumier and Rocheteau 2000: 121), who choose a midfield of Kopa, Giresse, Platini and Zidane, with Fontaine and Papin as strikers – noticeably all having made their name in the national team. For *France Football*'s jury of 34 players and managers he came only tenth in the French Player of the Century vote (*France Football*, 20 December 2000: 12).

What both French and English fans might agree on is the impenetrability and proud independence of the man, moulded by a strong sense of justice and injustice, and for whom football fame and fortune were never enough to fill a life that he chose to redirect at the age of 31. The French media, in the topical puppet show *Les Guignols de l'info*, chose to caricature him and his southern accent as the harmless philosopher-poet with a vacuous epigram for every occasion. In Britain his image has borne forever the marks inflicted by the press following his drop-kick at the fan insulting him on being sent off at the Crystal Palace ground – for which misdemeanour he served a half-season ban and community service.

Born in Marseille in 1966, Cantona emerged as a prospect far away from home, in the Auxerre youth coaching centre under the firm hand of Guy Roux. He made his debut in professional football with Auxerre in 1983, and moved on to Montpellier, Marseille and Nîmes, before moving briefly to Sheffield Wednesday in 1992, then winning English championships with Leeds, and Manchester United, where he was captain and the last vital piece of Alex Ferguson's jigsaw before retiring in 1997. His 45 international caps were won, and 20 goals scored, between 1987 and 1995.

David Ginola – Frog Prince

One judge on *France Football*'s panel picking the French Player of the Century, a former team-mate at PSG, was the only one to vote for Ginola (as the fifth of his five selections), claiming he was the most gifted of all his choices, but had not won enough medals. In his last three seasons with PSG he helped them win two French Cups (1993, 1995), a French Championship (1994) and a League Cup (1995) – the most prolific period in the club's history. He holds a unique double – Player of the Year in France in 1993/94 and in the English Premiership while playing for Tottenham in both the journalists and players polls in 1998/99 – an Anglo-French double that escaped both Glenn Hoddle, who won the French award playing for Monaco, but not the English one, and Eric Cantona, vice versa (Ridley 1998). His technical ability for Newcastle,

Tottenham or Aston Villa, for all of whom he scored some memorable goals, was never in doubt, but his British managers, as well as his former BBC TV commentary colleagues, were often frustrated by what they perceived to be his lack of desire to put in the last 10 per cent of effort that the Premiership demands. Opposition supporters and managers often accused him of diving and feigning fouls against him. His own fans, including new ones at Tottenham such as Salman Rushdie, were very quickly won over (Rushdie 2000: 123–124). However, after good starts at his new clubs he maybe lost the desire to turn it on week-in week-out.

His cultivation of an image of being above all a stylish player, well suited to advertising male beauty products on TV or on the catwalk and being part of the jet-set, did not help British managers love him. British football culture is too ingrained with the Protestant work ethic and working-class values. Born on the Côte d'Azur into a middle-class family of *fonctionnaires*, he had always been seen as a 'pretty-boy' player, the sort who allegedly carry a comb in their shorts. Having a mirror-image background to that of Kopa, his own take on this was to say: 'If I had been little and ugly, nobody would have doubted my qualities as a footballer' (Le Vaillant 1999). But he could not deny that he obviously enjoys the lifestyle and attention that his good looks have brought him.

French national team bosses had other doubts about him. He is best remembered in France for losing the ball while trying to attack rather than keeping hold of the ball by the opposition corner-flag in the last minute of the last World Cup qualifying match against Bulgaria in November 1993. This led immediately to the goal that eliminated Gérard Houllier's team from the 1994 Finals, and to Houllier's angry comment that Ginola's action was 'criminal'. Blame for France's elimination was no doubt unfairly heaped onto one man, and Ginola did play a further ten times for his country, but with Jacquet as manager looking for team players he never made the team for Euro 96 nor subsequent squads.

If he does have a horror of injustice, it is less inwardly directed than in Cantona's case; one way he has invested time in combating injustice is by stepping into Princess Diana's shoes when invited by the UN to work for the anti-personnel-mines campaign. A professional whose career depends on the skill in his feet can make a point about children who have lost one or both of theirs. It may be reading too much into his roving UN ambassadorship to suggest he is making up for some unease about his father working on torpedoes in the Saint-Tropez arsenal. If his pride has been hurt, especially in the World Cup affair, he has fought to regain respect for the sake of his family, who were hurt by the criticism he received. He says: 'I fight to please my nearest and dearest who shed tears when I was treated like dirt' (Le Vaillant 1999). In 2001, he engaged one of the most expensive and high profile British law firms to defend him against his manager's suggestion that he was overweight. Was he perhaps less confident he could rebut the charges by his performances on the pitch?

The New France: from Mekloufi to Zidane

Football, Immigration and Identity

French football, like sport in most societies, has not remained immune from major social conflicts within the nation. The key socio-cultural conflict of post-revolutionary France from 1789 to 1945 was the battle between Catholic France and secular France, and this was reflected in the development in France of competing football leagues. Football's integrative force proved stronger than this Franco-French quarrel and brought the federations and leagues together into a single national structure in the inter-war period. More recently football has reflected other major social issues: particularly those connected with immigration: multiculturalism, integration, racism.

The significance of the racial composition of the national team and of its link to immigration has been an issue certainly since the 1958 era. The senior French football writer of the time, Jacques Ferran, as Marks (1999: 47) recalls, wrote an article in *France Football* entitled 'Not to be confused: the French national team and French football'. In it he claimed that the most vital elements of the French national team (Kopa, the son of Polish immigrants, Fontaine, born to a Spanish mother in Marrakesh, and Piantoni, the son of Italian immigrants) did not constitute a coherent identity; the French team was 'une salade russe' [a Balkan salad], a hotchpotch of doctrines. Ferran's concern about the lack of footballing cohesion of this group of individualists cannot hide, Marks claims, a wider anxiety about French society. This is not an isolated comment. Beaud and Noiriel (1990: 95) identify two strains of French writing about immigration and football: criticism of the heterogeneity of styles associated with influences from outside France; and a contrasting view, particularly since the 1960s, that immigration has been seen as an element that enriches the national game, and that football acts as a 'melting pot' for immigrants' integration into French society (Marks: 1999: 48). We may characterise these approaches as the nationalistic and the multicultural.

Franco–Algerian Relations: Mekloufi and Political Symbolism

Whereas Kopa, born in France of Polish parents, aspired to be accepted as purely French and used football as a means of successful assimilation into French society, and was often portrayed as an example of how, in a meritocracy, hard work can lead to upward social mobility and success, one of his international colleagues chose to reject French identity and the chance to star in the 1958 World Cup. Rachid Mekloufi, born in French Algeria in 1937 (or 1936 – there is some doubt), was spotted by Saint-Etienne scouts in 1954, and came to France to play and turn professional. He won the world army football competition with France in 1957, represented the French national team four times, and appeared certain to be selected as a member of the French squad for Sweden. He and others were seen as a model of 'fraternal and successful integration of the indigenous Arabic population and the large settler community in a French Algeria' (Lanfranchi and Wahl 1996: 118). When, in April 1958, as part of the resistance to French colonial rule that turned into the Algerian War of Independence, the Algerian National Liberation Front (FLN) called on Algerian professional footballers in France to leave for Tunis where they were to set up an Algerian national team, Mekloufi and nine others heeded the call. Football was used as part of the Algerian struggle in other ways too: the withdrawal of ethnic clubs from colonial leagues, the bombing of football stadiums in Algeria and the execution of a leading political opponent at the French Cup Final.

For four years, up to the negotiated end to the war and Algerian independence in 1962, Mekloufi played against other African, Eastern European and Asian national teams, beating many. Once the independent (Marxist) Algerian State was in place Mekloufi was unable to earn his living there as a professional sportsman, and was accepted back in France, despite threats to his life from the OAS, the 'Secret Army' of former white settlers who had fled Algeria on independence, dispossessed of their property. In May 1968 as the political storm clouds were again gathering over Paris, ten years after his 'desertion', he received the French Cup as captain of Saint-Etienne from the hands of General de Gaulle, who had been brought back to power to end the Algerian War. The President congratulated the players with the words: 'La France, c'est vous.' [You are France]. Mekloufi went back to Algeria on retiring as a player in 1970 to become coach to the national team and rose, by 1990, to become President of the Algerian national Football Federation, but not without criticism on the way for having continued his professional career in France (Lanfranchi and Wahl 1996: 119). None the less, he has remained for many people a political symbol of the Algerian struggle for independence, but also of Franco-Algerian reconciliation. He acknowledged all he owed to the Saint-Etienne coach Jean Snella, and said his happiest moment had been winning the world army championship with the French team.

A Multicoloured France Challenged by the Extreme Right

If 1958 and 1968 were turning points in politics and society, as landmarks in the decolonisation process and in political stability as de Gaulle came into power, and in the liberalisation of social attitudes as a new society was heralded in the events of May, then May 1981 and the election of a socialist President was another step towards a more tolerant society and a less narrowly defined and defensive national identity. From our post-1998 perspective we can recognise the importance of the success of national teams of the 1980s in allowing the celebration in football of a multiracial aspect of French national identity. Under Mitterrand's presidency, left-wing values, less nationalistic, were more dominant politically, but were coming to be challenged from the extreme right by the new nationalism of Jean-Marie Le Pen, leader of the Front national, as economic crises and unemployment pushed parts of society to look for scapegoats in the immigrant communities. Mitterrand's France was represented by a team coming in part again from its immigrant communities. Under the leadership of Michel Platini, France's multiracial team could be celebrated as a distinctive aspect of French national style in contrast to their World Cup opponents. Writing in 1986 about the 1982 match against Germany, Démerin recalls the tricolours' multicoloured team representing 'France from Dunkirk to Tamanrasset', 'playing football as beautiful as a fireworks display', 'the technicolour of France versus the black-and-white of Germany' (Démerin 1986: 120–125). He describes the white face of the northern Frenchman Rocheteau and the bronzed features of Giresse from the south-west; the two players from French Africa: the copper-coloured face of Janvion from the Maghreb, the darker Tigana from sub-Saharan Africa (Mali); and the ebony of Marius Trésor from the French West Indies; and the Spanish origins of Hidalgo, Lopez and Amoros; and the three of Italian extraction, Ettori, Genghini, and Platini.

At about the same time as this celebration of diversity in the national team, after the brave World Cup semi-final defeat and then the European Cup success of 1984, *L'Equipe* interested itself in the origins of French football internationals and found that of the 660 individuals who had represented France since the beginnings of international matches at least 200 were of foreign extraction or from outside metropolitan France. At a time when immigrants made up over 10 per cent of the population and the workforce had 10–15 per cent of immigrants within it, *L'Equipe* found the most highly represented groups were: North Africans: 7 per cent; Italians: 6.5 per cent; Poles: 6 per cent; Spanish: 3 per cent; French Overseas Departments and Territories: 1 per cent. The range and diversity were most obvious in the 1980s teams. But, in Beaud and Noiriel's 1990 article, it was as if the immigrant origins of some of the 1958 team were being discovered for the first time.

The racial makeup of the national side raised political debate during Euro 96, when Le Pen declared the French team to be 'artificial'. He claimed certain players had chosen their nationality as a matter of expediency and that several 'visibly did not know the words of the *Marseillaise*'. Later reiterating his point, he drew attention to numbers of players who were sons of immigrants (*Le Monde*, 26 June 1996). The 1998 squad contained many of these players, and was often described as reflecting the 'cultural mosaic' of contemporary France. Several players were born outside metropolitan France: Lama in French Guyana, Karembeu in New Caledonia, Vieira in Senegal, and Desailly in Ghana. Several were born in France of parents born outside of metropolitan France (Guadeloupe, Algerian Kabylia, Armenia, Mongolia, Argentina, Portugal) (see Marks 1999; Hare 2003). As we have seen, the presence of players of diverse origin is nothing new for the French team, and as French football professionalised, it was immigrants more than any other members of the working classes who saw football as a means of social advancement (Mignon 1999: 86–87). The geography of the origins within France of these players reflected the geography of immigration and employment in their different eras: players of Italian extraction from the south-east and the east of France; Poles from the small mining towns and villages serving the heavy industry and mining areas of the north and east; newer immigrants from the poorer *banlieues* of major cities like Paris and Lyon. The ethnic diversity of the French side has simply reflected different eras of immigration in a country that for economic reasons (post-war reconstruction) and ideological choice (political asylum) has welcomed foreigners, and attempted to assimilate or integrate them into the Republican melting pot. One such was named Zidane.

Zidane and 'une France black-blanc-beur'

Since the two goals he scored in the World Cup Final on 12 July 1998, a balding French Kabyle named Zinedine Zidane has not only won a newspaper poll for the most popular personality in France, but is also, arguably, the best-known Frenchman in the world. He became, within France, the symbol of the new multiethnic society, as the French victory was used very widely as a metaphor for successful French integration.

His success, both on and off the pitch, is unparalleled. Born in Marseille in 1972, he attended the Cannes coaching academy, making his debut for Cannes in Division 1 just before his seventeenth birthday. He played for Bordeaux from 1992 to 1996, and was a finalist in the UEFA Cup. Moving to Italy, he acknowledges that he had to 'work like a sheep' to get much fitter in order to became the Zidane of 1998. He won two Italian championships with Juventus and was runner up in two European Champions Cup Finals. Often the star of French national teams' performances, his technical brilliance took the game to new levels. In 1998 he was the fourth Frenchman to become European Player of the Year (*Ballon d'Or*). Having moved to Real Madrid in summer 2001 for the highest transfer fee in history, nearly 500 million francs, he scored the unforgettable decisive goal in Real's Champions League victory in May 2002. His absence through injury for the first two matches of France's Korean campaign showed how much the national team relied on him.

Zidane, like Kopa in his time, is an obvious individual example of successful integration, but he also became a symbol of successful French integration in general. His family history is typical of many immigrants from North Africa: his father arrived from Algeria, in the Paris left-wing industrial belt in the 1960s, and moved to La Castellane in 1970, working as a warehouseman. In this poor Marseille estate his son learned to play football, becoming a local hero, serving as a model of social integration in an area where unemployment is 40 per cent. In 1998, from La Castellane to the Champs-Elysées, second-generation North African immigrants (*les Beurs*) chanted this shy and humble man's name. Girls wrote Zizou on their cheeks in lipstick. Greeting the team coach on the Champs-Elysées, Beurs waved Algerian flags alongside the French tricolour, showing their pride in their dual cultural identity. As historian Benjamin Stora remarked: 'This closes a chapter of French history because it shows one can remain faithful to an Algerian nationalist father and yet be for France, that one can be a Moslem and be fully French' (Graham 1998).

During the Finals, spectators experienced a rise in solidarity among French people from all cultural and ethnic backgrounds. Both President Chirac and his socialist prime minister, Jospin, promoted the metaphor of 'football team equals nation'. Discussion of the multiracial nature of the side moved from the sports pages to the front pages and was even covered abroad (Lichfield 1998; Desporetes 1998). The phrase '*black-blanc-beur*' was created on the pattern of the national colours (*bleu-blanc-rouge*) to describe the special Frenchness of the team and the nation's unity in diversity. The view that France was changing was expressed by demographer Michèle Tribalat, interviewed in *Libération* (Simonnot 1998). She saw in the gusto with which the multicoloured team sang the *Marseillaise* and in the joyful nationalism of supporters from all backgrounds a moment of identification with the nation. She compared the result of French republican integration of ethnic minorities with the German team of all-white faces and blond hair and no immigrant players of Turkish origin, concluding that the French system visibly opts for 'universalism' with an open nationality law whereas Germany's ethnic concept of the nation means Turkish children remain Turkish.

The French Republican approach to ethnic diversity has not been uncontroversial. A policy of 'assimilation' has generally been adopted. This means the cultural assimilation of ethnic minorities in a centralised, indivisible Republic, as opposed to the American notion of 'integration' meaning maintaining cultural difference yet still claiming a shared national project. The French approach has assumed traditionally that everyone can be French, but only by losing their distinctive community identities. Communitarianism has been rejected in favour of universalism, in principle, although issues such as the wearing of the Muslim headscarf in French State schools, for example, have been resolved in a fudge in relation to what previously might have been considered strict secular Republican nationalism. Following the oil crises of the 1970s and the subsequent economic difficulties of the mid-1980s, racism increased in France, along with alienation and social exclusion of children of first-generation immigrant families. Social problems of housing and schooling, rising inequalities, petty crime and antisocial behaviour, feelings of insecurity, and disillusionment with orthodox political parties that had failed to solve the problems, were seized upon by the extreme right. Le Pen helped set a political agenda where new nationality laws made it more difficult for children born in France of foreign parentage to become French. What the World Cup victory seems to have done is to provide a ready metaphor to discuss these issues: either the multiracial national team was presented as proof of integrated cultural and ethnic diversity contributing to a shared national project, or the solidarity of successful teamwork was highlighted as evidence of assimilated 'Frenchness' on the part of ethnically diverse players. Zidane was central to this political and social metaphor, and in this respect his celebrity has burrowed far deeper into the national psyche than his predecessors Kopa and Platini. The debate was not proof that the long-term problems of the *banlieues* had been solved.

Franco-Algerian Identity and the Deprived Suburbs post-1998

A senior British newspaper correspondent in Paris commented on the reactions to the World Cup victory from the President downwards as underlining France's hunger for good news (Graham 1998). A sense of depression, he felt, had hitherto deflected attention from areas where France has been a winner. This change of national mood and purpose seemingly went wider than those who saw the symbolism of Zidane as the central message of the World Cup. Patrick Mignon has on the other hand been more cautious in his interpretation. It was premature to talk of a victory for integration, of an inclusive nationalism, of a nation's improved self-image, of a defeat for the *Front national*, and of new attitudes towards immigrants in the deprived suburbs. He adds that the celebrations of 12 July were more symbols of an appeal for unity – since that unity was far from real (Mignon 1999).

Ironically, one of the areas that most typifies the problems of France's deprived suburban areas is the symbolically important area around the Stade de France. Much of the *département* of Saint-Denis is still an area of social deprivation, with a high proportion of immigrants of first or subsequent generations. High unemployment, low educational achievement, and other forms of social exclusion have, unsurprisingly, not been immediately improved by an urban regeneration effect that was one of the objectives in siting the national stadium in this northern Paris suburb. The honeymoon period following the World Cup victory could not obscure social reality for ever. The frustrations of the area are illustrated by the suspension of all matches in a local amateur football league in Saint-Denis in April 1999, following violence between players and among supporters. As reasons for this frustration Mignon (2000: 254) cites 'poverty, low expectations, racism, and the rise of communitarianism among football teams organised around ethnic origins', which contradicts the idea of the Republican melting pot.

One key event that tested the new France in general, and Saint-Denis in particular, was the organisation of the first-ever full international match between France and Algeria, at the Stade de France in October 2001, a full four decades after the Algerian War of Liberation. The watching French Prime Minister and Minister for Sport and millions of TV viewers were reminded that the distinct double identity of French Algerians and their place within French society are still issues. The match was built up as a moment of reconciliation between the two peoples and therefore another symbol of the new integrated France at peace with itself, but was brought to an untimely and embarrassing end by a pitch invasion – embarrassing that is for French football's officials and for the political establishment.

Before the event *Libération* presciently described the match as 'a matter of collective identity, not that of the French, whose thirst for identity had been satisfied by the triumphal 1998 epic, but the identity of Algerians by birth, by family connections or by tradition (i.e. living in France) who are having difficulty in finding their bearings between their country of reference [Algeria] which is in turmoil and their host country [France] where the road to integration is not free of obstacles and dead-ends' (Helvig 2001). The match attracted a huge number of spectators with North African connections, underlining the symbolic importance they attach to football as a site of identity formation. Outside the stadium, before the game, Franco-Algerian spectators living in the poor districts around the national stadium were reported as chanting that they were playing at home; then the French players were whistled during the warm-up and when their names were announced (with the exception of Zidane); the French national anthem was also copiously whistled; and finally, in the seventy-fifth minute, large numbers of young, (apparently) mainly second-generation North African immigrants ran onto the pitch, some carrying Algerian flags, past insufficient numbers of stewards. The events continued in the streets afterwards, as a few cars drove around with horns blowing and Algerian flags flying though wound-down windows, an ironic reminder of July 1998. (See reports in *L'Humanité*, *Le Monde*, *Libération*, and *Ouest-France*, 6 to 8 October 2001.)

The press quoted many older Algerian immigrants who have become integrated or have assimilated French aspirations and values as being deeply embarrassed by the behaviour of the second generation of immigrants. French officials and politicians appeared shocked or nonplussed. It is difficult to see the events as simply an expression of over-exuberance, since everyone knew full well that such an event was charged with so much political symbolism. In the security preparations for the match it might have been forgotten that before and during the Algerian war of liberation, football matches in colonial Algeria were key locations for anti-French demonstrations and indeed for violence (Fatès 2003). One interpretation of the actions of the young people from the poor suburbs is that they were a defiant affirmation of their Algerian roots, or indeed of their double attachment to the cultures of France and Algeria. What is worth underlining is that it was non-violent; there were few arrests. Regarding their identity as French citizens, however, they were no doubt expressing frustration that hopes for an end to exclusion and discrimination that the French World Cup victory had raised have thus far proved unrealistic. French society remains one where the Republican values of equality and solidarity are no more matched by social reality than in any other Western European country. These events tended to confirm Mignon's earlier conclusions that 'public intervention has been far too inadequate when football is located in its widest social context, and placed against a backdrop of serious social disadvantage' (Mignon 2000: 254).

Conclusion

Representing the national side has always seemed most important to French supporters. If football mattered, it had always been at international rather than club level. Cantona and Ginola might rightly be feted in England, but they will not be remembered with as much warmth in France as Papin or Blanc, because they did not shine as brightly when representing their country. Foreign stars playing for French clubs could reach cult status, like Stopyra or Waddle at OM, or Rai and Weah at PSG, but such status remained local.

If football does now matter in France, it is because it has gradually imprinted itself on the national consciousness as a vector of national values and identity through the national side. For many years the identity it seemed best to carry was one the French recognised in the figure of Astérix, a stylish and wily individualist capable of winning skirmishes but whose way of life remained under threat from the Roman Empire. Too many times the national team (or a national representative at club level) failed at the final hurdle, and could blame the fates. But perhaps playing with style was more important than winning. This was *L'Equipe*'s view in 1998: since France were not going to win, at least they must play time-honoured champagne football à la Platini. But since the World Cup victory French football teams are no longer automatically seen as an analogy for a supposedly tired nation, suffering from an inferiority complex, fearful of the challenges of modernisation and of social integration. It was through football that the French discovered they were not eternal losers. The 2002 World Cup squad and officials were criticised therefore for having lost – for having lost so tamely certainly, and to such mediocre opposition, but mainly for having lost, and heads had to roll.

The idea of a 'France qui gagne' may or may not prove more durable than the other metaphor represented by the national team of 1998 to 2000: that of a multicultural France at ease with itself. For a few months football was used to promote an inclusive and ethnically diverse view of the nation, that saw integration of the children of the new *banlieues* as possible. The team's multiethnicity corresponded to that of the new France and represented success rather than problems. One man more than any other symbolised this. French football had spawned other stars, also of immigrant origins, Kopa and Platini notably, brilliant footballers, who had also had to go abroad for their greatest achievements at club level. Yet they had never come to represent such a central social and political issue as did Zidane.

The complexities of post-colonialism have been articulated in France via football. Franco-Algerian relations in particular, which are the central trauma of post-Second World War France, have found expression from Mekloufi to Zidane through the national team. Mekloufi became a symbol of the struggle for separation and then of reconciliation between the two communities. After two generations of immigration from North Africa, Zidane became a symbol of successful integration into the Republic and of its progressive values of universalism and meritocracy. For a while French citizens could believe optimistically in the French approach to cultural diversity in the twenty-first century, until social realities of inequality and the threat of communitarianism and territorialism pushed their way into the news, and made them doubt again. It was again, however, via football that reconciliation and integration were supposed to be celebrated in the symbolic match in Saint-Denis between France and Algeria, and where the distance still to be travelled on all sides was revealed to a watching nation. Some of this lost ground might have been recovered if the national team had been able to renew the *black-blanc-beur* spirit by an impressive World Cup, but their spectacularly premature exit followed Jean-Marie Le Pen reaching the second round of the Presidential election, and France once again seemed to have its back to the wall. That all of these events from 1998 to 2002 should be mediated through television tells us something in general about its role in modern France, and in particular about its transformation of football from a local participatory event into a cross between a recurrent theme in the nation's public debate about its own identity and an audiovisual home-entertainment commodity. The next chapter will examine the symbiotic relations of television and football.

Note

1. Ball and Shaw (1996: 121) quote this *bon mot* by a reader of the *Independent* in 1995 (with apologies to Dorothy Parker). For an excellent chapter on Cantona see Edworthy (2002).

7

Television: Football as Spectacle and Commodity

In 1927, Ernest Chamond, Head of the Compagnie des Compteurs in the Paris suburb of Montrouge, met John Logie Baird, known in Britain as the inventor of television. Chamond had come over to London on one of his frequent cross-channel trips to see English League and Cup football matches. He was a football fan, and English football was recognised as being the best in the world at the time, since it was there that the modern game had been invented and professionalism had first developed. Chamond is a near-forgotten visionary: he immediately saw the commercial future of Baird's new invention as serving millions of people who wanted to watch sports events from their armchair, when it was impossible for them to get to the live event. Back in Montrouge, in his factory, which originally made metering equipment for water and gas, and then moved into electrical components, he immediately set up a new laboratory to investigate television transmission and reception, under the control of René Barthélemy, who was to become a famous name in the development of French television. Four years later the first public demonstration of television broadcasting took place in France between Montrouge and Ecole Supérieure d'électricité in Malakoff, a nearby suburb. Then, in 1935, it was following a visit to the Montrouge factory that the French Posts and Telegraphy Minister, Georges Mandel, set up the first public broadcasting system in France, transmitting from the Eiffel Tower (Lecoq 1997: 133).

Three-quarters of a century after Chamond's vision, the biggest sponsor of football, in both France and England, is television; and the owner of the biggest club in France, Paris Saint-Germain, is the subscription channel Canal+. Other media organisations are also involved in football sponsorship in France. Such are the stakes involved that the future of French digital television is tied to the selling of pay-per-view subscriptions to French football. The same may well be true of English Premier League football and BSkyB television. Certainly, the bankruptcy of ITV Digital, the key financier of England's other professional divisions, sent shock-waves through the media and football industries, not only in England, suggesting as it did that the financial links between football and television had made both industries very fragile.

This chapter shows how, in France, as in England, football has become crucial to the commercial success of television, and how television income became indispensable to modern football's *modus operandi*. The world financial instability of 2002 raised questions about the future viability of football's high spending based on TV income. For the present, football and television appear inextricably linked, symbiotically linked, just as the very creation of a television service in France is owed, in part, to an entrepreneur's passionate interest in football. A further point that will be argued is that the increasing commodification of football through the tool of commercial TV and pay-TV has moved at different paces in the two countries because of (a) the particular tradition of French statism and public service, and (b) the different speeds of development of national broadcasting systems.

Television and Football before Pay-TV

Before the advent of live pictures, newspaper and radio reporting created a football star system that shaped the shared folk memory of the game. Radio coverage developed by the end of the 1920s, although football's administrators were unsure whether its effect would be to take spectators away from the stadiums, or spread its popularity (Thomas *et al.* 1991: 112), a recurrent dilemma. But it is television that turned football from a local spectacle to a national one. The first live pictures were of the final of the French Cup in 1952 at Colombes, Nice vs. Bordeaux, followed in the same year by France vs. Germany (ibid.: 113). The League had seen crowds falling off over a number of years and banned television cameras from the stadiums from December 1955. An agreement to show some live matches was signed in 1961, and more stable relations achieved from 1972 onwards (ibid.: 113–114). The main successes of French club and national sides have coincided with the beginnings and later the high points of the era of free national terrestrial television; that is, before subscription or pay-TV prevented a fully national audience from seeing games at the same time. It was in the 1950s, with the innovation of European club competitions and France's unexpectedly good performance in the World Cup, that national interest was aroused in football as a vector of national values.

In the World Cup in Sweden in 1958, France played the early rounds in cities where there was no live television. Recordings took some days to come back to the minority medium of television. It was not until the semi-final that France appeared live. Poiseul (1998: 99) recalls that in the days preceding this eagerly awaited match the number of French homes owning television sets increased from 1 million to 1.2 million, with the semi-final attracting an estimated audience of 5 million viewers. The first occasion for the mass transmission of matches on French television was the Mexico World Cup of 1970 (Bourg 1986: 128).

It was via television coverage that the European exploits of Saint-Etienne, in the 1970s, caught the national imagination. So dominating the French domestic competitions between 1964 and 1983, 'les Verts' played in Europe almost every season, and as the French representative with the best chance of progressing, they captured the TV audience. The Saint-Etienne team had bravura and charisma, and their European matches had suspense, all the ingredients of good television, which showed their matches live. Developing more slowly than in Britain, French television could, by the end of the 1960s, reach a full national audience (Bureau 1986: 97–98) and had improved the notoriously poor quality of coverage since the 1960s (Wahl 1989: 324–326). In 1975 Saint-Etienne were losing semi-finalists and in 1976 losing finalists. In these two years especially, football had offered the national television audience regular episodes of their top club's European saga.

The next major footballing event to be followed on television, even more traumatic in the injustice of the French defeat, was Seville 1982 (see Chapter 6). Thirty million French television viewers sat entranced by the interminable drama. Such was the perceived importance of the match that a parliamentary debate was suspended to allow the députés to watch. The intensity of the match, its long drawn out conclusions, remembers Olivier Margot (Bureau 1986: 97–98), plunged a nation of television viewers into a state of shock, drained by the injustice of it all. Former Prime Minister Chaban-Delmas summed up the general feeling that the match would live in the collective memory for a long time (Poiseul 1998: 101).

Because the club sides of Reims in the 1950s, Saint-Etienne in the 1970s and Marseille in the late 1980s–early 1990s so dominated the French championship in their respective eras with no real home challenger, it was all the easier for the national public to identify with them as carrying national values in their European matches through the mediation of television. Historically, sport has been intimately associated with nation and place, but this is changing rapidly; now it carries audiences and advertising across national boundaries. It is one of the key agents of globalisation. And sport is a peculiarly mobile culture. Most cultural forms are limited in their ability to travel, most obviously by language, but sport has an extraordinary ability to communicate. It is therefore the obvious vehicle for multinational companies to use to sell their products and services. If the only genuinely global events are the Olympics and the World Cup, it can be argued that they have become global via television and that they have been hijacked by the forces of commercialism.

The commercialisation of the game would not have happened to the extent that it did without the presence of TV and its increased coverage of the game. TV offered (a) new advertising space for businesses, and (b) new technological developments which provide new ways of selling football as a product. So satellite TV, cable TV, and digital TV have brought with them subscription TV and pay-per-view, as well as bringing many more channels that need new programming to fill the screen time to attract viewers. Sport (and particularly football) is seen as an excellent marketing vehicle, an excellent instrument of direct and indirect advertising. And football has been able to fill this new screen time and sell the new channels since it became the dominant cultural form of the 1990s – replacing rock music as a purveyor of values to young people, especially to the difficult television audience of young men – on an international scale.

Income from television rights has transformed the finances of French soccer, just as it has in England with the advent of Rupert Murdoch's BSkyB. Advertising and sponsorship began in the late 1960s. An initial move by the FFF and the league in 1968 to sign a global contract for Vittel to sponsor Division 1 came unstuck when the Bordeaux club, whose chairman was head of the Bordeaux wine growers association, refused to wear the logo of a mineral water on their shirts (Bourg 1986: 106). Public service television, holding a monopoly of television channels in France at the time, initially objected to sponsorship on shirts as a form of illegal advertising, but eventually agreement was reached and revenue increased somewhat after the splitting up of the State television service into three competing but still publicly owned channels in 1975, financed by licence fee income supplemented by advertising income.

In France as in England the commercialisation of football took place in close symbiosis with changes in how television was distributed and sold. In the UK Murdoch and Sky's subscription TV eroded the BBC–ITV duopoly as providers of free-to-air terrestrial TV; in France the erosion of the State monopoly of public service free-to-air TV came in 1984 with the creation of Canal+, the first subscription TV company. Additionally, 1987 saw the privatisation of the top-audience channel TF1. There followed an immediate bidding-up of TV rights as Canal+ competed with TF1 for live TV football. The two major television companies were now dependent on audience: the one for selling subscriptions and the other for attracting advertising revenue.

More TV exposure also allowed greater income to football from sponsorship: a leap from 15 million francs in 1978 to 120 million in 1982 and 170 million in 1986, divided between the D1 and D2 clubs (Wahl 1989: 334). Advertisers and sponsors were of course interested in the huge TV audiences football could bring them, at least for high-profile matches: 30 million viewers for the World Cup semi-final France vs. Germany in 1982; 20 million viewers for the European Nations Cup Final France vs. Spain in 1984. The national team played only occasionally, however, and the European Cups were far from being weekly events in the 1980s. If audiences could be won for a weekly or twice-weekly diet of televised club football – which also required the league to agree – then that would take television and football onto a new level of symbiosis.

Canal+ and the Take-over of PSG

It was Canal+'s take-over of Paris Saint-Germain that heralded this new era in French football, as the first step towards a new dimension in football's commercialisation. Television offered football a major new source of revenue, and greater access to sponsorship and corporate interest. Until the mid-1980s, the whole of French television had remained a State-run monopoly. Advertising revenue did come into the three national channels, but they were essentially all run on public service lines. When Mitterrand's socialist governments decided it was politically expedient to inaugurate various forms of independent television between 1984 and 1986, they opted first for a subscription channel. Canal+ was to be chaired by President Mitterrand's personal friend and former director of his private office, André Rousselet, head of the advertising group Havas, with, as his executive director, Pierre Lescure who had a background in commercial radio. The initial remit was to be a film channel which showed large numbers of cinema films and invested in the French film industry. It indeed puts money into four out of five French-made films. But both of its *patrons* also had an interest in sport. They initially showed a number of minority sports such as American football, bullfighting, and indeed golf (a minority interest in France at the time) (Jeanneney 2001: 192–196).

Canal+'s interest in football was different from that of other business interests already investing in clubs, in that they foresaw a much more direct link between the business of football and their own business. They had seen OM dominate the French championship for three years with Bernard Tapie's money, which meant the French League lacked the week-to-week drama of true competition and the uncertainty of outcome, and therefore suspense, that can draw interest. Their strategy was to turn PSG, who had not done well in the late 1980s and early 1990s, into a big team capable of rivalling OM. Since Paris and Marseille were geographically and culturally the biggest potential rivals within French soccer, this would increase interest in soccer in general and attract more subscriptions for their coverage of football (Michel 1996). They invested in exclusive weekly live matches from 1992. As with the purchase of Tottenham Hotspur by the satellite dish manufacturer Alan Sugar in the same year, a company with a vested interest has a better chance of influencing future relations between football and television from the inside as chairman of a big league club than from the outside (see Conn 1997: 9–21).

In the face of PSG's 51 million francs of debts following the departure of Chairman Borelli, Canal+ presented its rescue plan in association with the City of Paris under mayor Jacques Chirac. The organiser of the take-over was the treasurer of the club Bernard Brochand, a former director of the advertising and travel agency Havas, and Chairman of DDB Needham International. On 31 May 1991 PSG was reborn, with Brochand as President, with a new structure. The Association sportive PSG held 51 per cent of the capital of the SAOS (the football club as such) whose chairman was the then Director-General of the television company, Pierre Lescure. Canal+ held 40 per cent of the capital, and the remaining 9 per cent was held by individuals (Halba 1997: 68). They gave free rein, as chief executive of the club, to Michel Denisot, a Canal+ presenter and hitherto chairman of the small Châteauroux club he had been successfully steering through the regional leagues into Division 2. As part of the deal a Canal+ company was also to hold the concession for the Parc des Princes stadium, and therefore sell in-stadium advertising, passing on a part of the income to the club (ibid.: 68). The Paris municipality also agreed to wipe the PSG slate clean of its debts. An annual budget of 120 million francs was fixed, of which 30 million was a municipal subsidy, 30 million from Canal+, the rest coming from season tickets, gate money, sponsorship and broadcasting rights. The use of the Parc des Princes as the home stadium, on the edge of Paris, in a smart district of the city and with relatively easy access on the metro system, automatically gave glamour and standing to the club, as well as providing space for large crowds, since, until the creation of the Stade de France in 1998, the Parc was the serving national stadium for football, rugby, and other sports.

Canal+ has been so successful overall that it has used its pay-TV expertise to spread its football-led strategy in a European expansion of pay-TV. It owns, either in whole or in part, similar channels in Italy (Telepiù), Spain, Belgium, Poland, and Holland. It fused in 1997 with the Dutch group Nethold that runs subscription channels in Denmark, Norway, Sweden and Holland, creating the biggest pay-TV company in Europe with 10 million subscribers (Jeanneney 2001: 195). Canal+ also invested in the Swiss club Servette. In the late 1990s the French channel was spending a quarter of its budget on its sports programming, for 8.6 per cent of its screen time. But for pay-TV the key figure is not the length of time viewers spend in front of their channel, it is the number of subscriptions sold, and football sold subscriptions.

The nation's top participation sport, football, has become its top TV sport. In the 1990s the biggest sporting draws on TV were, in order, World Cup matches, European Cup finals, French Cup finals, five-nations rugby, the final of French Open tennis, the Tour de France (Thomas *et al.* 1991: 114). Football's pre-eminence as high audience television has been recognised by advertisers being ready to pay 550,000 francs per 30-second advert in the TF1 France–Romania match in the European Nations Cup in 1996 (R.B. 1996a).

Reciprocally, football has come to rely on television-related income. The income from TV rights shared among D1 and D2 clubs quadrupled between 1991 and 1996. While income was only approximately a third of the TV revenue received by clubs in England, television rapidly became a principal source of income for French clubs. It brings in direct and indirect income that has become crucial to clubs like PSG. In its 1996/97 budget of nearly 280 million francs, 60 million came from paying spectators for matches in the domestic context, 30 million for gate receipts from participation in Europe, 34 million as a grant from the City of Paris, 15 million directly from television, 45 million from participation in a European competition from television rights, 70 million from its principal sponsors (who included Canal+), as well as the 300 companies who hired corporate hospitality boxes in the Parc des Princes. Fifteen million francs came from merchandising, a new phenomenon in France. There was room for expansion: the number of PSG shirts sold was only a tenth of the number sold by Manchester United. And participation in the European Champions League can double the income compared to playing in one of the other two European competitions (R.B. 1996b; Halba 1997: 68). By 1999 television was the source of 30 per cent of D1 clubs' income (Meignan 1999: 40) and by 2002 it had risen to 51 per cent (*LNF Infos*, 42 (March 2002): 6–7).

These developments, especially subscription TV, are part of the transformation of television viewing into an ordinary consumer act like any other – buying a TV programme product or a channel. Subscription changes the relationship between the viewer and the channel into one of customer and service provider. The logical extension of this philosophy is a choice of programme via pay-per-view. Pay-per-view football has become the latest incarnation of the TV sports product, and France was the first European country to reach this stage of TV development, in December 1996.

The Multi-channel Digital-TV Era

From the 1996/97 season, Canal+ offered a match-by-match pay-per-view service, extended since the opening of its digital satellite transmissions in 1997, widening the options for TV football fans in France. Its subsidiary CanalSatellite's pay-per-view service offered every single French D1 match simultaneously live on nine digital channels at a cost of 50 francs (£5) per match, 75 francs for access to all nine matches on a given evening, or a 'season ticket' for 950 francs (working out at 28 francs per match) payable in ten instalments (1999/2000 figures).

The French Football League signed a five-year exclusivity contract with Canal+ for pay-per-view covering 1996/2001. Sceptics like Guy Roux, who felt it would empty the stadiums, have since revised their opinion as crowds have in fact substantially increased in general *(Le Monde*, 15 June 1997). The three clubs most in demand on pay-per-view are PSG, Marseille, and Bastia. The first two have the biggest home following, the highest priced tickets, and probably the biggest national following, whereas the Corsican club has a TV audience for the enormous diaspora of Corsican exiles, and for its home supporters who can less easily cheaply travel away from the island.

The competing service called Multivision, available on cable and TPS, the digital satellite service in which TF1 is the main shareholder, is sharing coverage of the European Champions League with TF1, offering a choice of 12 matches per European night at 34 francs per session (Py 1997). There have been fears that too much football on TV has been eroding its attractiveness, and Canal+ dropped its prices in 1997 (Haget 1996: 36). After 15 years of exclusive coverage of French domestic league football, Canal+ agreed to end its determination to maintain exclusivity after its main commercial rival put in a strong bid to the League. Canal+ and TPS concluded a five-year agreement in summer 1999 to share coverage of domestic matches for five years (*Le Monde interactif*, 26 June 1999). Canal+ kept two matches played outside the standard times (Friday or Sunday evening, plus an early kick-off on Saturday evening), whereas TPS took one of the matches played on Saturday evenings. Everyone seemed happy, especially the League that had doubled its income over five years. Television income to the LNF in 2001/02 was 397 million euros (£250 million), 19 per cent of which went to Division 2. *Le Monde* concluded that the parent companies of each, Vivendi for Canal+, and Suez-Lyonnaise des Eaux, the Bouygues group and François Pinault for TPS, had decided to put an end to hostilities, since prices of various types of programming on digital TV had been rocketing as a result. French football's income from TV could be driven up no further. It is still lagging behind TV income across the Channel. English Premier League TV income alone was more than twice the amount coming to the two divisions in France (*LNF Infos*, 39 (November 2001): 2–3).

At the same time as Canal+ was having more general financial problems, and having to announce a drop in number of subscribers for the first time ever in 2001 (*Le Monde*, 7 February 2002), the subscription channel's interest in PSG started to appear very expensive, especially when a run of poor results since the late 1990s resulted in a number of changes of chairman and manager, and in deficits. The executive chairman has always been a member of the inner circle of Canal+ directors. Initially from 1991 Michel Denisot had led PSG in its most successful period. In March 1998 it was announced that he was to be replaced at the end of what was then a disappointing season that was causing discontent amongst the Parc des Princes public. In fact PSG went on to win the French Cup in Denisot's last match in charge. His successor Charles Biétry, founder and Director of Sport at Canal+, had apparently always wanted the job. He had a life-long interest in football, had almost played professionally, and had an irreproachable professional career in television production at Canal+. As *Le Monde* put it, Biétry had changed for ever the way football was presented on TV. However, PSG was eliminated in the first round of the European Cup Winners Cup. Biétry sacked the manager Giresse. Things did not improve and he resigned in December 1998, to be replaced by another member of the Canal+ inner circle, Laurent Perpère, who, in 2000, brought in former player and manager Luis Fernandez, who had appeared to be waiting in the wings (or rather in the Canal+ studios as an expert summariser) to manage his old club. The signing of Anelka began to look like an expensive mistake when he left the club in 2002 at a significant loss.

Canal+, like other big business owners, can get very twitchy when results do not go their way, especially perhaps since there have appeared other exclusively sports channels in digital television: Eurosport, L'Equipe-TV, Pathé-Sport, Infosport, and AB Sports. Additionally, clubs like OM have their own channel; not that these small channels can hope to afford to buy rights to show much live football. Rumours circulated in the press in February 2001 that Canal+ was seeking to sell its majority stake in PSG. An interest in one club now appears less important than an interest in managing the broadcasting rights of many more. In May 2001 a *rapprochement* between Canal+ (owned by Vivendi), RTL Group (Bertelsmann) and the Darmon group was announced in a joint venture to rival Kirch. Ninety per cent of its work would be in football, where it would manage the rights of 320 clubs around the world, more than 40 national football associations and leagues. *Le Monde* (23 May 2001) saw this as a way of gaining access to the very expensive but lucrative World Cup rights.

This new venture added the management of broadcasting rights to other aspects of Canal+'s interests at different points of football's 'chain of production'. It already produces and distributes television pictures of French D1 and the Champions League; it controls the richest club in France and sponsors certain others; it holds the contract from the City of Paris to manage a big stadium, the Parc des Princes; runs Internet sites for five professional clubs; runs Zidane's personal website; holds the exclusive image rights of a number of professional players such as Ronaldinho, the young Brazilian World Cup winner playing for PSG; and is getting into sports marketing. Canal+ is certainly the most powerful player within French football. In order to maintain viewers' interest in the French League it needs healthy competition between clubs. Just as it originally took over PSG to ensure a key rival to the then dominant OM, it reportedly intervened to help the struggling OM in 1995 and in 2001 (Potet 2001c, 2001d, 2001e). PSG and OM are the two clubs that have appeared most often on Canal+ (146 times each), since they are the most attractive to subscribers. In 1995, when OM had been relegated and was in financial difficulty, Canal+ paid an advance of 40 million francs (£4 million) on future rights to their European games; in 2001 when Bernard Tapie wanted to sell OM players to buy others, Canal+'s Swiss club Servette Geneva bought three OM players; Canal+ distributes OMTV via CanalSatellite and reportedly offered to buy into the Marseille club's channel since it was in deficit; and *Le Monde* also claims that Canal+ invested in Tapie's son's sports Internet company (Potet 2001e). This is not to say there is anything illegal in any of these deals, but simply that the subscription channel is putting itself into a position to control the future of French league football and therefore its hold over football television rights, which after all have remained the primary motivation for viewers subscribing to Canal+ (*France Football*, 25 July 2000: 48). Finally, as further evidence of the subscription channel's financial influence over French club football, Canal+ is encouraging a change in the big issue of the early twenty-first century, for European football leagues as a whole – namely, whether to allow individual clubs to be able to sell their own broadcasting rights or to retain the system whereby the League sells them *en bloc* on behalf of all clubs. *L'Equipe* reported (16 February 2001) that sums of up to 20 million francs (£2 million) had been advanced by Canal+ to certain French clubs as options on their future individualised television rights contracts (in Potet 2001c). If French football is very dependent on Canal+, the latter is very dependent on top flight French football or, rather, on its continuing ability to attract viewers.

Is this construction a house of cards? April 2002 saw major share-price fluctuations concerning Canal+'s parent company Vivendi-Universal, whose boss Jean-Marie Messier raised doubts about Canal+'s future direction by sacking chairman Pierre Lescure ostensibly because of the channel's poor financial results.[1] The bigger issue was not however Canal+'s financial problems but the parent company's over-stretching itself during Messier's buying sprees. When Vivendi's debt problem became impossible to hide, and subsequently stock market values collapsed more generally, Messier was very messily and publicly ousted as chairman. It became urgent to consider the status of all subsidiaries with poor financial results and Canal+ seemed likely to be sold. Equally, in the context of the sale, the channel's 90 per cent ownership of a heavily indebted football club that had stopped winning trophies or competing in the more lucrative European competitions seemed a liability it could do without. PSG was therefore put up for sale, with no result at the time of writing. This was a further indication of the fragility of the dependency of French club football on television.

Conclusion

Professional football has become crucial to the economics of television in England, France and world-wide, all the more so in the digital age, as suggested by satellite and cable television distribution companies' attempts to buy into football clubs. Football sells satellite dishes for subscription channels, and it gives commercial television and their advertisers 'parts of the national audience that other programmes cannot reach' (Critcher 1987: 142). A Eurodata TV study showed that of the 45 countries covered, in 13 it was a sporting event that had brought in the top audience of the year. Football was the top television sport in 13 out of 20 European countries covered. At the time France was somewhat of an exception (Eurodata 1998). However, the popular effect of 1998 World Cup mediated through television was to change that.

Earlier than in the UK French television institutions have embraced the new forms of payment that come with new broadcasting technology: subscription TV in 1984, and then two major digital TV platforms, CanalSatellite and TPS, and pay-per-view in late 1996 – which allowed French football to take the leap into blanket pay-per-view coverage of D1 football from the 1997 season onwards. In doing so they have missed out a phase in the history of televised football in England, that Barnett (1995) divides up into three eras:

1. The BBC monopoly period, with low facility fees being paid by TV to football, and when the public service principle of universal access was accepted.
2. The duopoly period when 'live and exclusive' matches reflected competition for access between BBC and ITV and when the value of TV rights rose.
3. The period following deregulation and the arrival of cable and satellite subscription TV.

In this latest era a new philosophy of sport comes to the fore, which provides a new revenue stream for football but which consists of buying up the rights and charging a direct subscription fee to viewers who want to watch matches, thus breaking the tradition of TV sport on universal access. In this era TV football has become a commodity. Barnett argues that revenue-hungry sports governing bodies have colluded with competitive commercial channels to 'sell their major events to smaller audiences for more money' (1995: 94). The result is that '[English] football is now handcuffed to television, but few can doubt which of the two is under arrest'. There are fears that the same is true of France – even if they have come to it via a different route.

What we have seen in France is a very short middle era of live league football on universal access: the onset of this era was delayed because of the late commercialisation of French TV; indeed, subscription TV started before TF1 was privatised. Public sector TV – where the public service ethos is still alive in France – has, since the mid-1980s, been financially squeezed out of football coverage through the competitive bidding up of rights fees by Canal+ and TF1, a competition won of course by the non-universal access channel. Although French international games have so far been protected for universal access TV by government decree, French football missed out on the opportunity of popularising the domestic competition through a long period of live universal access TV such as happened in England from the 1970s. At a time when TV fees were low, the French football authorities were afraid they would lose gate money as TV football competed with the real version. They therefore refused to allow club football to be shown live. The fear is that the French TV audience's interest in domestic club football is a fragile one, and that it may be transient. If so, the finances of both league clubs and Canal+ would be seriously compromised at a time when, for reasons external to football and to Canal+, the channel is under pressure. The crashes of Kirch in Germany and ITV Digital in Britain were because of financial over-stretching in buying football rights or of overestimating the potential audience. In both England and Germany there have been serious effects on clubs' financial stability. France may not be immune.

Broadcasting and football have promoted each other's growth and popularity symbiotically, if somewhat differently in each country. Firstly, French football finances are highly dependent on television, and particularly on one company, the Canal+ group. Secondly, for many fans, particularly those who have come recently to the sport, football has become essentially and exclusively a televisual experience. Certainly, by universal agreement, Canal+ has improved the coverage of football on TV – as seen in the technically excellent World Cup coverage. But it has also been instrumental, with TF1, in changing the way the game is experienced. The (partial) transformation of football into a televisual product, one element of home entertainment among others, is reflected in the ambitions of the head of Canal+'s sports coverage of the World Cup, Charles Biétry, for further improving television coverage: 'As long as the viewer is better off in the stadium than in his living room to watch a match, we will not have succeeded' (Biétry 1998, in McKeever 1999: 176).

Further questions arise that concern French football more directly. How do its links to television affect the values it carries? Are they transforming a live spectacle that once expressed community identity into a TV-mediated expression of commodity and commercial values? What issues of football's governance are raised by this for the sport's authorities and indeed for the State and public authorities, given the latter's traditionally close interest in sport? Issues of football's commercialisation and governance are addressed in the next chapter on football and business, politics and corruption.

Note

1. The dispute was seen by some as an attempt to rein in the channel's editorial independence and another round in the debate over the future of the French cultural exception (Webster 2002), which is another arena (cinema film production and distribution) where the French are attempting to defend specifically French approaches against the forces of global commerce.

8

Chairmen: Business, Politics and Corruption

It has already been suggested, in the chapter on coaches, that as a broad generalisation the key figure within French football clubs has, from the beginning, been the chairman, the *président du club*. While this has been a constant over the century of French football, there is not just one single model of club chairman. Previous analyses have suggested that the model of businessman chairman changed in the 1980s, reflecting broader changes in corporate practices over the twentieth century. Claude Bez and Bernard Tapie are cited as emblematic of both a new approach to the football business and the involvement of football and corrupt business practices. While these two larger-than-life characters may have changed the scale of business involvement in football, it will be argued that it is in the 1990s that clubs become part of modern big business in the shape of the big city corporate clubs of the twenty-first century such as Lyon under the chairmanship of Jean-Michel Aulas. For all these changes, the old-style small business chairmen do still exist in the smaller professional clubs. Old-style or new-style, the chairman remains in general the dominant figure within the club, but his involvement today may be only partly from the same motivations as the chairmen of old, and the outcomes sought may be different.

New Chairmen for Old? Nicollin and Urano

In the period of growth of football as a popular sport, after the First World War, many clubs were directed by industrialists and businessmen whose names remain associated with the success of the teams, often through the stadiums, as in the Stade Geoffroy-Guichard at Saint-Etienne. Bromberger recalls how chairmen would provide equipment, deal with transfers and bonuses (that were illegal until the professional era), and often give clubs a stadium, as in the case of the Guichard family (Bromberger *et al.* 1995: 180). In the 1920s, as football and other sports became more important for municipalities, and the teams became symbols of the whole town rather than of their founding firm, responsibility for most stadiums was taken by the municipality. The inter-war period was the era of the paternalistic chairman, wanting added value for the firm's image in return for his sponsorship. This was not uncontroversial. In the increasingly highly charged political atmosphere of the 1930s, of clashes between fascist leagues and trade union marches, the Marxist left was highly critical of the exploitation of football by the representatives of capitalism. They worried about the transformation of company clubs into clubs representing a town, and the consequent dilution of class consciousness as players came together from different social classes.

The influence of the founding firms remained, however, in the establishment of organisational structures of clubs along the lines of company hierarchies, where the operatives had to follow the orders of the management and bosses. Fridenson (1989: 53) discusses the paternalistic model of discipline of the Peugeot factory and the discourse of productivity in talking about the team. The importance of discipline and hard work was the ethos of teams until the 1970s. Faure and Suaud (1994b: 9–10; 1999: 67–75) show in some detail, and on the basis of interviews with former players, just how the paternalistic 'dictatorship of the chairman' operated as part of the structure of the game. He exercised personal power over the small number of club officials and over the players who were treated as part of a 'family' and whose 'life contract' committed them to total subordination to the fatherly authority of the chairman. The latter's authority was all the more legitimated as he was apparently committing himself to a gratuitous (and unpaid) task in the interests of the community, but which of course could give immense symbolic capital locally, and which was often the centre of a network of influence.

There was another model of chairman, that of Jean Clerfeuille (1959–69) and his successor at Nantes, Louis Fonteneau (1969–86). They were salaried managers within a local company, not entrepreneurs. Rather than using capital from their own company to run the club, like the Laurant brothers at Sedan, they acted, report Faure and Suaud (1994b: 14), out of a sense of integrity, responsibility and service as administrators of the club. Their authority rested on an image of competence and discretion. This model remained clearly a minority one.

Faure and Suaud (1994b) and Bromberger *et al.* (1995: 184–193) analyse the changes in chairmen that show that a new ethos was emerging in the 1980s. D1 clubs' wage bills increased from 141 million francs in 1980 to 645 million francs in 1988 (Bourg 1989: 163). Gate money did not increase, a doubling of town hall subsidies did not cover this increase, therefore deficits of clubs rose, and money came in from business. Importantly, the role of club chairman in these new circumstances attracted a new type of entrepreneur. Bourg (1986: 79) has shown that in the 1984/85 season, of the 20 D1 club chairmen, 17 were chairmen and managing directors of private companies, but not from the traditional industrial manufacturing sector. Rather they represented newer types of firm, media, advertising, construction firms, property developers, distribution. Marcel Leclerc (OM) was head of a sporting press group; Jean-Luc Lagardère (Racing) was chairman of Matra-Hachette (armaments, radio, press and publishing). In the new context, Bromberger's ethnographic study concludes that football clubs no longer embodied paternalism or the productivity and discipline of the factory, but a 'social project that matched the [new] spirit of the age' where organisation of work and industrial relations and objectives were conceived very differently. The values of professionalism replaced those of the voluntary sector (*le bénévolat*) that had hitherto been the cornerstone of clubs. Local notables putting time and effort into a hobby were being excluded and replaced by business managers wanting a return on investment. The clubs' business management was being professionalised, and merchandising introduced. The role of the 'association', its elected officers and its 'deliberative assemblies' was reduced. Bernard Tapie (OM) and Claude Bez (Bordeaux), examples examined below, are typical of the new chairmen of the 1980s. Tapie is quoted as saying: 'A football club should be run like a business' (*France Football*, 4 February 1986: 8, cited by Bromberger *et al.* 1995: 185). Lagardère said his involvement was not simply through 'personal passion' (Bromberger *et al.* 1995: 71). This new approach created a break between the club and the supporters who were active members of the association. The professionalisation of the sport and the transformation of the spectacle into a commodity fitted ill with the old legal framework of the non-profit-making association run by unpaid volunteers. Indeed, legal changes to the laws of sporting organisations were introduced in 1984 and 1992. New models of clubs had values of professionalism, expertise, competence, competitiveness, performance, the will to win. Sponsors in particular needed to see what they were getting for their money.

The new generation of chairmen that Bromberger calls the 'boss generation' (Bromberger *et al.* 1995: 188) sought permanent visibility and personal recognition in the media, whereas chairmen had previously stayed in the background. The football club became the means by which the chairman and his other companies got coverage and communicated their image. Appearance became all. Bromberger notes that ostentatious consumption, displays of wealth, and quickly earned fortunes became more acceptable within society (he quotes opinion polls, p. 188). Winning becomes more important than taking part. There is no room for sentiment such as might have given a place to Jean Tigana in OM's European Cup Final team of 1991 in his last season. Teams and clubs reflected therefore how one type of entrepreneurial logic had been replaced by another over the course of the twentieth century: the first based success on discipline, authority, hierarchy and discretion, the other on participation, consensus, risk taking, and appearance in the media. Business and management began using sporting metaphors rather than the other way round. Sportsmen began to be used to give team-building seminars in companies. 'Previously the team was compared to a company, now the company is compared to a team. Football, for a long time a belated reflection of the world of manufacturing industry, seems to have become in the eyes of business managers the vector of a new social project' (ibid.: 191). Football has become a modern myth that allows society to think about how best to live together.

This chronological distinction would be misleading if it were taken to mean that all the professional clubs suddenly changed structures and ethos, and that the old model of chairman disappeared over a couple of seasons. In some of the smaller clubs old-style chairmen still operate, some of whom have emerged fairly recently. Two such chairmen are Louis Nicollin, long-time boss of Montpellier, and a recent arrival, Pascal Urano of Sedan.

Louis Nicollin: 'my club is my passion'

As 99 per cent long-term owner of the Montpellier-Hérault Sports Club, 'Loulou' Nicollin regards it as more of a daughter than a mistress, but his whole approach to club chairmanship is reminiscent of bygone days. He employs his ex-players in his companies, and uses the term 'family' to describe the Montpellier club. *Libération* portrays him as a truculent, Gitane-smoking, old-style, overweight businessman and local notable, who is easily roused to fits of temper and whose business decisions regarding the club are more passionate than rational. He has been disinclined to share power with any other potential investor since he took over in 1974. He does, however, despite his own right-wing convictions, have to work with the local municipality and the long-standing socialist mayor Georges Frêche, who happens to be equally keen to use the football club to promote the town. Nicollin's own business is in refuse collection, and dependent on 300 municipal contracts in the region. He has used his sporting contacts in his businesses. He admits that 'if you go to a town to tender for a contract, and you are known through football, it does no harm' (*France Football*, 18 January 2002: 15). He was fined, on the island of Réunion, for trying to win the main town's refuse collection contact by giving 2 million francs to the local football club (Revault d'Alonnes 2001b). He also owns nearby Béziers rugby club.

Pascal Urano: a Throwback to the Traditional Chairman

When in November 2000 the CS Sedan-Ardennes found themselves on top of the French Division 1, it is open to speculation how the chairman Pascal Urano celebrated. In the previous season, on reaching the French Cup Final when still in Division 2, he took some friends to a restaurant to celebrate, so

L'Equipe recounts (7 November 2000: 8), but found the only free tables were in a back room already booked for the club's players. He simply took over the table, and the on-field heroes had to go to a player's flat to eat their pizzas. In the same article (Dupont 2000), as if to ram home the point that in Sedan what Monsieur Urano wants Monsieur Urano gets, we read that, on another occasion, to avoid waiting in a full restaurant he apparently paid the bill of a table of diners who were nearly finished on condition that they left immediately. He is, it would appear, as feared as the club's mascot, a wild boar.

To understand how smaller professional French clubs operate, anecdotes about personal characteristics, which easily turn into caricatures, are however less interesting than looking at the structures within which a chairman operates. The Sedan and Montpellier cases illuminate the long-standing tradition of a network of influences that tie together local politics, local business and local sport. In Urano's case he is at the centre of this network and appears to be one of the most powerful men in Sedan and the region. He became a successful businessman since unexpectedly having to take over the family construction business and give up his studies in 1980 at the age of 20. He built up the business from 200 to 500 employees and into five separate companies. He added to it the local Mercedes concession, opened with some pomp in 1996 in the presence of the Olympic judo gold medallist David Douillet, one of the most popular personalities in France, and Gérard Houllier, then National Technical Director of French football. Urano took a minor interest in the club in 1992, an interest that became more important as the club's financial problems worsened. *L'Equipe* claims he spent 25 million francs on the club between 1993 and 1999, and recounts a number of business operations that imply, fairly or unfairly, the possibility of bullying, cutting corners or even sharp practice, but which all bear witness to his ability to make things happen locally (Dupont 2000).

Among the details given are the following. Firstly, on relegation from Division 2 in 1995, the then chairman announced that he and Urano were both withdrawing from the club. Urano immediately, overnight and at his own expense, dismantled two television gantries that his companies had constructed. He was persuaded to stay with the club by the mayor, and became indispensable when in June 1998 he had to act as guarantor of the club's debts of almost 7 million francs to prevent them from losing their professional status and therefore being refused promotion back to Division 2 at an appeal hearing of the League's financial commission, the DNCG (see p. 168). He soon afterwards, *L'Equipe* reports, began employing one of the former members of the DNCG. Secondly, the same article recounts how his building of a new football stadium for the club in double-quick time was overshadowed by the manner in which the town council, on a technicality, overturned a first choice of tender to award the contract for its construction to a company that appears to have sub-contracted part of the work to Urano, who supervised much of the building. Sedan has fewer inhabitants than the number of seats in the new stadium, but a large stadium is necessary if the club wants to play in Europe. The building and maintenance costs to the local taxpayers are high. Whereas he had previously been a supporter of the right-wing mayoral candidate, he contributed financially to the victorious campaign of the outgoing mayor in 1995. Finally, Urano's companies are very influential bidders in local public procurement building contracts since he holds a near monopoly locally over the supply of the key construction material of gravel. Since his involvement in the construction of the stadium, he has become chairman of the club (September 2000). He has professionalised the running of the club, marginalising the unpaid volunteers who formerly helped during matches.

In the past, as in the case of Nicollin, there has generally been an element of passion as well as calculation in the involvement of small businessmen with football. In Urano's case though there is room for doubt in this respect, by his own admission. This son of an Italian immigrant seems to be a businessman through and through who finds it difficult not to be curious about the business side of everything. As he says: 'I can't enter a place without wondering if the shop is operating at a profit. When I go to the cinema, I calculate the turnover on the performance.' On the one hand he claims that he is not in football for the money, that it does not pay in normal commercial terms; on the other he states: 'The money is not a gift, it is an investment. I am not a philanthropist' (Dupont 2000). In under a decade, his involvement with Sedan has undoubtedly turned a small-town club in a not particularly well-off rural region, but with a footballing tradition, into a club that counts again within French football. He has professionalised it, and run it in a business-like way, but his relationships within the club recall an earlier tradition of chairman. His relationships with business and politics outside the club and the way he makes things happen (if *L'Equipe*'s details are taken at face value) appear to be based on the traditional clientelism, deals and networks that have long characterised French politics and business.

The Modern Businessman Chairman: the Bez–Tapie Era

The three names of club chairman best known to fans in the modern era are Roger Rocher of Saint-Etienne, Claude Bez of Bordeaux and Bernard Tapie of Marseille. They all appeared to be successful businessmen and contributed enormously to the successes of their club. All ended up in jail for corrupt practices. The latter two have been credited with changing how French football clubs are run.

Roger Rocher took over as chairman of AS Saint-Etienne in the glory years from 1961 to 1982. He was old-fashioned in his relations with his players, intolerant of any questioning of his authority. He fell partly because results eventually stopped coming, and because of his age and his policy of buying star players rather than relying on the youth scheme favoured by manager Herbin. Internal disputes over policy led to rumours of a slush fund and under-the-counter payments to players (*l'affaire des caisses noires* – Rocher's 'war chest' as he preferred to call it). The AGM of the association in December 1983 was a rowdy eight-hour session full of insults and was the beginning of the end of Rocher, who, along with others on both sides of the dispute, were charged with fraud. A number of players (including Platini) and manager Herbin were found guilty of taking illegal payments. In 1991 Rocher, who had already spent four months in preventative detention, was found guilty on appeal and condemned to three years in jail, with the remaining 32 months suspended. He was given a presidential pardon later in the year, and died in 1997. The Saint-Etienne finances never really recovered, and the club has never recaptured its former glories.

Claude Bez and the Modernisation of the Football Business

Under the leadership of mayor Chaban-Delmas, Bordeaux led the way among French cities in using the modern football business and in making the club a symbol of the city and the region on the national and international stage (see Chapter 3). The person who made it happen was Claude Bez, chairman of Girondins de Bordeaux from 1978 to 1990. Under his leadership the club was undoubtedly, in the 1980s, the dominant force in French football: French champions three times and European semi-finalists twice. He saw that the financial side of sport was turning into big business, and so he brought in modern business methods to run the club on the model of Barcelona or Juventus. His methods were subsequently copied elsewhere in France. He used the tools of marketing, commercialisation, sponsorship, advertising, and set about creating a modern image for the club and indeed for himself, as a larger-than-life, Bentley-driving cavalier leader, with immediately recognisable drooping moustaches. As unpaid chairman, Bez spent 15 hours a week on club business. Bourg judges that it was the glory and recognition that motivated him (1986: 75–76). Bez saw money as a means, not as an end in itself: 'The basis of my personal philosophy is power. And money, for me, is just the instrument of power' (interview in *France Football*, 27 October 1984, cited in Faure and Suaud 1994b: 15). In football terms this led to a policy of buying success, the quick fix rather than relying long term on developing a club by producing players through a youth policy.

As the boss of a successful chartered accountancy firm, he came into the club executive as (unpaid) treasurer in 1974 at the age of 33; six months later he was vice-president; and he became chairman four years later. At his first meeting with mayor Chaban, he promised him a great team, but added it would cost the city a lot of money (Rousseau 1999). One of his key innovations was as a pioneer in the sale of television rights. As chairman of the top club of the time he broke an agreement to alternate European rights between TF1 and Canal+, thus changing the balance of power between clubs and TV channels, and beginning the rise in television income for French clubs. He also increased sponsorship income from corporate sources, in the case of Bordeaux from Opel cars. This new income allowed him to buy international players. He changed relationships with the supporters, setting up official supporters clubs, club shops for merchandise, and increasing the numbers of season ticket holders. The club was the first to install private boxes for a new kind of audience (in 1986). In the 1980s Bordeaux had the biggest municipal grant of all French clubs, the biggest advertising income, and the highest gate receipts (Bourg 1986: 146).

His relations with his players elicited tributes on his death in 1999, saying he had been a 'man of his word' (from Battiston, Platini, and Trésor). This suggests that his man-management style was in the old-fashioned manner of the family club. He also knew how to attract publicity by theatrical gestures. As a protest against the Federation's suspension of his goalkeeper, he picked his smallest and best outfield player Alain Giresse in goal for the next match.

His influence in French football went wider than his club. He was instrumental in Platini replacing Henri Michel as national team selector in 1988, such was his power within the Federation and League at the time (Rousseau 1999). His highly publicised personal feud with Bernard Tapie attracted much publicity and comparisons with *Dallas*'s unscrupulous businessman character J. R. Ewing (*Le Nouvel Observateur*, 11 October 1990, cited by Rousseau 1999). The feud of these two heavyweights was perhaps inevitable given the historic rivalry between the two major cities of the south, but it gained venom over the surprise transfer of Bordeaux star Giresse to OM in 1986. Bez also accused Tapie of trying to bribe one of his players, whereas Tapie accused Bez of having his hand in the till.

His downfall came following an early exit from the European Cup in the first round in 1985/86. This was expensive given that the club's budgetary calculations were based on greater income from this lucrative competition, and so began the financial destabilisation of the club. The disclosure of ten million francs of tax debts in 1989 was followed in November 1990 by the publication by mayor Chaban of an internal audit revealing a deficit of 242 million francs. Charged with fraud, tax problems, and irregularities regarding transfers and the organisation of matches, he resigned, was convicted and sentenced in June 1995 to three years in prison (two of them suspended) and a fine of 2 million francs. The charges of fraud concerned his personal affairs as well as his stewardship of Bordeaux. He was due to appear in court again in 1999, but he was already an ill man and died of a heart attack.

Bernard Tapie, Football and Politics as 'Soap'

Just as the transition of Bordeaux had its political dimension, so, with other clubs, some politicians have attempted to harness themselves to successful teams for political gain. Most national politicians in France keep their local base, often as mayor of a medium or large town, where clientelism and the old-boy networks are important political tools. The links between local municipal politics, tendering for local public works contracts, and the occult financing of political parties and election campaigns have more and more come into the open as the courts have felt freer from national political pressures. Add to this the complexities of football finances within the strait-jacket of the 1901 law, and it is no wonder that some prominent individuals have over-reached themselves and suffered the inevitable consequences of trying to accommodate football, business and politics. The most prominent example has been Bernard Tapie, who entered local and national politics via business and sport rather than the other way round.

Born in 1943, he was listed as fifty-second richest person in France in 1988, worth at least 0.8 billion francs (£80 million) (Frémy and Frémy 1991: 1860). After dabbling in the pop industry, he had set up a holding company in 1979 and became a wealthy tycoon. He specialised in taking over firms in difficulty: la Vie claire (1980), Toshiba France (1982), Wonder batteries, Wrangler France, Kickers, Soft Mazda (1984) and turning them temporarily at least into going concerns. In other words he was an asset stripper. He enjoyed an ostentatiously flamboyant lifestyle, and moored his yacht in Marseille harbour. He came into politics having been invited by the long-term mayor of Marseille, Gaston Defferre, a key government minister and baron of the Socialist party, to become chairman of OM in April 1986. As seen in rival right-wing Bordeaux, a successful local club was important for local politics. Tapie's millions could just do the trick – he offered to put aside 500 million francs per year from his business group to invest in OM (Bourg 1986: 78).

At first he was successful on all three fronts: football, business and politics. From seventeenth and twelfth in 1985 and 1986 respectively, OM finished second to Bordeaux in Tapie's first full season as chairman and won the championship five times in a row from 1989 onwards, and the European Cup in 1993. As a self-made business man with political ambitions but no local base, Tapie recognised in the city of Marseille an unrivalled opportunity to establish political roots, with the mayor's office as the final goal with Defferre's blessing. His notoriety was already worth millions of francs in publicity for the club. His TV appearances turned him into a guru of modern business management. As the only politician of the left willing to take on Jean-Marie Le Pen in TV debates, his self-confident, man-of-the-people gift of the gab made him both the darling of the political left and a favourite with voters. He stood for parliament and was elected in 1989 in a constituency near Marseille after his 1988 defeat had been annulled by the Constitutional Council. He was re-elected in 1993. He became minister for cities in the Bérégovoy government of 1992/93. He is credited with being pushed by Mitterrand to lead a left-wing Radical list in the European elections of 1994 to ruin Michel Rocard's chances of taking over the Socialist Party on Mitterrand's eventual retirement, and was an MEP until 1997. For a while he was even spoken of as a possible left-wing candidate for the presidential election when Jacques Delors withdrew. However, by then, it was too late, since his business affairs had begun to fail and he was under corruption charges in his position as chairman of OM.

Initially, he had inflated the transfer and salary market by buying in top international players and managers. He knew he could use his political protection to persuade the nationalised banks to back him. He bought Adidas in 1990. He openly spoke of image being everything. 'A company's health is measured not only by its economic performance, but by the quality of its industrial relations, which are good if people are proud of what they are doing. Sporting success is a guarantee in this respect. People can fully identify with it' (Bourg 1986: 78). Tapie created his own commercial structure of which he was the majority shareholder, but retained the Association 1901 for the club in order to remain within the FFF rules. As in the case of Bordeaux, problems came from banking too early on success in Europe. The pressure to succeed was such that it appears that at the end of the 1992/93 season, in order to ensure winning the championship and therefore continued presence in Europe, bribes were offered to Valenciennes players, one of whom (Jacques Glassmann) was so outraged that he revealed the approach, and was eventually listened to. The affair finally went to court, and to appeal, but Marseille ended up being punished by relegation on top of bankruptcy, and Tapie left the club in December 1994. He was banned from French football for two years. (For details, see Assouly 2000; Bordenave 2001; Gattegno 2001.)

Tapie and other club officials were investigated, and charged in the criminal courts with bribery and suborning a witness, false accounting regarding the OM finances and regarding his Testut company, and for tax evasion over his yacht. The affair was dragged out until after the presidential election – national politics *oblige*, and then further on appeal. Tapie was sentenced to prison terms on all four of the counts, ineligibility for public office for three years, a five-year ban from business activity, and huge fines. (See *L'Equipe*, 4 April 2001: 2, and Bordenave 2001, for summaries of his judicial history.) By then he was already bankrupt and had lost his political credibility. And that seemed to be that, but Tapie and the world of football in Marseille are curious creatures. Robert Gildea sums them up quite neatly:

> Both he and his football team were corrupt, but his corruption was seen as somehow thumbing his nose at the establishment. The fact that the courts confiscated his yacht and furniture for tax evasion and the Crédit Lyonnais pursued him for debts only served to confirm his Robin Hood status with his have-not supporters. He was the antithesis of the 'governmental' socialist Michel Rocard: in revolt against the taxman, the big banks, the judicial system, a tribune of the people emerging from the ruins of the classic Left . . . Tapie was politics as soap, now up, now down, but always fighting back and always in the public limelight. (Gildea 1997: 200)

Gildea could have added that in Marseille being anti-establishment meant also being anti-Paris, which added to Tapie's attraction. He was emblematic of a new form of demagogic politics and a new form of unscrupulous, winning-is-everything running of a football club. Politically he benefited from and in the end contributed to the political alienation of a French electorate that has become very sceptical about the motivations and morality of its traditional political class.

He emerged from prison in July 1997 having spent in total no more than 165 days behind bars. He appeared in a Lelouch film, wrote a novel with a football setting, was engaged for a radio talk show then a TV talk show (on satellite channel RTL9), and played the Jack Nicholson role in *One Flew Over the Cuckoo's Nest* on stage in a touring company. However, in the northern suburbs of Marseille, where footballing success is more important than establishment politics, such was OM's plight that there were calls from the terraces for the miracle worker's return, and such was the owner's desperation that he called in Tapie as Director of Football and prospective saviour of the club. Tapie was called chairman Louis-Dreyfus's final card – the Swiss boss of Adidas had already sunk £90 million of his own money into OM (Chaumier and Rocheteau 2001: 276). This sum had risen to £100 million by the end of season 2001/02 (Henry 2002). Tapie believes he still has a political constituency and a political future once his political ineligibility ends in 2003, and that he can convince the courts that the Crédit Lyonnais bank diddled him out of millions in the sale of Adidas in 1993, which wrongly led to his bankruptcy. As *Le Monde* commented, he has not forgotten how his sporting victories prepared his political success, and how both guaranteed his business continuity and the confidence of public sector investors and of the nationalised bank, the Crédit Lyonnais (Gattegno 2001).

He started his comeback by stepping back into football, but few believe that is an end in itself. Success did not immediately follow, and maybe the links between sport, business and politics are no longer quite the same as they were. Or are they? What shocked many outside football is that following an apparent clean-up of the game after the Bez and Tapie affairs, and the setting up of the DNCG (see p. 168) to prevent football clubs running on deficits, there were so few protests from inside the game at Tapie's return. The World Cup win had been a breath of fresh air for the game, along with the values of modesty, integrity and hard work attributed to coach Aimé Jacquet. *Le Monde*'s editorial of 5 April 2001 considered the return of 'chancers' into the game as a step in the wrong direction. The murky affairs of OM continued when, after prolonged internal wrangles and restructuring, and interventions by chairman Louis-Dreyfus to get to the bottom of what he called 'Mafia-like practices within the club', the public prosecutor's office announced in April 2002 an investigation into possible links between OM and organised crime (*Le Monde*, 16 April 2002). Tapie left the club, chairman Louis-Dreyfus restructured the management, and nothing came of the investigation, which was dropped.

Regulating the Business Side: Sports Legislation or Self-Regulation?

Over the years, but in the 1980s particularly, changes in the economic and ideological climate and the changing relationship between sport and business (and its abuse) persuaded the football authorities and government to amend the legislation regulating professional sports clubs. Government became aware of the business restrictions imposed on clubs within the framework of the 1901 law, and legislated on the organisation of professional sport in 1975, 1984, 1992, 1999 and 2000. The 1984 and 1992 reforms aimed to reinforce the economic aspect of professional sport, whereas the Buffet law of 2000 drew a line in the sand regarding further deregulation of clubs' business activities. The major innovation of the football authorities, the new financial regulatory body, the DNCG, was a means by which the Federation retained control of the professional clubs.

La loi Mazeaud (1975)

In 1975 the right-wing Youth and Sports Minister Pierre Mazeaud spelled out the implications of French law for professional sport when there was an attempted break-away of a professional league from the French Basketball Federation. He confirmed, for football and other sports, that professional clubs were subordinate to their sports federation. France is unique in Europe in terms of the State's tutelage over sport. The State was determined to maintain its power over sport to keep it in the public domain and to protect it from the laws of the free market, and to maintain close financial and fiscal scrutiny over professional sports clubs and players. The law stated that sports clubs must be constituted either (as before) under the law of 1901 regulating non-profit-making associations or under business law as a *société d'économie mixte*, a mixed public and private company. The SEMS (*société d'économie mixte sportive*) allowed a local authority to hold a minority of shares in a company, but with a risk of losing money. The sports association (alone or in conjunction with the local authority) must hold the majority of capital and voting rights. Its accounts were subject to closer scrutiny under the law. Very few clubs took up the new option. The financial state of football did not improve. The most famous post-war club, Reims, went bankrupt in 1978, after Red Star, Rouen and Rennes. The collective debts of the remaining professional football clubs reached 90 million francs by 1983, therefore threatening the budgets of the local authorities that sponsored them, at which point government decided to look again at the laws regulating professional sport (Faure and Suaud 1999: 40).

La loi Avice (1984) and its Modifications

The next sports law, the *loi Avice*, and its later modifications were intended, as Faure and Suaud interpret it (1999: 40–41), to ensure a more rigorous control of clubs' financial management. It forced professional sports clubs with an annual turnover of more than 2.5 million francs to constitute themselves into a SEMS or into a SAOS (*société anonyme à objet sportif*). In an SAOS the club's original association must hold one-third of the shares in order to have a blocking minority, so the amateur club still remained in principle in control of the professional team. The SAOS is otherwise much like a limited liability company, but cannot pay out profits to shareholders. The change was none the less unpopular with the sports traditionalists supporting the autonomy of French sport and its separation from business values. Most big clubs became SAOS by the end of the 1990s.

Bernard Tapie got round the legislation by creating a *société de participation* of which he was the major shareholder (60 per cent), the club 39 per cent and the city 1 per cent. To hide this structure not recognised by the Federation, the association still existed and looked after day-to-day matters.

The right-wing governments of 1993–97 recognised that local authority subventions to professional clubs were illegal, for clubs that were trading commercially in the form of SAOS or SEM, which was almost all. Henceforward they could only get sponsorship from French regional authorities (Echégut 1994: 21). The Sports Minister of the later left-wing government, Mme Buffet, managed to delay the implementation of this. Private investors could henceforward buy two-thirds of the capital, although the ban on paying dividends was a serious discouragement

La DNCG (Direction Nationale de Contrôle de Gestion)

A government decree of April 1990 set up a body, the DNCG, to scrutinise the administrative and financial management of football clubs under the control of the FFF. It is a financial regulator made up of independent financial experts who examine the accounts of all professional clubs to prevent them from going too far into the red. It is a means of self-regulation, since it reports to the Federation, and has been interpreted as an attempt by the latter to exert control over the big clubs (Faure and Suaud 1999). The League only has one-fifth of the votes in the general assembly of the FFF, where the whole French 'football family' is so heavily represented as to ensure the domination of the governing body by representatives of the amateur game. One of the DNCG's instigators was Noël Le Graët, then chairman of the small Division 2 club, Guingamp. The strength of the anti-commercial lobby that he represented in the early 1990s, even among professional league clubs, is further shown by his election to the chairmanship of the League management body in 1991. His platform was based on opposition to the entry of economic liberalism and free enterprise into football. The existence of the DNCG underlines the theoretical control of the FFF over the League, since the DNCG can prevent a club from buying players, or even strip a club of its professional status and indeed relegate it from Division 1 and/or Division 2 into Division 3 (the National), as happened to Toulouse in 2001. Faure and Suaud (1994b: 24–25) criticise this body as being in hock to the amateur game and to the small clubs, therefore having a vested interest in preserving the *status quo*. Its effect, as Eastham (1999: 75) shows, was gradually to wipe out Division 1 clubs' debts – at least until the 2001/02 season. It is criticised, however, by the bigger clubs as stifling their ability to compete with major clubs in England, Spain and Italy who have no such regulator to prevent them from speculating in the transfer market and running up huge deficits. Its longer term authority *vis-à-vis* the bigger clubs may be questioned in the light of 2002 figures regarding the deficits of OM in particular. On average, salaries more than doubled over six years to 2001 and French clubs' transfer dealings showed a deficit. The total debts of the D1 clubs for the season 2000/01 had risen spectacularly to 53 million euros (over £30 million), most of which were attributable to PSG and OM, especially the latter who accounted for 72 per cent of the deficit. OM has been in deficit since 1995/96. The DNCG threatened the club with relegation but withdrew it on presentation of a letter of credit by OM's chairman, Robert Louis-Dreyfus, the owner of Adidas, which is a huge sponsor of football in France and the world (see Hare 1999b). PSG's accounts also showed a deficit for the third year running, but the club has, so far, been protected by Canal+. As *L'Equipe* (13 March 2002: 6) commented, the DNCG had been much more heavy handed with less fashionable clubs. One might add that Adidas, in its sponsorship contracts with league clubs, and Canal+, with its TV money, are vital to the financial equilibrium of French football as a whole. OM and PSG are also the only two French clubs represented among the top European clubs that formed the G14 group in September 2000 as a lobbying group *vis-à-vis* UEFA and FIFA.

The lois Buffet (1999 and 2000)

In her 1999 and 2000 legislation the communist sports minister went another step along the way to allowing professional clubs to become limited companies, but not as far as the League wanted. Various elements of the law and its decrees upset the whole of the French sports movement, as represented by the CNOSF as well as the UCPF. Mme Buffet's aims were to regulate the relationship of professional sport with society as a whole and with amateur sport. In particular she wanted to bring the trend towards the domination of sport by business values under some form of democratic control. For her, sport was an area where 'money must not be able to dictate its own laws' (Bezat 2000). The preamble of her bill justified this by referring to the public service mission of sport, its contribution to social cohesion, its part in the struggle against social inequality, and the need to democratise physical exercise and sport. The sports federations were defined as the key tools through which the State could ensure that sport's public service mission was carried out. (See *LNF Infos,* issue 21, October 1999: 4–5.)

A new type of company was created, the SASP *(société anonyme sportive et professionnelle)*, which ten D1 clubs adopted in 2001/02, as an alternative to the SAOS. This means a club can operate as a limited company with various constraints. It allows dividends to be paid to shareholders, and chairmen of clubs to be paid a salary for the first time, but its shares cannot be bought and sold on the Bourse. Whereas in a SAOS the non-profit-making association must hold a blocking minority of one-third of shares, in a SASP it may give up its shares. But the registration of the club with the FFF is still held by the Association, which also owns the name, the brand and other distinctive signs of the club. The Association is responsible for the amateur section of the club and the company for the professional section, but they share responsibility for 'la formation' (youth training) (Potet 2002; Bourzat and Breillat 2001).

The law also reinforced the regulation concerning young players who were to be obliged to sign an initial three-year contract with the club whose academy they were trained in. Players' agents were to be regulated and would have to register with the FFF. They would not be allowed to sign contracts with players under the age of eighteen. Two controversial parts of Mme Buffet's legislation concerned television rights. First a 5 per cent top slice off television rights paid to football, rugby, tennis and other sports was to go annually to the FNDS to finance amateur sport, which the UCPF estimated at a loss of 100 million francs per year to football clubs (Potet 2001f). Even more seriously in the eyes of the big professional clubs, by law the sports federations were deemed to own all television rights for their sport, with the ability to delegate them in part to professional leagues or clubs. This was in a sense the key to Mme Buffet's attempt to claw back control over sport from the big business interests that she saw as taking it over to the federations and hence to publicly accountable authorities.

In late 2001 the professional football club chairmen, feeling the new laws had simply given with one hand and taken more way with the other, appealed to Brussels, citing European competition law in an attempt to regain control over these rights. As evidence, they commissioned a report by Deloitte and Touche on the restrictive laws under which French clubs operate compared to other European clubs. The report claims that French clubs have lost ground economically on English, Italian, Spanish and German clubs, and that the reasons are structural: they no longer own their TV rights nor their image rights, nor their registration with the FFF (which is now owned solely by the club's non-profit-making association). They cannot trade their shares on the stock exchange. They are penalised by higher taxes and social costs than elsewhere. The gap in turnover for French and other European clubs has widened since 1995 (Potet 2001f; Mislin 2001). After the change of government in 2002, the new sports minister, the former fencing champion J.-F. Lamour, appeared more sympathetic to the business needs of professional clubs.

Modern Corporate Involvement: J.-M. Aulas

The movement for change within French professional football is being led by chairmen of the bigger clubs, headed by the ones that have come as close as the law will allow to becoming true businesses, and by Jean-Michel Aulas of Lyon in particular. It was not a coincidence that these same big league clubs, in the same year (1990) as the creation of the Federation's financial regulator of professional clubs, set up their own Union of Professional Football Clubs (UCPF). They have ambitions for it to take the place of the present League Management Committee as the real employers' representative body, which would mean cutting themselves off unilaterally from the rest of French football.

The involvement of major private finance in the big clubs has happened in the 1990s. Most of the big-budget clubs are owned or controlled by major companies: PSG (owned by Canal+, and ultimately by Vivendi-Universal), Lyon (controlled by the media group Pathé), Marseille (by the sport and leisure equipment company Adidas), Bordeaux (owned by the television channel M6, and indirectly by the media group CLT-UFA), Strasbourg (by the American sports management group McCormack), Rennes (controlled by the Pinault-Printemps-Redoute distribution and luxury goods group), and Nantes (by la Socpresse of the Hersant/*Figaro* press group). Two further big clubs are Monaco (under the control of the royal family) and Lens (that has managed to spread its ownership around local companies). This situation recalls what Le Graët was warning against in 1991 when he foresaw, if business values were given their head, professional football being limited to the 'Paris region and the three or four big metropolises where there are multinational companies' with no clubs in the provinces (*Libération*, 13 March 1991, cited by Faure and Suaud 1999: 47).

The involvement of big business has coincided with the increase in money coming into football from television rights, sponsorship and merchandising, and from increasing Europeanisation of football through the Champions League, a competition forced on UEFA by the richest European clubs. The new competition replaced the old European (Champions) Cup, where only one team per country (the reigning league champions) could compete. The new competition is open to three or four clubs from the bigger countries (i.e. those with lucrative television audiences) and operates on a mini-league system (until 2003 two successive mini-leagues) before a brief knock-out stage. Since there is no risk of an early exit, this structure guarantees more games for a club and for every national television company that buys the TV rights. UEFA has control over the distribution of TV income and guarantees huge pay-outs for the clubs. In the 1999/2000 season, all 32 participating clubs were guaranteed approximately £1.9 million, plus bonuses for wins and draws, for the first stage matches alone. Playing in the second group stage would bring in over £1 million to a club, even if all matches were lost. The eventual winner could expect overall at least £10 million income from UEFA (Mislin 1999). This has significantly increased the number of games played: in 1976 Saint-Etienne needed only eight matches to qualify for the final; from 1999 the system required 16. Overall 157 matches were played (and televised somewhere) in the 1999/2000 competition. European participation is a much bigger part of a club's life in every sense.

Jean-Michel Aulas: 'a businessman in the world of football'

The chief spokesperson for the neo-liberal approach to football is the influential Jean-Michel Aulas, who took on the chairmanship of an indebted Olympique Lyonnais in 1987 when the club was going nowhere in Division 2. Two seasons later they were promoted as champions. In the meantime they have become financially the healthiest club in the league, a regular in European competitions, with the best overall record in the French league since the mid-1990s, and have finally won the Division 1 championship in 2002, thus fulfilling Aulas's declared ambitions and expectations. On investing in the Brazilian striker Sonny Anderson in 1999 he announced his intentions of winning the championship within three years and to be one of the big names in Europe. His success in sporting terms has been equalled or bettered by his rising to the top of the leadership structures of professional clubs. He imposed himself on the LNF executive by his competence and the clarity and ambition of his views, becoming part of the executive committee, first as treasurer, then as first vice-president and kingmaker to the new puppet president Gérard Bourgoin in 2000, finally ousting the latter in April 2002 when he proved too much of a loose cannon. He is the real leader of the professional league, as well as being one of the key people in the UCPF, which he described as the 'Club Chairmen's Union' ('syndicat') (*Libération*, 13 January 1991, cited in Faure and Suaud 1994b: 25). He also was crucial in the setting up of the Groupe Europe, a lobby group bringing together 12 French clubs that regularly play or have ambitions to play in Europe. He has become in his 15 years' involvement in French professional football the key leader of the 'modernisation' movement, and the lightning conductor for attacks by all those opposed to the arrival of business values in sport, including Minister Buffet and 'archaic' representatives of small clubs and amateur clubs.

Aulas has no background in football, but made his reputation and money through his very successful business career. Coming from an academic family in Lyon, he turned to business having studied economics and computing. He owns 34 per cent of a computing company he founded (CEGID), that has 1,400 employees and a turnover of a billion francs (£100 million). He played sport at a high level in his youth (Division 1 handball) until he suffered a back injury on the ski slopes. His company sponsored Alain Prost in Formula 1. Then a former OL chairman asked him to take over the club. Bernard Tapie helped in the process (Aulas had shares in Tapie holdings). He also took advice from Claude Bez, in whom he recognised 'great qualities'. Rather like these two football businessmen, Aulas calls himself an entrepreneur, a risk taker; he needs to win. He is considered by many to be ambitious, authoritarian, able to take difficult decisions, a natural leader, but is thought cold in human relations, thriving on conflict and challenges, hard working (to the detriment of his family life), and able to keep a lot of different balls in the air at a time. Compared to the jovial Nicollin who can share a beer with his supporters clubs, Aulas is less expansive, and more ill at ease outside the boardroom in which he shines. There was a time when he was thought to have political ambitions regarding the

Lyon Town Hall, but he is not a member of any political party (Ramsay 1999: 6–8).

He has brought his business practices and his contacts to his involvement in club football. He is proud of having run OL on business lines without going into deficit, knows how much elimination in the preliminary round of the Champions League cost them in 1999 (40 million francs), and generally wants more control of the business he runs for OL, whether it be in taking over the management of the stadium or buying it from the city council or even building another, getting control over television rights for individual clubs, being able to raise money through being listed on the Bourse, or having a fairer taxation regime. He was able to bring into the club as biggest shareholder (34 per cent) the chairman of media group Pathé, Jérôme Seydoux (Barth 2000b). There is less discussion of decisions on the League representative body now he is one of the small executive group; he does not like wasting time because of administrative blockages that get in the way. In short, he operates as a 'businessman in the world of football' (Chassepot 2002).

The demand for professional football to be run more like a business, to allow it to compete on equal terms with clubs from other countries, did not begin with Aulas, but he is now leading this debate with the French and European authorities, using consultants like Deloitte and Touche to bolster the arguments. As an elitist, he believes that without the inequalities that come with the creation of an elite, every club will stay small (Barth 2000b). His solutions are to remove any kind of sporting exception and to bring football into line with European-wide business law: 'The only solution to the problem of finding money is the Bourse [the French Stock Exchange]. If Lyon was quoted on the Stock Exchange, that would allow the club to raise 45 million euros [£30 million], which would allow us to run a deficit of as much again' (Rousseau 2002: 6). 'As soon as I solve the problem of television rights and the Bourse, I can run a budget of 900 million francs [£90 million] within two years. We shall then be the equivalent of Juventus or Real Madrid' (Chassepot 2002).

Conclusion

The 1980s saw a change in the values represented within football. The big clubs began trying to buy success by resorting to financial deficits, borrowing against future success, rather than by relying on long-term club and player development. The type of chairman that embodied this approach – Claude Bez or Bernard Tapie – was merely a more modern version of the traditional chairman, just as new forms of enterprise based on financial and other services were replacing traditional forms of manufacturing industry as the basis of the French economy. Small clubs who could not afford to adopt this approach – Faure and Suaud put their local club Nantes in this category – were forced to invest in long-term development and *formation*. They argue that these two approaches were due less to individuals than to a club's structurally dominated position in the world of football. They had no choice but to incarnate a certain type of value, which, it so happens, can be portrayed as occupying the moral high ground. A club that relies on coaching and player development is seen as more respectable than one that goes for the quick fix. This division within club policies sets up a set of related value judgements. It corresponds to the traditional distinction between professional values and amateurism, between the importance of results and a desire to entertain, between win at all costs and the traditional Coubertinian sporting value of taking part being more important than winning (sport for sport's sake). The devotion and altruism of the huge numbers of unpaid volunteers running amateur sport working for the good of the community were often contrasted to the practices of those club officials who had hit the headlines for apparently lining their own pockets through their involvement in professional football. From this moral high ground, legitimated by the 'failures' and the corruption of Bez, Tapie and others, those in positions of power within the Federation (elected in large measure by the grass-roots amateur game) have consistently opposed the desire of the big league clubs to operate in a more deregulated business environment as ordinary profit-making limited companies, which they have consistently condemned as threatening sport's integrity. The long-term Chairman of the Federation, Claude Simonet, elected in 1994, having been a member of the DNCG from 1992, came from a club that relied on *formation* (he was vice-chairman of Nantes), and has always been a staunch defender of the community of interest between the amateur and the professional game and the contribution of the *bénévoles* (Faure and Suaud 1999: 31–34). The Federation was always supported in this approach at the highest level of government over the five years as Minister for Youth and Sport of Mme Marie-George Buffet, a key member of the Communist Party, itself indispensable to the left-wing coalition of the Jospin government of 1997–2002. Indeed Mme Buffet was an even stronger opponent of change than the FFF. The heavy defeat suffered by the left in the 2002 elections removed this ideological opposition to a more free-market approach.

The defenders of amateur values and of the key involvement of the voluntary sector and of notions of public service in football have generally been able to maintain their influence in the institutions of governance of the Federation and until recently on the executive of the professional league. Faure and Suaud (1994b: 24) point out that there has been an objective alliance between the smaller professional clubs and representatives of the amateur leagues who are also attached to the *status quo* in a system that perpetuates their domination in footballing terms by other bigger clubs, but ensures the funding that allows them to survive. The push for change is coming from the self-styled Union of Professional Football Clubs, the big clubs that have already benefited from the investment of large amounts of private money (from media companies and sports management and sports equipment companies). The UCPF challenge the Federation's version of the self-governance of football (which has been given added legal backing by Mme Buffet's legislation). They point to rules that operate in society at large (and particularly in European Union law) but not in football, and reject the idea of sport's exceptionalism. At the same time they claim that fully professional management is the best way to ensure the survival of French professional football as competitive in the new European-wide game. The big French clubs cannot ignore the Europeanisation of football, where the key rewards, both sporting and financial, are to be had. The traditional values of French football that survived throughout the twentieth century are under threat from what Faure and Suaud see as the next stage of the professionalisation of football. This 'complete professionalisation' can only happen through a breakaway of the top clubs from the Federation and therefore from the rest of football. Given the relationship of sport and the State in France, where the latter delegates responsibility for running sport as a public service to the sport's federation, this split could only happen with political blessing. The 2002 elections will be seen as having been critical in this respect, as will the almost simultaneous debacle of the World Cup, which will be discussed in the final chapter.

9

Conclusions: French Exceptionalism vs. Commodification

The strengths and weaknesses of French football are very specific to its cultural and structural differences from its European neighbours, to its situation as an exception that it often finds itself defending in the face of increasing globalisation, standardisation and neo-liberalism (as the French call the ideology of the global free-market). Traditionally the French have believed in regulation, public service values and the importance of the State in intervening to guarantee the common good. An obvious strength is the State-backed youth coaching system that produces excellent young players. It is precisely this system that is in danger from the neo-liberalism of EU law, which has allowed the brawn drain of French internationals out of the domestic league.

This concluding chapter attempts to evaluate the strengths and weaknesses of French football and to tie them in to what is specific to the French approach to its football culture, and more widely to French culture and values in general. But first it presents the latest twist in the saga of the French national team and the fall-out from a 2002 World Cup performance that was variously described as a 'debacle' and a 'fiasco'.

What went wrong in Korea?

The bare facts are that France, in its World Cup group stage, lost its opening match to Senegal, drew the second match with Uruguay, and lost the final game to Denmark, thus becoming the first World Cup holder to be eliminated at such an early stage of the finals. France had scored not a single goal, despite having the top goalscorers of the English, Italian and French leagues in the squad. Inquests offered explanations that went from criticising players' hubris and complacency, to saying it was just something that happens in sport. France had played no competitive matches for too long having qualified automatically as cup holders. The players, representing top foreign clubs in European competitions, were tired from too much football, especially as the World Cup began earlier than usual to avoid the monsoon season. The players had been poorly prepared at the INF where the Federation had spent too much time involving them in sponsorship deals. France's tactical system was now too well known and depended on the ball always going through Zidane, and Zidane missed two of the matches through an injury sustained in what some called an unnecessary friendly match against Korea. The right replacements for Zidane were not available: Pires was missing through injury; Carrière had been left at home. The squad had been insufficiently renewed since 1998: the defenders were all over 30. There was no communication between coach Lemerre and the team. There was no 'patron' on the field, a vital role previously filled by Deschamps. Captain Desailly did not have the temperament of a leader, and had spent too much time on his own business affairs. Henry was played out of position and his frustration got him sent off. Trezeguet hit the underside of the bar and there was no Russian linesman . . .

Back at home, defeat was taken calmly, there were no outbreaks of hooliganism or riots in the streets. Italian reactions to elimination, blaming unfair refereeing, were much less reserved. Jean-Michel Normand (2002) saw the collective Gallic shrug of the shoulders as evidence of a detachment that meant that football had not taken mature root in the French national psyche. 'We get ourselves worked up if we win, but in defeat we think about other things because life goes on.' Perhaps he got it right by saying French football culture is still that of the occasional supporter ('supporteur de circonstance') rather than of a nation truly passionate about sport.

A key effect of France's early elimination from the 2002 World Cup was on the debate about the future direction of French professional football, since it completed a swing in the balance of power between the big professional clubs and the FFF, in two ways. Firstly, the national team's poor performance weakened the influence of the DTN *vis-à-vis* the professional clubs, as evidenced by the DTN candidate for new national team coach being overlooked. Secondly, in its attempts to hold sway against the professional game, the FFF had hitherto been supported by the amateur league and its values. However, officials of the amateur game had become increasingly frustrated about the lack of income coming their way from the FFF whose income had been increasing rapidly, for example from sponsorship rights for the national team. Unfortunately the FFF's expenditure had increased as fast as its income. An official 2001 *Cour des comptes* report had criticised the lack of transparency of the FFF's financial management and its poor management in general. FFF chairman Simonet's position was also weakened since he could no longer counter criticisms by holding up the national team's success as the ultimate justification that all was well in French football.

In Simonet's personal case bad publicity was generated by news of his 'celebrating' France's defeat against Senegal in an expenses-paid meal in the Seoul Sheraton by indulging his taste for hugely expensive French wine – a bottle of Romanée-Conti costing 4,800 euros (£3,200) (*Le Monde*, 9 July 2002). This embarrassing faux-pas apart, he had earlier made the mistake of renewing Roger Lemerre's contract as national team coach before the start of the World Cup finals, prematurely, thus making it harder and more expensive to sack him afterwards. When the press was expecting Lemerre to resign gracefully, Simonet appeared indecisive and was unable to persuade him to go quietly. In July the amateur league representatives defeated Simonet's budget proposals at the annual general meeting of the FFF. He declined to resign. He was forced to look for support on the FFF executive from the big professional clubs. It was no surprise when in late July, once Lemerre had gone back to the DTN, Simonet awarded the position of national team coach not to Raymond Domenech of the DTN, the Under-21 national team coach, but to a candidate from the professional game, the championship winning Lyon coach Jacques Santini. Santini was paradoxically strongly backed by his club chairman, J.-M. Aulas, who had not really got on with his championship-winning coach. A disagreement on policy had already led Santini to relinquish the post of coach for that of technical director at Lyon.

The League began to use its greater freedom of manoeuvre. Its official magazine signalled the antipathy between the League and the FFF by pointing out that the strengths of French football lay in the League and not the national team since 19 out of 23 Bleus played abroad, whereas 19 out of 23 Senegalese played in the French D1, most of whom had emerged from French club academies, and that two Brazilian World Cup winners played for PSG and Lyon (*LNF Infos*, 45 (June 2002): 10–11). During the summer, as if to cock another snook at the FFF and the Ministry, the League announced a change of image, with strong symbolic value. Firstly, the LNF was to change its name to incorporate the word 'professional' and become known as Ligue de football professionnel (LFP). The second innovation was attaching the name of a sponsor to the official title of the two professional divisions: now known as Ligue 1 Orange and Ligue 2 Orange. Given the public service nature of sport and its governing bodies, whose power to run the sport is delegated to them by the State, this association of commerce with the name of a football competition for the first time was significant, and, symbolically, has moved French football a step nearer the situation of professional tennis for example, which is run quite separately from the national federation.

Jean-Michel Aulas had a lot to be pleased about by the end of the summer. His club were champions and had qualified directly for the lucrative Champions

League, he had influenced the appointment of the new national team selector-coach and taken his salary off his club's budget, and had struck a blow for the growing independence of the League. The new sports minister had also declared he would consider reforms in the ownership of club registrations and logos and of television rights, even if he was in no hurry to change the law about quotation of professional clubs on the Stock Exchange. There remained the issues of clubs' use of 'their' stadiums, and the lowering of social costs on players' salaries – which the League intended to raise at the earliest opportunity.

Another effect that may yet have repercussions on French football income is that TF1, the television channel that bought exclusive rights to the 2002 and 2006 World Cups for 168 million euros (£112 million), saw its share price fall by 3.3 per cent after France's draw with Uruguay and is estimated to have lost up to £20 million or 2 per cent of annual advertising income. Its calculations of break-even point had been a semi-final place for France. Time will tell how much this will affect the FFF's future TV income for the national team.

Domestic Fragility in the Global Football Economy

In seasons 2000/01 and 2001/02 no French club reached the quarter-finals of a major European competition. This had not happened since 1989. In the UEFA standings French clubs had still been second to Italy in 1996. In 2002, with Spain ahead of Italy and England and Germany fourth, France was a lonely fifth in the hierarchy of European club football (Vierne 2002). The club ranking affects the number of clubs invited from the different countries into the Champions League – which, given the lucrative rewards coming from participation, is likely to consolidate existing inequalities.

One of the obvious explanations of the relative weakness of French domestic football and its achievements in European tournaments is the exodus of players, which had risen to over a hundred potential first-team players by the season 2001/02. Since the 1990s, as national sporting protectionism has been broken down by the Europeanisation and liberalisation of more and more domains of social life, France has been brought face to face with its semi-peripheral position within the global economy of professional football as it has seen its best players poached by core European footballing nations.

Player Costs and the Post-Bosman Exodus

The exodus began in earnest at the start of the 1996 season following the European Court of Justice's so-called Bosman ruling of December 1995. This confirmed that the law on free movement of workers within the Single European Market applied to football, thus destroying clubs' protectionist contracts and the retain-and-transfer system. Thereafter players could leave a club without a transfer fee once their contract had expired. Initially, individual national football authorities could still impose a transfer fee for movement between clubs within the same national Football Association, so in effect the ruling encouraged movement between European nations and encouraged the import and export of players (Miège 1996: 75–79). The end of the 1996 season, following the shop window for international players provided by the European Nations Championship in England, saw a large number of top players moving club. Either they were out of contract and were able to offer their services free of transfer fee, and therefore negotiate far higher wages from a new club, or clubs were more inclined to sell contracted players and claim a transfer fee before the contract was up.

French clubs were in a weak position in terms of offering competitive wages compared to European neighbours, for structural reasons. In addition to their low attendances, and lower income in all respects, France imposes high employment costs and corporate taxes on all employers, including professional football clubs. High French labour overheads (what the French call social costs) relative to other European economies is a general constraint for French companies. The whole of the French national health and social security system, plus the retirement pension system, is financed, not from the central state budget (except where there is a deficit) but from contributions from employers and workers as a percentage of salary. The French health service is good and is heavily used, so it is costly, and pensions have gone up in line with wages rather than, as in Britain since the 1980s, only in line with prices. National insurance contributions are therefore very high in France, for both workers and employers. The NI contributions of employer and worker add to the total labour cost. Studies comparing the tax and NI overheads for players and clubs in the five major European football countries show France is the odd one out, and suffers a net handicap *vis-à-vis* other European clubs, which explains the difficulty of retaining French players or indeed attracting top European players. French income tax is lower for married players with two or more children, but not for single men or married ones with one or no children. It should be borne in mind, therefore, that the examples quoted in Tables 9.1 and 9.2 of unmarried childless players were chosen by the players' union and the LNF clubs to show the disparity with the rest of Europe at its greatest.

The figures in Table 9.1 show how high social costs penalise French employer clubs compared to those in its major competitors. They show that, in 1996, a *net* monthly salary of about 50,000 francs received by a player cost a French club over three times as much due to tax and social costs. A similar net salary cost German and Spanish clubs just over twice the amount received by the player, and British and Italian clubs just under twice. This means that in order to ensure

Table 9.1 *European comparisons of player employment costs (1996). The example used is of an unmarried player with no dependent children – on a base of a gross monthly salary of 100,000 francs (£120,000 p.a.)*

	France	Germany	Spain	Italy	UK
National Insurance deductions	15,937	5,085	960	1,740	1,440
Employer's contributions	55,150	5,085	5,158	3,610	10,200
Net income before income tax	84,063	94,915	99,040	98,260	98,560
Monthly income tax payable	34,130	49,030	47,870	41,395	36,084
Player's net monthly income after income tax	49,933	45,885	51,170	56,865	62,476
Total cost of above salary to club	155,150	105,085	105,158	103,610	110,200
Net salary as percentage of total cost to club	32.2%	43.7%	48.7%	54.9%	56.7%
Total cost to club as percentage of player's net salary	310.7%	229.0%	205.5%	182.2%	176.4%
Relative cost to club at base of 100	**100**	**73.7**	**66.1**	**58.6**	**56.8**

Source: The table combines an Arthur Andersen study and a French study by M. Bérard (1997), first published in the French players' union Newsletter as 'Clubs professionnels de football: une comparaison européenne', *Profession Football*, 22, (October–November 1996), and reprinted in 'Economie du sport', *Problèmes économiques*, 2503 (15 January 1997): 29–31.

an equivalent salary to Marco Simone (the one major star to be attracted to the French league in 1997/98), PSG had to find half as much again as his previous Italian employer to cover the extra social costs and taxes.

French clubs have in the meantime increased their income from spectators and from television rights in absolute terms, but more recent figures show that they have not caught up in comparative terms. They are still at a serious structural disadvantage in their ability to finance top players' salaries. The Deloitte and Touche study (Table 9.2), commissioned in 2001 by the LNF, showed first of all that the gap had considerably widened for the big clubs in terms of turnover. The top five English and top seven Italian teams had turnover approaching twice that of the top five French clubs, and the top five Spanish and German clubs had turnovers of one-third more than the French. Secondly, the effect of social and tax costs on employment had not improved. Taking these into account for player costs in 2001, a French club had to pay 100 euros for every 58 euros paid by an English or Italian club to ensure the same net take-home pay for players. To employ international players, the gap between French and other European clubs has therefore widened since 1996. French clubs are falling behind in their ability to attract or retain top stars.

Table 9.2 *European comparisons of player employment costs (2001). The examples used are of an unmarried player with no dependent children – on a base of a net take-home pay of an international class player, an average D1 player, and a good D2 player (in euros)*

	France	Germany	Spain	Italy	UK
Net annual take-home salary for international class player	1,800,000	1,800,000	1,800,000	1,800,000	1,800,000
Gross annual salary	4,302,184	3,675,687	3,442,621	3,354,776	2,986,487
Total cost to club	5,728,891	3,682,519	3,453,090	3,370,741	3,341,879
Relative cost to club at base of 100	**100**	**64.3**	**60.3**	**58.8**	**58.3**
Net annual take-home salary for an average D1 player:	219,590	219,590	219,590	219,590	219,590
Relative cost to club at base of 100	100	66.7	61.8	62.0	59.0
Net annual take-home salary for a good D2 player:	96,513	96,513	96,513	96,513	96,513
Relative cost to club at base of 100	100	74.1	67.5	70.5	63.0

Source: Deloitte and Touche report to LNF (in G. Mislin, 'Les clubs français face à la concurrence européenne', *LNF Infos*, 40 (December 2001): 2–5)

In view of the unequal bargaining and remunerating power of French clubs, as seen in Table 9.2, it is not surprising that many top French players left for Italy, England, Spain and Germany. Estimates of players contracts in 1997 showed, with salaries, bonuses and advertising contracts included of the 19 top French earners, only five were playing in France: four at PSG and one at Monaco (Perrot 1997: 46). Estimations of monthly salary in the 2001/02 season showed Desailly at Chelsea and Vieira at Arsenal both earning 2 million francs (£200,000) net, Barthez at Manchester United earning 1.6 million francs net, and Zidane at Real Madrid earning between 3.3 and 4 million francs net per month. The top earner at PSG, the Nigerian Okocha, earned a salary of 1.1 million francs. The top French player's monthly salary at PSG was 0.7 million francs (Ambrosiano 2002a: 34–35).

The Youth Exodus

The deskilling of French football has been even more keenly felt by the loss of the most talented products of its youth academies. The issue that worries French clubs more than anything is how to retain young players in France until the end of their training period, which is considered to be beyond the age of majority. The cost to a club of youth training is considerable, and yet there have been a number of cases of young players leaving their academies to join foreign clubs for little or no compensation to the club that has invested in them. The new club Charter and the Buffet laws have attempted to oblige young players to sign a three-year contract with the club that has trained them, but the post-Bosman laws make it difficult legally to prevent a young player going abroad, even before their eighteenth birthday provided the parents accompany them. Nicolas Anelka was one of the first to be poached when still a *stagiaire* (apprentice) aged seventeen – from PSG by Arsène Wenger for Arsenal for half a million pounds. As part of the Paris apprentice system he was earning 3,800 francs per month (approx. £5,000 per year) at the time. PSG tried to keep him by offering to put him on a bit more than the standard starting salary according to the Professional Footballers Charter. He bid them up, but the salary overheads of French clubs and social costs meant that Arsenal could beat their offer. Anelka's move set a worrying precedent. He is a product of the National Football Institute at Clairefontaine, where he trained from age 12 to 15, before entering the PSG Centre de Formation. His departure is against the French Federation's Professional Footballers Charter agreed between the Players Union and French clubs. But the Charter is only valid between French clubs (Ramsay 1997). What was most galling to the French club was that Arsenal sold Anelka on two and a half years later to Real Madrid for £22 million. The fact that PSG bought back Anelka from Spain in 2000 for about the same price was ironic, but suggested at least that the top French clubs were doing their best to catch up with their neighbours. To add insult to this irony, Anelka then had to be sold to Manchester City in 2002 for little more than half that fee.

A further example that was called 'shameful' by the president of the LNF again involved Wenger. Jérémie Aliadière, not quite sixteen, left his *préformation* at Clairefontaine to go to London with his parents and sign a seven-year contract with Arsenal in 1999 (Butterlin 1999). There is a fear that France's semi-peripheral position within the global football market is transforming it into a nursery country, feeding the major footballing nations, in a new form of colonisation. There have already been agreements between clubs that officialise this kind of relationship. Arsenal entered into a five-year agreement with Saint-Etienne in 1998 to exchange trainees (see Eastham 1999: 72–73). As part of an agreement with Le Havre, in 2001, Liverpool signed the two top scorers from the French World Cup winning under-17 side, Anthony Le Tallec and Florent Sinama-Pongolle, with a view to their joining Liverpool in 2003 (Labrunie 2001c). Summer 2002, a slack year for transfers throughout Europe because of financial uncertainties, none the less saw 17 more players leaving the French League for English clubs, including a number of Senegalese who had impressed in the World Cup, such as El-Hadji Diouf from Lens to Liverpool. Lille lost key players Cygan to Arsenal and Bruno Cheyrou to Liverpool, and cash-strapped PSG sold Distin, Anelka, E. Cissé, B. Mendy and Okocha (*France Football*, 6 August 2002).

Strengths and Weaknesses of French Football

The major weaknesses of French football have been related to its late and incomplete professionalisation, its small number of modern metropolises and the lack of interest in football in the capital city until recent years, its lack of an ingrained supporter tradition and the financial weakness of its major clubs that some chairmen have been tempted to overcome by sharp practice and corruption. Its recent strengths have come from its long-term interest in football as an international phenomenon, its State-backed coaching systems that have produced many technically gifted young players and influential coaches, and recent support from domestic media companies and the bigger French private companies.

Football entered the French national consciousness late compared to other European nations. It was imported by Anglophile French elites and by English and Scots exiles in the late nineteenth century and the early twentieth, and remained an amateur game until the 1930s. Since it remained amateur it was not dropped by the middle classes and remained less class defined than in Britain. Its popularity between the wars in small industrial towns also meant that it was adopted for their factory teams by industrialists, whose pressure led the football authorities to accept professionalism. The model of the professional club therefore tended to reflect the paternalistic structures and family values of the small factory. The strength of the professional game long reflected the socio-economic geography of France's first (partial) industrialisation as football was adopted as a way of promoting local and regional identity in small industrial towns dotted across the country.

The Second World War and Occupation was a set back for its development, to the extent that the professional game had to begin again after the Liberation. This is part of the explanation for the term 'incomplete professionalisation' that has been coined to describe the organisation of football in France. Another factor was the availability of middle-class players who wished to play part-time in the pre- and post-war periods. Dominant British social values could happily allow the growth of football to depend on individual initiative, and its organisation and regulation could be left to autonomous bodies operating independently of the State and local government as businesses. In post-1944 France, on the other hand, football's governing structures and clubs have been shaped by the French State's concept of the public service and voluntary community service (*le bénévolat*), and by Republican interventionism, as opposed to laissez-faire individualism. From the 1990s onwards this has been a bone of contention between the professional League and the French governing body, the FFF, whose authority has had official State backing, since the State delegates its authority to the federations to organise sports in its name. The State and local authorities have taken the notion of public service seriously by regulating and financing sports facilities and sports clubs, including professional football clubs, to a greater extent than in the rest of Europe, thus reflecting the dominant view that amateur and professional sport are essentially part of the same 'movement' or the same 'family' and should remain so. This continuity between grass-roots and elite sport is another factor in football's incomplete professionalisation.

Whereas small or medium-sized towns still make themselves felt in the top two divisions, none the less, in the contemporary era of multinational companies, sports sponsorship, and global commercialism, French football is dominated by the big city clubs. The interests of the local authorities, with their executive mayors, coincide with those of the more ambitious city clubs, who share a desire to count on a European or even global level as the context of the nation-state loses its primacy. The French clubs with the biggest budgets are now from the major conurbations of Paris, Lyon, Marseille, Bordeaux, and the north of France, where Lens's supremacy is being challenged by Lille, in a battle between the old industrial club and the modern city club. Small town clubs are not generally attractive to major sponsors. European regional capitals on the other hand are part of a much bigger network of interests. France's weakness in this sense is that it has fewer big conurbations than England or Germany. Paris of course is on an altogether bigger scale than the provincial cities, and another weakness for football has been that Paris was a post-war football desert until the late 1970s when PSG was implanted and, with serious political and commercial support, became the biggest French club of the 1990s.

French clubs have only recently attracted numbers of spectators that remotely compare with other major European footballing countries. This followed remarkable growth in the popularity of the game in the 1990s as television coverage heightened the sport's profile and French club teams and, more especially, the national team made their mark in international competitions.

There are, however, great differences between the best supported and the worst. Football support has not had a tradition to build on, except in one or two of the old-style clubs like Saint-Etienne and Lens, or in Marseille where its local economic and psychological particularities found expression in support of the successes and failures of OM. Traditional lack of passion compounded by competition from new lifestyles in the newly affluent 1960s was overcome in the 1980s by a new form of fandom as militancy, as a search for an identity that was not an inherited one. Supporter cultures still reflect influences from Britain and Italy. Relatively innocuous but highly visible forms of 'hooliganism' have been associated with PSG fans, who had to invent themselves and their Ultra fan culture from the late 1970s into the 1980s. French club football is still more fragile in its implantation and less consistently successful at European level than its neighbours.

Historically France has made an important contribution to the development and organisation of football as an international and world game – beyond its importance as a world footballing power. French administrators and journalists took leading roles in the organisation of the world-governing body FIFA, the creation of a World Cup, a European Nations Cup, and a European club championship. This is reflected in the interest taken by French governments in using sport as a tool of international diplomacy, a way of expressing French grandeur and expertise. This official attitude to sport pre-dated Gaullism and still lives on after de Gaulle, for example in the very Gaullist organisation of the 1998 World Cup, in its planning, its execution and its objectives, which went far beyond a desire for success on the pitch.

The key factor in French footballing success in recent years is generally recognised to be French coaching systems, that have produced a generation of highly talented players and managers. The systems include youth training in the INF and in professional clubs, the development of national and regional youth training centres for thirteen to fifteen-year-olds in the 1990s by Gérard Houllier as National Technical Director, and the interest and support of the State in the systematic training of coaches using a highly centralised system of qualifications. Fortuitously, in the post-Bosman era, products of this highly selective elite schooling found that they could go abroad to perfect their skills and toughen their resolve while earning far more money than French clubs could pay. Through this trend French clubs have each lost an average of five or six potential first team players who now earn their living in other European leagues. This phenomenon undoubtedly helped the French international side by honing their competitiveness and experience while playing in the top European competitions, at least until the proliferation of games got the better of some players' fitness and sharpness.

The most idolised coach in France was of course the World Cup winner Aimé Jacquet, who along with Zinedine Zidane had to bear the burden of becoming national icons. Around both of them in their different ways the media built ideological constructions about the meaning of the 1998 World Cup victory as a political fable that promoted the idea of the complementarity of old and new values in the new 'France qui gagne' and the success of French-style integration. The World Cup victory became a means of shedding a national inferiority complex and rejoicing in a modern ethnically diverse national identity. Players had achieved hero status in France before, and always by performances for 'les Bleus' rather than for club sides, since football had imprinted itself on the national consciousness as a vector of national values and identity through the national side. Raymond Kopa and Michel Platini achieved heroic status in this way in their time, but their status was also enhanced by their performances in clubs in Spain and Italy, as if they were regarded as French ambassadors representing their country abroad. While dominating their eras, their significance was of a lesser order than that of Zidane. They had helped establish in the nation's mind the idea that playing with style was more important than winning, an idea that Jacquet's side dispelled. Zidane was arguably no more exceptional a player than his two illustrious predecessors, but to some, as a symbol of a multicultural France at ease with itself, and to others a role model of what could be achieved in a socially fractured society, he came to represent the central social and political issues of post-colonial France. He articulated through football the trauma of Franco-Algerian relations and the hope of reconciliation.

Modern footballers have become stars through television, and the impact of the 1998 World Cup was mainly a television-led phenomenon. This was not exclusively so, since in 1998 quality newspaper coverage of the event was important in forming opinion. However, the large number of big screens in cities across France allowed a sense of the imagined national community to take on some reality as thousands gathered to experience the matches together. In a real sense television has changed the way football is experienced. It has certainly brought football to many for the first time. But, in the era of pay-TV, football is becoming for most people a home entertainment commodity. What was a live spectacle expressing local community identity has been transformed into a television-mediated expression of commodity and commercial values. Football has become crucial to the commercial success of television, just as television has made itself indispensable to the economics of football. Football sells subscriptions for Canal+ and advertising for TF1, who in turn have made football clubs and players rich. Exclusive television rights are the key new revenue stream that has turned football into a huge business. Canal+ in particular has a huge stranglehold on French club football, owning PSG, dominating television rights and involving itself in many other aspects of football's production line. The question is, since the French TV audience's interest in football is a recent and perhaps fragile one, can Canal+'s finances, which for reasons extraneous to football were showing for the first time in 2002 signs of fragility, withstand a loss of audience interest. Equally, can French football stand a sudden loss of television income?

The business side of French professional football has had its many ups and downs. The 1980s saw a new set of values enter clubs with a new generation of businessmen chairmen. They tried to buy success by using modern business methods, at the same time as using football to promote the image of their own companies, and of any other companies willing to pay to use football's image. They felt that commercial success would inevitably follow success on the pitch. To achieve this, OM at least was prepared to use bribery. Success of a kind was achieved, domestically and in Europe. By the 1990s French club football had certainly reached a level where it was for the first time in history more or less comparable with any in Europe as measured in European competitions. However, the most prominent chairmen, Bez and Tapie, those responsible for the success of Girondins de Bordeaux and OM, fell from their pedestals and were convicted of corruption. It may be said, as a (dangerous?) generalisation, that the new businessmen chairmen of big city clubs seem more interested in business success than in success on the field, or rather they feel that business success is a prerequisite for footballing success, which is measured by and rewarded by success in Europe. Their recipe for business success is a level playing field with their European opponents in terms of being able to operate according to the same trading rules as any other business, in other words to complete the professionalisation of French football. In this struggle they have had serious opponents: the football establishment dominated by amateur values and ministers who have been keen to protect French sport's social role and 'public service mission'. Neither of the latter have been able to contemplate a break between grass-roots sport and professional sport. Hence Minister Buffet, even more reluctantly than her predecessors, would only grant legal company status to professional clubs if hedged around with a number of constraints to prevent the profit motive from becoming the key factor within sport. The defenders of the traditional values of French football that survived throughout the twentieth century are resisting the next stage of the professionalisation of football. So entrenched are the positions that it may take a revolutionary change such as a breakaway from the French Federation by the big professional clubs. The sociologist Michel Crozier, in his book *La Société bloquée* (1970) demonstrated that in many domains of French society evolutionary reform was more difficult to achieve than explosive changes of a radical nature. If his thesis is applied to football, it may appear that such a revolutionary break is just around the corner, or may already have started. The twelve months following the start of the 2001/02 football season saw many harbingers of change: the post-September 11 stock-market falls, the reminder of the problems in the *banlieues* in the France–Algeria 'friendly', the shock of the French elections when the extreme-right appeared to matter again politically, the World Cup debacle in Korea, and the missed opportunities for celebrating the 1998 spirit. National optimism and self-confidence within French football and French society in general took a knock. Does this herald retrenchment or radical change?

Vive la Différence?

The State, in France, has been the key guarantor of sporting values against the intrusion of market forces. It has given key support to the football establishment. FFF officials have usually been able to claim a double source of authority: one from below through elections from within the 'football family', the other from above by delegation from the State. Their position has been further legitimised by the voluntary and apparently altruistic nature of their involvement in a mission that is recognised by the State as a public service. Faure and Suaud describe their situation as one of structurally determined self-interest, leading to a perpet-uation of the *status quo*. They point to 'the hijacking' of public money in the way that public funds have been distributed to sport, giving football 42 per cent of the total local authority funds going to sport when football has only 17 per cent of all registered sports practitioners. Within this funding given to football, 70.7 per cent went to the elite side of the sport and only 15.5 per cent to amateur clubs in structural grants, 5.7 per cent to 'formation', and 3.7 per cent to events (official Ministry figures for 1992, cited in Faure and Suaud 1999: 242). This has been an incentive for the small professional clubs to remain objective supporters of the *status quo*. The big clubs and the small clubs were divided by the issue of youth coaching and the exodus. By supporting a more liberal and deregulated approach the big clubs will inevitably accelerate the youth exodus that the smaller clubs, the Federation and the Ministry want to stop. However, the big clubs are generally more often 'buying clubs' rather than 'clubs formateurs', so they have comparatively less interest in 'formation'.

Whereas professional football clubs have become part of the entertainment industry, and there is an enormous gap in practice between the worlds of amateur and professional football, the governance of the sport retains the notion of a pyramid with grass roots at the bottom and the elite at the top, and an unbroken continuity between the two. At the same time, as Faure and Suaud put it (1999: 244), understandings of the notion of 'professionalism' within French football have not evolved as in other domains where the term connotes 'competence' and 'reliability'. The FFF and the Ministry are suspicious of the business values associated with professional football; they are seen as a danger to the public service mission of sport. The UCPF on the other hand want to be recognised as 'professionals' rather than feeling mistrusted and 'de-professionalised'; they want the freedom to run their own affairs. The professional clubs have thus decided to contest the domestic French interpretation of 'sport as an exception'. They are challenging the internal laws of the way sport is organised by having recourse to the notion that everyone is equal before the law. As the President of the UCPF, Gervais Martel (chairman of Lens) declared: 'We do not want to be given lessons in right and wrong: amateurism is not a sufficient guarantee of good conduct, professionalism is much more professional than people imagine. In a word, we want to be considered like adults capable of being in charge of our own destiny' (Martel 1993, quoted in Faure and Suaud 1999: 248).

France is the country that has protested most loudly against the effects of globalisation in terms of the economy and in terms of culture and language, and invented the idea of 'l'exception culturelle'. The struggle within French football between the governing body and the Ministry on the one hand and the big professional clubs on the other may usefully be seen in these terms. It is a battle between those whose power is exercised in and is dependent on the national context and who believe in an 'exception sportive', and those who have to operate within the commercial realities of the world of professional football and wish to be free to operate according to the rules of the global marketplace. Since club football at the elite level now operates in a European not to say global dimension, and since professional football is now clearly subject to European competition law and to employment laws on freedom of movement within the EU (the Bosman ruling), the French approach to sport and to the dependent position of its professional football clubs finds itself in contradiction with European law which rejects the notion of the 'sporting exception'. The belief in the role of the Republican State as both protector of the rights of the individual and the ultimate judge of the public interest and of public good is so ingrained into French culture that it is difficult to accept that a national sports governing body or a professional football league could derive its own legitimacy from its intrinsic activities (Faure and Suaud 1999: 254–256). France is a highly centralised ('Jacobin') State, whereas Germany is highly decentralised. France is highly statist whereas Britain is highly libertarian. French traditional culture finds it difficult to accept that sport can essentially be dependent on individual initiative and its organisation and regulation left to autonomous bodies operating independently of the State. The current debates within French football, then, go much deeper than issues to do with sport. They go to the heart of French society and culture, and the notion of French exceptionalism. How long will this 'différence' manage to live on? In his perceptive analysis of 'The French Exception', Andrew Jack described France as 'a modern country trying to wrest itself from a post-war corporatist straitjacket . . . while its private sector has changed in recent years, the same cannot be said of its public sector' (Jack 1999: 277–278). Jack might also have included the voluntary sector in his judgement on the public sector. Despite all predictions of its forthcoming demise, the French exception has none the less proved remarkably durable.

Appendix

Table A.1 *Structure of French Football Leagues at Senior Level (2002/03)*

National competitions (professional and semi-professional):

Championnat de football professionnel Ligue 1 (20 clubs from 2002/03, previously 18)
Championnat de football professionnel Ligue 2 (20 clubs)
  These two divisions are run by the Ligue de Football professionnel (LFP, previously LNF).
Championnat national (20 clubs)
  A three-up, three-down promotion/relegation rule operates between the top three divisions. A club relegated into the National may retain its professional status for two years.

Amateur competitions:

Championnat de France Amateur 1 (CFA1)
  Four regional pools of 18 clubs, each winner gaining promotion to the National.
Championnat de France Amateur 2 (CFA2)
  Eight regional pools of 16 clubs (reserve teams of professional clubs play in the CFA).

Regional leagues:
22 *'Ligues' in Metropolitan France*:
  Alsace, Aquitaine, Atlantique, Auvergne, Basse-Normandie, Bourgogne, Bretagne, Centre, Centre-Ouest, Champagne-Ardenne, Corse, Franche-Comté, Languedoc-Roussillon, Lorraine, Maine, Méditerranée, Midi-Pyrénées, Nord-Pas de Calais, Normandie, Paris-Ile de France, Picardie, Rhône-Alpes;

---

9 *'Ligues' in Overseas departments and dependencies*:
  Wallis et Futuna, Guadeloupe, Guyane, Martinique, Nouvelle-Calédonie, Réunion, Mayotte, St Pierre et Miquelon, Polynésie française.

Each regional league has four divisions:
  Division d'Honneur (14 clubs)
  This is the top league at regional level; winners are promoted into CFA2.

The lower divisions of a regional league are:
  Division d'Honneur régionale (pools A and B by area),
  Promotion d'Honneur (3 area pools),
  Promotion de ligue (5 district pools).

District leagues:
102 *districts*
  They correspond roughly to the administrative *département* structures. Most of France's 20,000 amateur clubs play at his level, in different divisions:
In each district league the divisions are called:
  Excellence; Première division; Promotion Première Division; Promotion 2ème Division; 3ème Division.

Company football:
  There is also a *Championnat national du Football d'entreprise*: for company teams, also playing by *Région* and *District*, and a *Coupe nationale d'entreprise*).

Source: FFF web site http://www.fff.fr/

Table A.2 *Structure of French football by Age Group (2002/03)*

Age group structures:
  Débutants: 6–7 years
  Poussins: 8–9 years
  Benjamins: 10–11 years
  13 ans (or *Minimes*): 12–13 years
  15 ans (or *Cadets*): 14–15 years
  17 ans (or *Juniors*): 16–17 years
  Seniors espoirs: 18–20 years
  Seniors: 18–34 years
  Seniors-Vétérans: 35 years and over

Youth Competitions:

Championnat national des 18 ans
  A separate national competition for youth sides of professional clubs
  and others, organised into four regional groups of 14 clubs.

Challenge Gambardella
  National cup competition for clubs at Junior level – 16–17 years old.

Championnat national des 16 ans
  National competition for youth sides, organised into six regional groups
  of 12 clubs.

Championnat fédéral des 14 ans
  A competition for youth sides, organised into ten regional groups of
  12 clubs.

Challenge Lucien-Poinsignon
  National cup competition for selections of 14–15 year olds (*Cadets*)
  representing each Ligue.

Coupe nationale des Poussins
  National competition for 8–9 year olds – open to club sides.

There are also various Regional and District competitions at 18, 17, 15
and 13 years of age; and at *Benjamin* level: various 9-a-side and 7-a-
side competitions).

Sources: Thomas *et al.* (1991: 68–70) and FFF web site http://www.fff.fr/

Table A.3 *Structure of Women's Football in France (2002/03)*

National women's competitions:

Championnat de France féminin D1
   National league of 12 clubs – the top four play off in a further challenge cup phase, le Challenge de France.

Championnat de France féminin D2
   Two regional groups of ten clubs.

Championnat de France féminin D3
   Four regional groups of ten clubs.

Coupe fédérale féminine 16 ans
   Under-17s in 12 regional groups of four clubs.

Coupe nationale des 16 ans

Coupe fédérale féminine 13 ans

Challenge des Districts 13 ans à 7
   Under-14 teams playing seven-a-side.

There are also various regional and district level and youth competitions.

Source: FFF web site http://www.fff.fr/

Bibliography

'Affluences: Nouveau record historique!', *LNF Infos*, 35 (May 2001).

'L'Afrique des coaches français', *France Football*, 2881 (26 June 2001): 36–38.

Alvis, I. (1994), 'Communication: privilégier les habitants', *Le Monde* (28 February): 2.

Ambrosiano, M. (2002a), 'Qui sont les vrais gagnants du foot business?', *Grand Stade*, 2 (February): 30–46.

—— (2002b), 'OM Milan AC 1991. Et l'élève dépassa le maître', *Grand Stade*, 2 (February): 98–101.

Anderson, B. (1983), *Imagined Communities: Reflections on the Origins and Spread of Nationalism*, London: Verso.

Andreff, W. and J.-F. Nys (1997), *Economie du sport* (3rd edn), Paris: PUF.

Armstrong, G. and R. Giulianotti (eds) (1997), *Entering the Field: New Perspectives on World Football*, Oxford: Berg.

—— (1999), *Football Cultures and Identities*, London: Macmillan.

Arnaud, L. and P. Arnaud (eds) (1996), 'Le sport: jeu et enjeu de société', *Problèmes politiques et sociaux* (*Documentation française*), 777 (13 December).

Assouly, A. (2000), 'Scandal on the Canebière', in Rühn (ed.) (2000b): 225–236.

'Au Top 50 JDD, « Zizou » le préféré des Français', *Journal du dimanche* (6 August 2000): 1, 30.

Augustin, J.-P. (1990), 'La percée du football en terre de rugby', *Vingtième siècle* (April–June): 97–109.

Authier, C. (2001), *Foot-business*, Paris: Hachette Littératures.

Baddiel, D. (2000), 'Unjust rewards: Harald Schumacher's foul on Patrick Battiston, World Cup 1982', in Rühn (ed.) (2000b): 37–41.

Ball, P. and P. Shaw (1996), *The Umbro Book of Football Quotations*, London: Ebury Press.

Barcilon, R. and S. Breuil (1997), *Sport et télévision 1991–1996. Bilan de six années de régulation*, Paris: CSA (Les Etudes du CSA).

Barker, C. (1997), *Global Television. An Introduction*, Oxford: Blackwell.

Barnes, J. (2000), 'Terms of endurance', *Guardian Saturday Review* (26 August): 1, 3.

Barnett, S. (1990), *Games and Sets: the Changing Face of Sport on Television*, London: British Film Institute.

—— (1995), 'Sport', in A. Smith, *Television. An International History*, Oxford: OUP, 85–96.

Barth, E. (2000a), 'Marseille: les gradins de la colère', *Le Monde* web (15 January).

—— (2000b), 'Pour Jean-Michel Aulas, «l'inégalité de l'élitisme» est une fatalité', *Le Monde* (29 February): 30.

—— (2000c), 'Le Paris Saint-Germain s'est donné les moyens de ses ambitions', *Le Monde* (28 July): 19.

—— (2000d), 'La défaite face au PSG accentue le climat de crise à l'OM', *Le Monde* (14 October).

Baup, E. (2001), [Interview], *France Football* (2 January): 8.

Bayeux, P. (1996), *Le Sport et les collectivités territoriales*, Paris: PUF.

Beaud, S. and G. Noiriel (1990), 'L'immigration dans le football', *Vingtième siècle* (April–June): 83–96.

Benamou, G.-M. (1998), 'Le hussard de la France qui bouge', *Evénement du jeudi* (16–22 July): 3.

Berthou, T. (1999a), *Dictionnaire historique des clubs de football français, Tome 1: Abbeville – Montpellier*, Créteil: Pages de Foot.

—— (1999b), *Dictionnaire historique des clubs de football français, Tome 2: Mulhouse – White-Rovers*, Créteil: Pages de Foot.

Bertrand, O. (2001), 'Les patrons de Lyon font du foot leurs affaires', *Libération* (11 October).

Bezat, J.-M. (2000), 'Un texte moins consensuel que les précédents', *Le Monde* (1 February).

Biétry, C. (1996), [Interview], 'L'argent du football rallume la guerre des chaînes', *Le Monde* (14–15 April): 4.

Blair, O. (2000), 'A Geordie conquers the heart of the South of France: Chris Waddle plays for OM', in Rühn (ed.) (2000b): 158–166.

Blaquart, F. (2001), 'Qu'est-ce que la préformation?', *Fédération française de football website* (pages on 'Formation'), http://www.fff.fr/

Boniface, P. (ed.) (1998), *Géopolitique du football*, Paris: Editions Complexe.

Bordenave, Y. (2001), 'Le «banni» n'a toujours pas honoré toutes ses créances', *Le Monde* (5 April): 27.

Borja, J. and M. Castells (1997), *Local and Global: The Management of Cities in the Information Age*, London: Earthscan.

Bouchard, J.-P. (2001), 'Paris-SG. Maman, j'a raté ma saison 2', *France Football*, 2874 (8 May): 22–32.

—— and A. Constant (1996), *Un Siècle de football*, Paris: Calmann-Lévy.

—— and J. Harscoët (2001), 'Périls en la demeure', *France Football*, 2874 (8 May): 33.

Bourcier, B. *et al.* (2001), 'Comment devenir un vrai pro?', *Planète Foot*, 97 (March): 12–24.

Bourdieu, P. (1980), 'Comment peut-on être sportif?', *Questions de sociologie*, Paris: Editions de Minuit, 173–195.

—— (1999), 'The State, economics and sport', in Dauncey and Hare (eds) (1999b): 15–21.

Bourg, J.-F. (1986), *Football Business*, Paris: Olivier Orban.

—— (1989), 'Le marché du travail sportif', in W. Andreff (ed.) (1989), *Economie politique du sport*, Paris: Dalloz.

—— (1991), 'Aspects économiques des relations entre le sport et la télévision', *Médiaspouvoirs* (July–September).

—— (1994), *L'Argent fou du sport*, Paris: La Table Ronde.

—— (1997), 'Le prix de la performance', *Problèmes économiques*, 2503 (January): 10–13.

—— and J.-J. Gouguet (1998), *Economie du sport*, Paris: La Découverte.

Bourzat, N. and J.-C. Breillat (2001), 'De l'EUSRL à la SASP en passant par la SAOS', *LNF Infos*, 33 (March): 5–7.

—— (1996), 'Le mouvement sportif regrette le désengagement financier de l'Etat', *Le Monde* (12 November): 22.

Bozonnet, J.-J. (1998), 'Aimé Jacquet, le plus glorieux des humbles serviteurs du football', *Le Monde* (12–13 July): 16.

Brochen, J.-M. (2000), 'L'opposition se ligue', *France Football* (4 July): 24.

—— (2001a), 'Un changement d'ère', *France Football* (27 March): 6–7.

—— (2001b), 'Deschamps: « Monaco, quel cadeau! »', *France Football* (27 July): 4–7.

—— (2001c), 'Aston: « C'est par le journal que j'ai appris ma sélection »', *France Football* (25 December): 17.

Brohm, J.-M. (1992), *Sociologie politique du sport*, Presses universitaires de Nancy.

—— (1998), *Les Shootés du stade*, Paris: Editions Paris-Méditerranée.

—— (2000), 'La loi de la jungle, stade suprême du sport', *Le Monde diplomatique* (June): 26–27.

Bromberger, C. (1998), *Football, la bagatelle la plus sérieuse du monde*, Paris: Bayard Editions.

—— A. Hayot and J.-M. Mariottini (1987), 'La passion pour le football à Marseille et à Turin', *Terrain*, 8 (April).

—— A. Hayot and J.-M. Mariottini (1995), *Le Match de football: ethnologie d'une passion partisane à Marseille, Naples et Turin*, Paris: Editions de la Maison des Sciences de l'Homme.

Broussard, P. (1990), *Génération supporter, enquête sur les ultras du football*, Paris: Laffont.

Bruna, E. (2001), 'Les supporters du PSG ont enfin la parole', *Le Parisien* (9 April): 2–3.

Bureau, J. (ed.) (1986), 'L'amour foot. Une passion planétaire', *Autrement*, 80 (May).

Butterlin, J.-M. (1999), 'A nous le petit Français', *L'Equipe* (27 January): 7.

Caffin, V. (2000), 'Le championnat de tous les records', *Journal du dimanche* (30 July): 17.

Caja, J., M. Mouraret and A. Benet (1996), *Guide de la préparation au brevet d'éducateur sportif 1er degré* (5th edn), Paris: Vigot (collection Sport et Enseignement).

Callède, J.-P. (2000), *Les Politiques sportives en France. Eléments de sociologie historique*, Paris: Editions Economica.

Castells, M. (1996), *The Rise of the Network Society*, London: Blackwell.

'Le championnat 2000 jugé par son public', *France Football* (7 January 2000).

Chassepot, P. (2002), 'L'incorrigible Monsieur Aulas', *Le Journal du dimanche* (17 February): 25.

Chaumier, D. (2001), 'La statue déboulonnée', *France Football* (27 March): 3.

—— and D. Rocheteau (1997), *Le Guide du football 1998*, Paris: Editions de la Lucarne.

—— and D. Rocheteau (1999), *Le Guide du football 2000*, Paris: Editions de la Lucarne.

—— and D. Rocheteau (2000), *Le Guide du football 2001*, Paris: Editions de la Lucarne.

—— and D. Rocheteau (2001), *Le Guide du football 2002*, Paris: Editions de la Lucarne.

—— *et al.* (2000), 'Jacquet: « Je prépare le football de demain »', *France Football*, 2848 (7 November): 4–11.

Chemin, M. *et al.* (1998), 'La saga Jacquet. Itinéraire de l'entraîneur des Bleus. D'ouvrier-footballeur à coach bâtisseur', *Libération* (11 July): 6–8.

'Clubs professionnels de football: une comparaison européenne', *Profession Football*, 22 (October–November 1996), reprinted in 'Economie du sport', *Problèmes économiques*, 2503 (15 January 1997): 29–31.

Coakley, J. and E. Dunning (eds) (2000), *Handbook of Sports Studies*, London: Sage.

Collinot, J.-F. (1997), *Créer son association*, Toulouse: Editions Milan (Essentiels Milan).

Colombani, J.-M. (1998), 'La parabole Jacquet', *Le Monde* (14 July): 1, 14.

Conn, D. (1997), *The Football Business. Fair Game in the '90s?*, Edinburgh: Mainstream Publishing Projects.

Crevoisier, J. and G. Houllier (1993), *Entraîneur: compétence et passion*, Paris: Albin Michel, new edn 2000.

Critcher, C. (1987), 'Media spectacles: sport and mass communication', in A. Cashdan and M. Jordin (eds), *Studies in Communication*, Oxford: Blackwell.

Crozier, M. (1970), *La société bloquée*, Paris: Editions du Seuil (Points Politique).

CSA (1997), *Sport et télévision 1991–1996. Bilan de six années de régulation*, Paris: Etudes du CSA.

Dalloni, M. and C. de Chenay (1997), 'Mme Buffet remet en cause les projets de son prédécesseur', *Le Monde* (27 June): 26.

Dauncey, H. (1999), 'Building the finals: facilities and infrastructure', in Dauncey and Hare (eds) (1999b): 98–120.

—— and G. Hare (1998a), 'Jouer dans la cour des grands: France 98', *Modern and Contemporary France*, 3 (August): 339–350.

—— and G. Hare (eds) (1998b), 'Sport, society and popular culture in twentieth century France', *Modern and Contemporary France*, 3 special issue (August).

—— and G. Hare (1998c), 'Télévision et commercialisation du football', in Lenoir (ed.) (1998): 265–280.

—— and G. Hare (1999a), 'The coming of age: the World Cup of France 98', in Armstrong and Giulianotti (eds) (1999): 41–51.

—— and G. Hare (eds) (1999b), *France and the 1998 World Cup: the National Impact of a World Sporting Event*, London: Frank Cass.

—— and G. Hare (2000), 'World Cup France 98: metaphors, meanings, and values', *International Review for the Sociology of Sport*, 35 (3) (September): 331–347.

Defrance, J. (1995), *Sociologie du sport*, Paris: La Découverte (Repères).

Delaunay, P., J. de Ryswick, J. Cornu and D. Vermaud (1997), *100 ans de football en France*, Paris: Editions Atlas/Editions RMC.

Demazière, D. *et al.* (1998), 'La fabrication des « Sang et Or »: organisations et engagements des supporters lensois', in Lenoir (ed.) (1998): 227–239.

Démerin, P. (1986), 'Séville', in Bureau (ed.) (1986): 120–125.

Desporetes, G. (1998), 'L'exploit des Bleus convertit la France au culte du ballon. Hommes, femmes, blancs, blacks, beurs . . .', *Libération* (10 July): 2.

Dhers, G. and D. Revault d'Alonnes (2002), 'Six pistes pour un échec. Usure, défense défaillante, choix de l'entraîneur . . .', *Libération* (12 June): 3–4.

Dine, P. (1995), 'The tradition of violence in French sport', in R. Gunther and J. Windebank (eds), *Violence and Conflict in Modern French Culture*, Sheffield: Sheffield Academic Press, 245–260.

—— (1996), 'Un héroïsme problématique – Le sport, la littérature et la guerre d'Algérie', *Europe*, 806–7 (June–July): 177–185.

—— (1997a), 'Sport, imperial expansion and colonial consolidation: a comparison of the French and British experiences', in F. van der Merwe (ed.), *Sport as Symbol, Symbols in Sport*, Sankt Augustin (Germany): Academia Verlag, 63–69.

—— (1997b), '*La France qui gagne*: the institutions and institutionalisation of French sport', in R. Jones, *Sports Institutes, Sports Academies and National Sporting Identities*, British Network of the International Society for Comparative Physical Education and Sport, 24–38.

—— (1997c), 'Peasants into sportsmen: modern games and the construction of French national identity', in P. Dine and I. Henry, *The Symbolism of Sport in France*, Stirling: Stirling French Publications (5).

—— (1998a), Entries on 'Sport' and 'Sports funding', in A. Hughes and K. Reader (eds), *Encyclopedia of Contemporary French Culture*, London: Routledge.

—— (1998b), 'Sport and the State in contemporary France: from *la Charte des Sports* to decentralisation', in Dauncey and Hare (eds) (1998b): 301–311.

—— (1999), 'Breton sport', in G. Jarvie (ed.), *Sport in the Making of Celtic Cultures*, Leicester: Cassell/Leicester University Press, 112–130.

—— (2001), *French Rugby Football: a Cultural History*, Oxford: Berg.

'Dix villes mobilisées pour la Coupe du monde 1998', *La Gazette des communes*, 9 June 1997.

Dufour, J.-P. (2001), 'Le stade Grimonprez-Jooris va être rénové et agrandi', *Le Monde* (22 May).

Duhamel, A. (1985), *Le Complexe d'Astérix. Essai sur le caractère politique des Français*, Paris: Gallimard.

Duke, V. and L. Crolley (1996), *Football, Nationality, and the State*, New York: Addison-Wesley Longman.

Dumazedier, J. (1962), *Vers une civilisation du loisir*, Paris: Le Seuil.

Dunning, E. (1998), *Sport Matters: Sociological Studies of Sport, Violence and Civilisation*, London: Routledge.

—— P. Murphy and J. Williams (1988), *The Roots of Football Hooliganism: an Historical and Sociological Study*, London: Routledge and Kegan Paul.

Dupont, R. (2000), 'Urano, le sanglier des Ardennes', *L'Equipe* (7 November): 8.

Eastham, J. (1999), 'The organisation of French football today', in Dauncey and Hare (eds) (1999b): 58–78.

Echégut, A. (1994), 'Charles Pasqua dénonce l'aide des collectivités locales au sport professionnel', *Les Echos* (16 March): 21.

—— (1997), 'Mondial 1998: une facture de 9,4 milliards', *Les Echos* (4 December): 54–55.

—— (1998), 'La France a montré son savoir faire', *Les Echos* (13 July): 39.

'Economie du sport', *Problèmes économiques*, 2503 (15 January 1997).

Edworthy, N. (2002), *Football Stories. Bad Boys and Hard Men*, London: Channel 4 Books.

Ehrenberg, A. (1991), *Le Culte de la performance*, Paris: Calmann-Lévy.

Elias, N. and E. Dunning (1986), *Quest for Excitement. Sport and Leisure in the Civilising Process*, Oxford: Blackwell.

Ernault, G. *et al.* (2000), 'Les Trophées du siècle', *France Football* special issue (26 December).

Eurodata (1998), *1997: une année de sport dans le monde*, Eurodata TV-Médiamétrie, 1998, cited in G.R., 'Le monde entier est dingue de sport', *Le Journal du dimanche* (31 May 1998): 15.

Fatès, Y. (2003), 'Football in Algeria: between violence and politics', in G. Armstrong and R. Giulianotti, *Football in Africa*, Basingstoke: Palgrave, forthcoming.

Faure J.-M. and C. Suaud (1994a), 'Les enjeux du football', *Actes de la recherche en sciences sociales*, 103 (June): 3–6.

—— (1994b), 'Un professionnalisme inachevé. Deux états du champ du football professionnel en France, 1963–1993', *Actes de la recherche en sciences sociales*, 103 (June): 7–25.

—— (1999), *Le Football professionnel à la française*, Paris: PUF (Collection Sociologie d'aujourd'hui).

Ferran, J. and E. Maitrot (1997), *Sport: la télévision a-t-elle tous les droits?*, Paris: Télésatellite Publications.

Ferré, J. *et al.* (1998), *Dictionnaire des APS*, Paris: Amphora.

Ferré, P. (2000), 'Morlans: « On ne s'improvise pas entraîneur »', *France Football* (14 November): 20–21.

—— (2001), 'Hanot, le talentueux touche-à-tout', *France Football* (25 December): 20–21.

Finn, G. P. T. and R. Giulianotti (eds) (2000), *Football Culture. Local Contests, Global Visions*, London: Frank Cass.

'Foot-télévision, le mariage de raison', in Chaumier and Rocheteau (1997): 297.

'Football, sport du siècle' (1990), *Vingtième siècle*, 26 Special issue (April–June).

Fourastié, J. (1979), *Les Trente glorieuses: ou, La Révolution invisible de 1946 à 1975*, Paris: Fayard.

Frémy, D. and M. Frémy (1991), *Quid 1992*, Paris: Laffont.

Fridenson, P. (1989), 'Les ouvriers de l'automobile et le sport', *Actes de la recherche en sciences sociales*, 79 (September).

Gattegno, H. (2001), 'Le but en or de Bernard Tapie', *Le Monde* (15–16 April): 8.

Giddens, A. (1985), *The Nation-State and Violence*, Cambridge: Polity Press.

—— (2001), *Sociology* (4th edn), Cambridge: Polity Press.

Gildea, R. (1997), *France since 1945*, Oxford: OUP (first published in 1996).

Giulianotti, R. (1999), *Football. A Sociology of the Global Game*, Cambridge: Polity Press.

—— (2000), 'Built by the two Varelas: The rise and fall of football culture and national identity in Uruguay', in Finn and Giulianotti (eds) (2000): 134–154.

—— and J. Williams (eds) (1994), *Game without Frontiers: Football, Identity and Modernity*, Aldershot: Avebury.

Graham, R. (1998), 'Tonique for the nation', *Financial Times* (18 July).

Grandemange, S. and S. Cazali (2002), 'Une saison financièrement difficile', *LNF Infos*, 42 (March): 6–9.

Gravier, J.-F. (1958), *Paris et le désert français*, Paris: Flammarion.

Haget, H. (1996), 'Télé: l'indigestion de foot', *L'Express* (26 December): 36.

—— (1998), 'Vas-y Mémé', *L'Express Le Magazine* (4 June): 8–11.

Halba, B. (1997), *Economie du sport*, Paris: Economica.

Hall, S. (1992), 'The question of cultural identity', in S. Hall, D. Held and T. McGrew, *Modernity and its Futures*, Cambridge: Polity Press.

Hare, G. (1995), 'Communications strategy, cultural tourism and the vitality of the small rural commune: the case of Fontvieille (Bouches-du-Rhône)', *Francophonie*, 12 (December): 28–33.

—— (1997), 'The broadcasting media', in J. Flower (ed.), *France Today* (8th edn), London: Hodder and Stoughton, 218–245.

—— (1999a), 'Towards demassification of French television in the twenty-first century', *Modern and Contemporary France*, 7 (3): 307–317.

—— (1999b), 'Get your kit on for the lads: Adidas versus Nike in France 98', *SOSOL (Sociology of Sport On-Line)*, 2 (2).

—— (1999c), 'Buying and selling the World Cup', in Dauncey and Hare (eds) (1999b): 121–144.

—— (2003), 'Is French football still French? Globalisation, national identity, and professional sport as spectacle and commodity', in *Shifting Frontiers of France and Francophonie* [Selected papers of ASMCF Annual Conference, 30 August–1 September 2000, Leicester University] forthcoming.

Hélal, H. and P. Mignon (eds) (1999), 'Football, jeu et société', *Les Cahiers de l'INSEP*, 25, Paris: INSEP-Publications.

Helvig, J.-M. (2001), 'Editorial: Identité collective', *Libération* (6–7 October).

Henry, M. (2002), 'Tapie à mi-temps à l'OM en attendant moins', *Libération* (26 March).

Hobsbawm, E. and T. Ranger (1983), *The Invention of Tradition*, Cambridge: Cambridge University Press.

Holt, O. (2001), 'Soccer gets a French lesson', *The Times [Supplement]* (15 February): 4–5.

Holt, R. (1981), *Sport and Society in Modern France*, London: Macmillan.

—— (1994), 'La tradition ouvriériste du football anglais', *Actes de la recherche en sciences sociales*, 103 (June): 36–40.

—— (1998), 'Sport, the French and the Third Republic', in Dauncey and Hare (eds) (1998b): 288–300.

——, J. A. Mangan and P. Lanfranchi (eds) (1996), *European Heroes. Myth, Identity, Sport*, London: Frank Cass.

Hopkins, S. and J. Williams (2001), 'Gérard Houllier and the New Liverpool "Imaginary"', in J. Williams, S. Hopkins, and C. Long (eds), *Passing Rhythms. Liverpool FC and the Transformation of Football*, Oxford: Berg, 173–194.

Humphries, A. [director] (2001), *Football Stories: Confessions of a Football Manager*, Channel 4 (2 July).

Jack, A. (1999), *The French Exception. France – Still so Special?*, London: Profile Books.

Jacques, M. (1997), 'Worshipping the body at the altar of sport', *Observer* (13 July): 18–19.

Jacquet, A. (1999), *Ma Vie pour une étoile*, Paris: Laffont.

Jeanneney, J.-N. (2001), *L'Echo du siècle. Dictionnaire historique de la radio et de la télévision en France* (2nd edn), Paris: Hachette/Arte/La cinquième.

Jeffries, S. (2001), 'Sport fever "turns the French into cretins"', *Observer* (29 April): 21.

Késenne, S. (1996), 'L'affaire «Bosman» et l'économie du sport professionnel', *La Revue du marché unique européen*, 1; reprinted in *Problèmes économiques*, 2503 (15 January 1997): 6–10.

Kopa, R. and B. Meunier (1996), *Planète football*, Paris: La Sirène.

Kote, G. van (1994), 'Les clubs sportifs redoutent la perte des subventions municipales', *La Tribune* (1 April).

Labrunie, E. (2001a), 'Sous une mauvaise étoile, le Red Star fait ses adieux au football professionnel', *Le Monde* (19 May).

—— (2001b), 'Battu à Lens, Lyon s'offre une discorde entre chefs', *Le Monde* (30 July).

—— (2001c), 'Les responsables français s'inquiètent de la fuite des apprentis champions', *Le Monde* (4 October).

Lagarde, F. (2002), 'Les concours financiers des collectivités territoriales aux clubs professionnels', *LNF Infos*, 42 (March): 2–4.

Laget, S. and J.-P. Mazot (1997), *Le Sport français. Les 200 exploits qui ont fait l'histoire*, Paris: Solar.

Landrin, S. (2001), 'Les ambitions mesurées du nouveau maire de Lyon', *Le Monde* (28 November).

Lanfranchi, P. (1994), 'Mekloufi, un footballeur français dans la guerre d'Algérie', *Actes de la recherche en sciences sociales*, 103 (June 1994): 70.

—— and A. Wahl (1996), 'The immigrant as hero: Kopa, Mekloufi and French football', in Holt, Mangan and Lanfranchi (eds) (1996): 114–127.

—— and A. Wahl (1998), 'La professionalisation du football en France (1920–1939)', in Dauncey and Hare (eds) (1998b): 313–325.

Larcher, C. (2000), 'Batteux, le père spirituel de la profession', *France Football*, 2855 (26 December): 44.

Laroche, A. (2001), *Tapie et l'OM. La vérité*, Paris: Plon.

Lawrence, A. (2000a), 'Calling time on Wenger', *Observer Sport* (13 August): 12.

—— (2000b), 'The French evolutionary: Arsène Wenger', in Rühn (ed.) (2000b): 201–210.

Leclair, J.-P. (1997), [Interview with] 'Gianni Agnelli', *L'Equipe magazine*, 815 (15 November): 74–78.

Lecoq, G. (1997), 'Le couronnement de la télé, ce fut le sacre de Reims' [Interview with Georges de Caune], *Les Ecrits de l'image*, 16: 129–133.

Lenoir, R. (ed.) (1998), 'Football et sociétés', *Sociétés et représentations*, 7 Special issue (December). [Selected papers from CNRS Conference 'Football et cultures', May 1998, Paris.]

Le Vaillant, L. (1999), 'David Ginola, 32 ans, footballeur et mannequin', *Libération* (26 May).

Lichfield, J. (1997), 'Sport: cup plans proceed despite scandal', *Independent* (4 January): 23.

Loret, A. (1996), *Génération glisse*, Paris: Editions Autrement.

Losson, C. and O. Villepreux (1998), 'Il y a une footballisation de la société' [Interview with Christian Bromberger], *Libération* (12 May): 22.

Lupiéri, S. (1996), 'Les fédérations sportives bousculées par l'argent', *Alternatives économiques*, 141 (October); reprinted as 'Les fédérations sportives françaises en pleine mutation', in 'Economie du sport', *Problèmes économiques*, 2503 (15 January 1997): 27–29.

MD (2000), 'Au PSG, Nicolas Anelka a bouclé la fort rémunératrice boucle de ses transferts', *Le Monde* (23 July).

Machenaud, V. (1999), '[Interview with] Elie Baup', *France Football*, 2788 (14 September): 5.

Maguire, J. (1999), *Global Sport*, Cambridge: Polity Press.

Maitrot, E. (1995), *Sport et télé. Les liaisons secrètes*, Paris: Flammarion.

Mandard, S. and O. Zilbertin (2000), 'Le sport dans la course à la technologie', *Le Monde Supplément interactif* (6 September): I–III.

Margot, O. (1986), 'Les moments forts du football à la télévision', in Bureau (ed.) (1986): 97–98.

Marks, J. (1999), 'The national team and French national identity', in Dauncey and Hare (eds) (1999b): 41–57.

Marseille, J. (1990), 'Une histoire économique du football en France est-elle possible?', *Vingtième siècle* (April–June): 67–72.

Martel, G. (1993), [Interview in] *Profession football. Bulletin d'informatio de l'UCPF*, 8 (November/December).

McIlvanney, H. (1996), *McIlvanney on Football*, Edinburgh: Mainstream.

McKeever, L. (1999), 'Reporting the World Cup: old and new media', in Dauncey and Hare (eds) (1999b): 161–183.

Meignan, G. (1999), 'Foot et télé: la fuite en avant des droits de retransmission', *L'Expansion* (18 February): 38–42.

Mendras, H. (1988), *La Seconde Révolution française 1965–1984*, Paris: Gallimard.

Michel, C. (1996), 'Le PSG version Canal+ capitalise sur le football', *Sport's magazine*, 20 (March): 88–89.

Miège, C. (1993), *Les Institutions sportives*, Paris: PUF.

—— (1996), *Le Sport européen*, Paris: PUF.

Mignon, P. (1990), 'Supporters et hooligans en Grande-Bretagne depuis 1871', *Vingtième siècle* (April–June): 37–47.

—— (1994), 'New supporter cultures and identity in France: the case of Paris Saint-Germain', in Giulianotti and Williams (eds) (1994): 273–297.

—— (1995), 'La Violence dans les stades: supporters, ultras et hooligans', *Les Cahiers de l'INSEP*, 10.

—— (1998), *La Passion du football*, Paris: Odile Jacob.

—— (1999), 'Fans and heroes', in Dauncey and Hare (eds) (1999b): 79–97.

—— (2000), 'French football after the 1998 World Cup: the State and the modernity of football', in Finn and Giulianotti (eds) (2000): 230–255.

—— and G. Truchot (2001), 'La France sportive: premiers résultats de l'enquête "Pratiques sportives 2000"', *STAT-Info (Jeunesse et sports)*, 1 (1 March): 1–8.

Mislin, G. (1999), 'Deux coupes pour une nouvelle ère', *LNF Infos*, 20 (September): 4–5.

—— (2001), 'Les clubs français face à la concurrence européenne', *LNF Infos*, 40 (December): 2–5.

Morlans, J.-P. (2001), 'Qu'est-ce que la Direction technique nationale?', *Fédération française de football website (pages on 'Formation')*, http://www.fff.fr/

Normand, J.-M. (2002), 'Y a pas péno. Supporteur de circonstance', *Le Monde supplément Mondial* (27 June): vii.

Nussle, P. (1986), 'Jouons "à la française"', in Bureau (ed.) (1986): 24–25.

Parker, G. (1993a), 'Montpellier ou la maïeutique mercatique – from identity to reality. The art of wishful thinking', *Modern and Contemporary France*, new series 1 (4): 385–396.

—— (1993b), 'Le marketing territorial – communication et identité régionale', in M. Kelly and R. Böck (eds), *France: Nation and Regions*, Southampton: ASMCF, 154–167.

Penverne, A. (2000), [Interview re: Batteux] 'C'était un révolutionnaire', *France Football*, 2855 (26 December): 45.

Perrot, R. (1997), 'Les 19 premiers salaires', *Evénement du jeudi* (24–30 April): 46.

Pickup, I. (1999), 'French football from its origins to Euro 84', in Dauncey and Hare (eds) (1999b): 22–40.

Pierrat, J.-L. and J. Riveslange (2002), *L'Argent secret du foot*, Paris: Plon.

Pion, P. (2001), 'Quel est le rôle d'un Conseiller Technique Départemental (CTD)?', *Fédération française de football website (pages on 'Formation')*, http://www.fff.fr/

Pociello, C. (1999), *Sports et sciences sociales. Histoire, sociologie et prospective*, Paris: Vigot (Collection Repères en éducation physique et sport).

Poiseul, B. (1992), *Football et télévision, 1 Sophismes et vérités; 2 La télévision des autres*, Paris (2 vols).

—— (1996a), *Canal+ L'aventure du sport*, Paris: Editions Editoria.

—— (1996b), 'Sport: la télévision a-t-elle tous les droits?', *Les Ecrits de l'image*, 13 (December): 150–152.

—— (1998), 'Football, roi du monde', *Les Ecrits de l'image*, 18 (Spring): 98–104.

Polley, M. (1998), *Moving the Goalposts. A History of Sport and Society since 1945*, London/New York: Routledge.

Poste, la (1997), 'Le sportif de haut niveau', *La Poste et vous*, 2 (October): 19.

Potet, F. (1998), 'Le RC Lens veut reprendre le flambeau des Verts', *Le Monde* (9 December).

—— (2000a), 'Un rapport parlementaire réclame davantage de démocratie dans les fédérations', *Le Monde* (23 May): 28.

—— (2000b), 'Sedan bâtit ses succès sur les failles du football français', *Le Monde* (14 November).

—— (2001a), [Interview with Guy Roux], *Le Monde* (3 May).

—— (2001b), 'Jean-Michel Aulas veut porter plainte à Bruxelles contre la FFF', *Le Monde* (2 November).

—— (2001c), 'Canal+ investit quasiment tous les secteurs du football professionnel', *Le Monde* (29 November).

—— (2001d), 'Quand Sport+ jouait les intermédiaires dans le transfert du Brésilien Dill', *Le Monde* (29 November).

—— (2001e), 'L'OM, club très apprécié par la chaîne cryptée', *Le Monde* (29 November).

—— (2001f), 'Les clubs pro poursuivent à Bruxelles leur offensive contre le ministre des sports', *Le Monde* (21 December): 27.

—— (2002), 'Pierre Blayau plaide pour une transformation de la Ligue en société', *Le Monde* (28 March).

Pretti, R. (2001), 'Un bon «client» pour les médias', *France Football* (27 March): 7.

Psenny, D. (2000), 'Le football reprend ses droits', *Le Monde supplément Radio et Télévision* (30–31 July): 4–5.

Puillet, B. *et al.* (1999), *Histoire de l'AS Saint-Etienne*, Paris: Cahiers intempestifs.

Py, D. (1997), 'La guerre des tarifs', *Le Monde (*15 June).

R.B. (1996a), 'Télévisions: la pub aime le foot', *Les Echos* (26 November).

—— (1996b), 'PSG, premier club français et premier client de JCD', *Les Echos* (26 November).

Ramella, F. and J. Touboul (1998), 'De la folie joyeuse', *L'Equipe* (11 May): 3.

Ramsay, A. (1997), 'Au PSG, personne ne comptait sur moi. [Interview with Nicolas Anelka]', *Sport's magazine*, 30 (March): 38–40.

—— (1999), 'Aulas, histoire d'une ambition', *France Football* (10 August): 6–8.

—— (2000), 'Black star: the unforgettable Roger Milla', in Rühn (ed.) (2000b): 175–182.

Raspaud, M. (1994), 'From Saint-Etienne to Marseilles: tradition and modernity in French soccer and society', in Giulianotti and Williams (eds) (1994): 103–127.

Rethacker, J.-Ph. (2000), 'Auxerre: the ultimate youth academy', in Rühn (ed.) (2000b): 18–23.

Revault d'Alonnes, D. (2001a), 'Les évolutions de Carrière. Le meneur de jeu s'est imposé à Nantes', *Libération* (14 May).

—— (2001b), 'La danseuse du ventripotent. Louis Nicollin gère le Montpellier-Hérault (D1) en paternaliste', *Libération* (11–12 August).

—— (2002), 'Les sponsors tirent sur la carte bleus. Le budget de parrainage de l'équipe de France a doublé depuis 1998', *Libération* (27 March).

Ridley, I. (1998), 'Ginola's double vision', *Observer Sport* (27 December), 5.

—— (1999), 'French evolution feeds the flow at Highbury', *Observer Sport* (10 January).

—— (2000), 'Houllier first among equals', *Observer Sport* (13 August): 13.

—— (2002), 'Bunkering down with Houllier. Europe provides a perfect incentive for Liverpool manager's return', *Observer Sport* (7 April).

Rivoire, X. and D. Ortelli (2002), 'Born in France, made in England', *Observer Sport Monthly*, 21 (January): 16–25.

Robrieux, Ph. (2002), 'Pierre Chayriguès le « Pierrot de Saint-Ouen »', *Le Monde* (12 June).

Romain, D. (2001), 'Les chiffres qui font hurler les grands clubs', *Le Parisien* (20 December): 25.

Ross, I. (1999), 'Houllier unveils hard streak', *Guardian Sport* (28 August): 3.

Rousseau, D. (1999), 'La mort de Claude Bez. La fin d'un chapitre', *L'Equipe* (27 January): 6.

—— (2002), 'Les comptes virent au rouge', *L'Equipe* (13 March): 6.

Rühn, C. (2000a), 'Blood and gold: the best supporters in France', in Rühn (ed.) (2000b): 255–261.

—— (ed.) (2000b), *Le Foot. The Legends of French Football*, London: Abacus.

Rushdie, S, (2000), 'Frenchy but chic – David Ginola', in Rühn (ed.) (2000b): 123–129.

Russell, D. (1997), *Football and the English*, Preston: Carnegie Publishing.

Saint-Martin, E. (1998), 'Dix villes sur le pied de guerre', *Le Point*, 1320 (3 January): 60–62.

Samson, M. (2000), 'Le Stade-Vélodrome, terrain de jeu politique', *Le Monde* (1 December).

Sassen, S. (1991), *The Global City: New York, London, Tokyo*, Princeton: Princeton University Press.

Schlesinger, P. (1991), *Media, State, Nation*, London: Sage.

Scotto, M. (1997), 'La ville de Strasbourg cède au privé un club de football en bonne santé', *Le Monde* (20 February): 29.

—— (1998), 'L'Alsace et la Lorraine privées de Coupe du monde', *Le Monde* (5 June): 25.

Simonnot, D. (1998), 'Ce jour est magique, il incarne l'idéal du creuset français', *Libération* (15 July): 5.

Sinet, V. (2002), *Coupe du Monde 1938. La Coupe du Monde oubliée*, Saint-Cyr-sur-Loire: Editions Alan Sutton.

Slack, T. (1998), 'Studying the commercialisation of sport: the need for critical analysis', *SOSOL (Sociology of Sport On-Line)*, 1 (1).

Sowden, P. (1997), 'Stade Auxerrois, la maison d'en face', *France Football* (19 December): 10–11.

Sperling, D. (1991), *Le Marketing territorial. La communication des régions*, Paris: Editions Milan-Midia.

'Sport et télévision' (1988), *Dossiers de l'audiovisuel*, 18 (March–April).

'Le sport à l'aube du numérique' (1998), *Dossiers de l'audiovisuel*, 77 (January–February).

Sugden, J. and A. Tomlinson (eds) (1994), *Hosts and Champions. Soccer Cultures, National Identities and the USA World Cup*, Aldershot: Arena (Popular Cultural Studies 4).

—— (1998), *Who Rules the People's Game? FIFA and the Contest for World Football*, Cambridge: Polity Press.

Taylor, D. (2001), 'Royle's reign cut short by costly crew of drinkers and stinkers', *Guardian* (22 May): 32.

'La télévision remplit les stades de foot', *Le Monde* (15 June 1997).

Thibert, J. and J.-P. Rethacker (1996), *La Fabuleuse Histoire du football*, Paris: Editions de la Martinière.

Thomas, R. (1991), *Histoire du sport*, Paris: PUF (2nd edn 1997).

—— (1993), *Le Sport et les médias*, Paris: Editions Vigot (Collection Sport et Enseignement).

—— (1996), *Sociologie du sport* (2nd edn), Paris: PUF.

——, J.-L. Chesneau and G. Duret (1991), *Le Football*, Paris: PUF.

Tomlinson, A. (1994), 'FIFA and the World Cup. The expanding football family', in Sugden and Tomlinson (eds) (1994): 13–33.

Toulet, M.-P. (2000), 'Tradition, modernity and post-modernity in French football. The evolution of French football as seen through a comparison of RC Lens and Girondins de Bordeaux', M.Litt. dissertation, Newcastle University.

Tournier, P. and J.-Ph. Rethacker (1999), *La Formation du footballeur. Comment devenir un professionnel*, Paris: Editions Amphora.

Tshitenge Lubabu Muitubile, K. (1998), 'Légendes du football: Roger Milla, les rugissements d'un Vieux Lion indomptable', Radio France Internationale web site [http://www.rfi.fr/Kiosque/Mfi/Sport/130798-7.html].

'Un nouveau secteur économique: le sport', *Problèmes politiques et sociaux*, 581 (1 April).

Urbini, P. (1986), 'Traquenards', in Bureau (ed.) (1986): 99–100.

Vidacs, B. (2000), 'Football in Cameroon: a vehicle for the expansion and contraction of identity', in Finn and Giulianotti (eds) (2000): 100–117.

Vierne, J.-J. (2002), 'Un bilan européen désastreux', *France Football* (15 March): 12–13.

Vuori, I. *et al.* (1997), 'Inventaire économique d'un phénomène de société', extract from report *Le rôle du sport dans la société: santé, civilisation, économie*, Conseil de l'Europe, 1995; reprinted in *Problèmes économiques*, 2503 (15 January): 1–5.

Wagg, S. (1984), *The Football World: a Contemporary Social History*, Brighton: Harvester.

—— (ed.) (1995), *Giving the Game Away: Football, Politics, and Culture on Five Continents*, Leicester: Leicester University Press.

Wahl, A. (1989), *Les Archives du football*, Paris: Gallimard.

—— (1990a), *La Balle au pied. Histoire du football*, Paris: Gallimard (Découvertes).

—— (1990b), 'Le mai 68 des footballeurs français', *Vingtième siècle* (April–June): 73–82.

—— and P. Lanfranchi (1995), *Les Footballeurs professionnels des années trente à nos jours*, Paris: Hachette (Collection La Vie quotidienne).

Walvin, J. (1994), *The People's Game: the History of Football Revisited*, Edinburgh: Mainstream.

Watrin, D. (1998), *Le Sport français face au sport 'business'*, Paris: Editions Amphora.

Weaver, P. (2001), 'Wenger the last of the small spenders', *Guardian* (16 May): 30.

Weber, E. (1970), 'Pierre de Coubertin and the introduction of organised sport into France', *Journal of Contemporary History*, 5 (2): 3–26.

—— (1971), 'Gymnastics and sports in *fin-de-siècle* France: opium of the classes', *American Historical Review*, 76 (February): 70–98.

Webster, P. (2002), 'Stars fight back to save TV channel', *Guardian* (18 April): 12.

Whannel, G. (1992), *Fields in Vision: Television, Sport and Cultural Transformation*, London: Routledge.

Whittell, I. (2001), 'French evolutionary who teaches patience', *Observer Sport* (18 February): 9.

Williams, J. and S. Wagg (eds) (1991), *British Football and Social Change. Getting into Europe*, Leicester: Leicester University Press.

—— and R. Taylor (1994), 'Boys keep swinging: masculinity and football culture', in T. Newburn and B. Stanko (eds), *Just Boys Doing Business?*, London: Routledge.

Williams, R. (2000a), 'Wild things', *Guardian* (12 August).

—— (2000b), 'How French cut the mustard', *Guardian Sport* (2 September): 2.

—— (2001), 'From the pits to the peaks', *Guardian* (16 May): 30.

Index